OCR GCSE

Religious Studies B
Philosophy & Applied Ethics

Applied Ethics

Vicky Bunting · Jane ___ ___on
Opinderjit Kaur Tak___ ___on Mayled
Debbie Newton · Ca___ ___od

Series Editor: Janet ___
Series Consultant: ___ ___led

www.heinemann.co.uk

✓ Free online support
✓ Useful weblinks
✓ 24 hour online ordering

01865 888080

Official Publisher Partnership

OCR AND HEINEMANN ARE WORKING TO___ ___ ___PPORT FOR YOU

Heinemann is an imprint of Pearson Education Limited, a company incorporated in England and Wales, having its registered office at Edinburgh Gate, Harlow, Essex, CM20 2JE. Registered company number: 872828

www.heinemann.co.uk

Heinemann is a registered trademark of Pearson Education Limited

Text © Pearson Education Limited 2009

First published 2009

13 12 11 10 09
10 9 8 7 6 5 4 3 2 1

British Library Cataloguing in Publication Data
A catalogue record for this book is available from the British Library

ISBN 978 0 43550151 8

Edited by Helen Kelly and Sarah Christopher
Reviewed by Richard Gray and Imran Mogra (Birmingham City University)
Proofread by Tracey Smith
Project managed and typeset by Wearset Ltd, Boldon, Tyne and Wear
Original illustrations © Pearson Education 2009
Illustrated by Chris Coady, Alasdair Bright and Wearset Ltd
Picture research by Q2AMedia
Cover photo/illustration © Lukasz Witczak/iStockphoto
Printed by Rotolito, Italy

Acknowledgements
The author and publisher would like to thank the following individuals and organisations for permission to reproduce photographs:

Page 2 ClassicStock/Alamy. Page 4 Tobi Corney/Riser/Getty Images. Page 6 Ashwini Bhatia/Associated Press. Page 8 Dmitriy Shironosov/Dreamstime. Page 11 Pascal Genest/Istockphoto. Page 13R Jason Burtt/Silverringthings. Page 13L Jonathan Player/Rex Features. Page 14 Biju/Alamy. Page 16 Michael Pettigrew/123RF. Page 17 Sven Hoppe/Shutterstock. Page 18 Blend Images/Alamy. Page 19 David Grossman/Alamy. Page 20 Exotic eye/Alamy. Page 21 Charles O. Cecil/Alamy. Page 23 Israel images/Alamy. Page 25 Nathan Benn/Alamy. Page 28 Christine Osborne/ Photographersdirect. Page 32 Nik Wheeler/Sygma/Corbis. Page 34 Monkey Business Images/Dreamstime. Page 36 Sean Sprague/ Alamy. Page 38 Norma Joseph/Alamy. Page 41 Phototake Inc/ Alamy. Page 43 www.nikoartwork.com. Page 47 Steve Lindridge/ Alamy. Page 48 Mika/zefa/Corbis. Page 49 Dario Mitidieri/ Reportage/Getty Images. Page 50 STR/Associated Press. Page 52 Mikhail Nekrasov/Shutterstock. Page 54 Ed Kashi/Corbis. Page 57 Jennifer Leigh Sauer/Photonica/Getty Images. Page 58 Jgroup/ BigStockPhoto. Page 62 Eddie Gerald/Alamy. Page 63 Mark Boulton/Alamy. Page 64 Sanjay Rawat. Page 66T Rex Features. Page 66B Viviane Moos/Corbis. Page 71 Gideon Mendel/Corbis. Page 72 David J. Phillip/Associated Press. Page 73 Hartlepool Museum Service, Cleveland, UK/The Bridgeman Art Library. Page 74L Matthew Butler/Rex Features. Page 74R Les Stone/Sygma/Corbis. Page 76 Nevada Wier/Corbis. Page 77 Friedrich Stark /Alamy. Page 78 Km Chaudary/Associated Press. Page 79 Grapheast/Alamy. Page 80 Tony Kyriacou/Rex Features. Page 81 Sanjeev Gupta/epa/ Corbis. Page 82 STR New/Reuters. Page 85 Israel images/Alamy. Page 86 Andy Aitchison/Corbis. Page 87 Robert Spencer/Associated Press. Page 92 Stephen Hird/Reuters. Page 94 Jorge Adorno/ Reuters. Page 98 Tim Page/Corbis. Page 99 Ciniglio Lorenzo/Corbis Sygma. Page 100 Sgt Albert Eaddy/U.S. Army. Page 103L Matthew Polak/Sygma/Corbis. Page 103TR Associated Press. Page 103BR Stewart Cook/Rex Features. Page 104 Jayanta Shaw/Reuters. Page 105 Rex Features. Page 106 Channi Anand/Associated Press. Page 108 Ilyas J Dean/Rex Features. Page 109 Sinan Isakovic/ Shutterstock. Page 110 Javarman/123RF. Page 111T Helene Rogers/ Art Directors & Trip Photo Library. Page 111B Studio DL/Corbis. Page 112 Magnus Johansson/Reuters. Page 114 Chuck Savage/ Corbis. Page 117 Helene Rogers/Art Directors & Trip Photo Library. Page 122 Nyul/Fotolia. Page 124 Hulton-Deutsch Collection/Corbis. Page 126 David Hoffman Photo Library/Alamy. Page 127 Pascal Deloche/Godong/Corbis. Page 129 Gopal Chitrakar/Reuters. Page 130L Hugh Sitton/zefa/Corbis. Page 130R Image Source/Jupiter Images. Page 131 Photofusion Picture Library/Alamy. Page 132 Arcaid/Alamy. Page 135 Baldev/Corbis. Page 136 2d Alan King/ Alamy. Page 138 Alex Wong/Getty Images. Page 139 Distinctive Images/Shutterstock. Page 140R Helene Rogers/Art Directors & Trip Photo Library. Page 140L Comstock Select/Corbis. Page 141 Ron Sachs/CNP/Corbis. Page 142 Associated Press. Page 143 Hanan Isachar/Corbis. Page 145 Associated Press. Page 146R Vivek Sharma/Alamy. Page 146L Douglas E. Curran/AFP/Getty Images. Page 147 Helene Rogers/Art Directors & Trip Photo Library. Page 148 Christine Osborne/www.worldreligions.co.uk. Page 152 Adrees Latif/Reuters. Page 155 Paul Gauguin/The Bridgeman Art Library/ Getty Images. Page 156 The Kobal Collection. Page 158T Ron Sachs/Rex Features. Page 158B Annie Robert. Page 159 SNAP/Rex Features. Page 161 Universal/Everett/Rex Features. Page 162 Richard T. Nowitz/Corbis. Page 164 Helene Rogers/Art Directors & Trip Photo Library. Page 166 Sipa Press/Rex Features. Page 167 Francis Dean/Rex Features. Page 168 Richard Levine/Alamy. Page 169TR Greg Baker/Associated Press. Page 169MR Capital Pictures. Page 169BL Raheb Homavand/Reuters. Page 170 Trent Warner/Rex Features. Page 172 Photos 12/Alamy. Page 174 The Ronald Grant Archive.

The authors and publisher would like to thank the following for permission to use copyright material:

Bible scripture quotations taken from The Holy Bible, New International Version Anglicised Copyright © 1979, 1984 by International Bible Society. Used by permission of Hodder & Stoughton Publishers, a division of Hachette (UK) Ltd. All rights reserved. 'NIV' is a registered trademark of International Bible Society.

UK trademark number 1448790.

Scripture quotations in Judaism sections reprinted from TANAKH: THE HOLY SCRIPTURES: THE NEW JPS TRANSLATION TO THE TRADITIONAL HEBREW TEXT, © 1985 by the Jewish Publication Society, with the permission of the publisher.

p.68 Edward Conze, *Buddhist Scriptures*, Penguin, 1959.

Every effort has been made to contact copyright holders of material reproduced in this book. Any omissions will be rectified in subsequent printings if notice is given to the publishers.

Introduction

A note for teachers

This student book has been written especially to support the OCR Religious Studies Specification B, Units B603: *Ethics 1 (Relationships, Medical Ethics, Poverty and Wealth),* and B604: *Ethics 2 (Peace and Justice, Equality, Media).* The book covers all six religions within the specification: Buddhism, Christianity, Hinduism, Islam, Judaism and Sikhism. It is part of an overall series covering the OCR Specification B, which comprises:

- three Student Books: this book, a companion book on Philosophy, which also covers all six religions, and a book covering Christian Philosophy and Applied Ethics – further details on pages viii and ix.
- a Teacher Guide: covering Buddhism, Christianity, Hinduism, Islam, Judaism and Sikhism – further details on pages viii and ix.

Who are we?

The people who have planned and contributed to these books include teachers, advisers, inspectors, teacher trainers and GCSE examiners, all of whom have specialist knowledge of Religious Studies. For all of us the subject has a real fascination and we believe that good Religious Studies can make a major contribution to developing the skills, insights and understanding people need in today's world. In the initial development of this series, Pamela Draycott lent us her expertise, which we gratefully acknowledge.

Why is Religious Studies an important subject?

We believe that Religious Studies is an important subject because every area of life is touched by issues to do with religion and belief. Following a Religious Studies GCSE course will enable students to study and explore what people believe about God, authority, worship, beliefs, values and truth. Students will have opportunities to engage with questions about why people believe in God and how beliefs can influence many aspects of their lives.

Students will also explore why members of a particular religion may believe different things. In lessons students will be expected to think, talk, discuss, question and challenge, reflect on and assess a wide range of questions. As young people growing up in a diverse society studying religion will help them to understand and relate to people whose beliefs, values and viewpoints differ from their own, and help them to deal with issues arising, not only in school, but in the community and workplace.

The study of religion will also help students to make connections with a whole range of other important areas, such as music, literature, art, politics, economics and social issues.

The specification for OCR B Philosophy and/or Applied Ethics

The specification outlines the aims and purposes of GCSE. The content to be covered is divided into six different Topics. The book's structure follows these Topic divisions precisely:

Unit B603: Ethics 1

Topic 1: Religion and human relationships

Topic 2: Religion and medical ethics

Topic 3: Religion, poverty and wealth

Unit B604: Ethics 2

Topic 1: Religion, peace and justice

Topic 2: Religion and equality

Topic 3: Religion and the media

The Topics focus on developing skills such as analysis, empathy and evaluation, which will enable students to gain knowledge and understanding of the specified content.

In following this specification students will have the opportunity to study Philosophy and/or Applied Ethics in depth and will learn about the diversity of religion and the way in which people who believe in a religion follow its teachings in their everyday lives.

This book covers everything students will need to know for the examination and shows them how to use their knowledge and understanding to answer the questions they will be asked.

Changes to the specification

The specification has changed dramatically according to the developing nature of education and the need to meet the demands of the world for students. The new specification will be taught from September 2009 onwards. The main changes that teachers and students should be aware of include the following:

- The Assessment Objectives (AOs) have changed, with a 50% focus now given to AO1 *(Describe, explain and analyse, using knowledge and understanding)* and a 50% focus to AO2 *(Use evidence and reasoned argument to express and evaluate personal responses, informed insights and differing viewpoints)*. Previously, the balance was 75% to 25% respectively. There is more information on this on pages x and xi.
- There is an increased focus on learning *from* religion rather than simply learning *about* religion, and explicit reference to religious beliefs is now required in answers marked by Levels of Response.
- Levels of Response grids have been changed to a new range of 0 to 6 marks for AO1 questions and 0–12 marks for AO2 questions. The complete grids are reproduced on pages x and xi.
- Quality of Written Communication (QWC) is now only assessed on parts (d) and (e) of each question.
- There is now a greater choice of Topics within the specification including Religion, reason and revelation and Religion and the media.

Why did we want to write these resources?

We feel strongly that there is a need for good classroom resources that take advantage of the changed Assessment Objectives which:

- make the subject lively, interactive and relevant to today's world
- encourage students to talk to each other and work together
- challenge students and encourage them to think in depth in order to reach a high level of critical thinking
- train students to organise their thoughts in writing in a persuasive and structured way, and so prepare them for examination.

The book has many features which contribute towards these goals. **Grade Studio** provides stimulating and realistic exercises to train students in what examiners are looking for and how to meet those expectations. **Exam Café** provides an exciting environment in which students can plan and carry out their revision.

Of course learning is about more than just exams. Throughout the book you will find **Research Notes**, which encourage students to explore beyond the book and beyond the curriculum. All of these features are explained in more detail on the next two pages.

What is in this book?

This student book has the following sections;

- the **Introduction**, which you are reading now
- the six **Topics** covered in the specification
- **Exam Café** – an invaluable resource for students studying their GCSE in Religious Studies
- **Glossary** – a reference tool for key terms and words used throughout the book.

Each of the above is covered in more detail in the text below.

The six Topics

Each Topic in this book contains:

- a Topic scene-setter including a look at the key questions raised by the Topic, and the key words associated with those questions (**The Big Picture**)
- two-page spreads covering the **main Topic content**
- exam-style questions with level indicators, examiner's comments and model answers (**Grade Studio**).

These features, which are explained more fully in the following pages, have been carefully planned and designed to draw together the OCR specification in an exciting but manageable way.

The Big Picture

This provides an overview of the Topic. It explains to students **what** they will be studying (the content), **how** they will study it (the approaches, activities and tasks) and **why** they are studying it (the rationale). It also includes a **Get started** activity, often linked to a picture or visual stimulus, which presents a task designed to engage students in the issues of the Topic and give them some idea of the content to be studied.

Develop your knowledge

This lists the **key information**, **key questions** and **key words** of the Topic. At a glance, it allows students to grasp the basic elements of knowledge they will gain in the study of the Topic. It is also a useful reference point for reflection and checking information as it is studied.

Main Topic content

The main content of each Topic is covered in a number of two-page spreads. Each spread equates to roughly one lesson of work – although teachers will need to judge for themselves if some of these need more time.

Each spread begins with the learning outcomes, highlighted in a box at the top of the page, so that students are aware of the focus and aims of the lesson. The text then attempts to answer, through a balanced viewpoint, one or two of the key questions raised in **Did you know?**. The text carefully covers the views of both religious believers and non-believers. It is also punctuated with activities that range from simple tasks that can take place in the classroom to more complex tasks that can be tackled away from school.

A range of margin features adds extra depth and support to the main text both for students and the teacher.

- **For debate** invites students to examine two sides of a controversial issue.
- **Must think about!** directs students towards a key idea that they should consider.
- **Sacred text** provides an extract from the sacred texts of the religion to help students understand religious ideas and teachings.
- **Research notes** provide stimulating ideas for further research beyond the material covered in the book and in the OCR specification.

Activities

Every Topic has a range of interesting activities which will help students to achieve the learning outcomes. Every two-page spread has a short starter activity to grab students' attention and to get them thinking. This is followed by a development section where the main content is introduced, and a plenary activity, which may ask students to reflect on what they have learnt, or may start them thinking about the next steps.

All activities are labelled AO1 or AO2 so you can tell at a glance which skills will be developed.

What is Grade Studio?

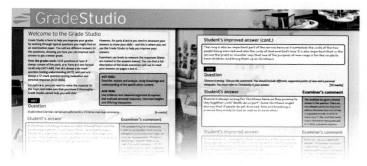

Everyone has different learning needs and this section of the book gives clear focus on how, with guidance from the teacher, students can develop the skills that will help them to achieve the higher levels in their exam responses.

Grade Studio appears as boxes within each Topic, as well as a two-page spread at the end of every Topic. It includes tips from the examiner, guidance on the steps to completing a well structured answer, and sample answers with examiner comments.

What is the Exam Café?

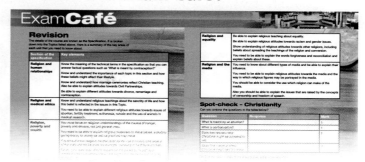

This is the revision section of the book. Here students will find useful revision tools and tips on how to get started on their revision and exam preparation. Students will also find assessment advice, including examples of different types of questions and samples of frequently asked questions. A useful **revision check list** allows students to review each Topic's content and explains where to find material in the book that relates to the exam questions.

Exam Café also has:

- sample student answers with examiner's comments
- help on understanding exam language, so students can achieve higher grades
- examiner tips, including common mistakes to be avoided.

For the Student: ActiveBook CD-ROM

In the back of this book is an ActiveBook CD-ROM. This contains an electronic version of the book, with easy-to-use and intuitive navigation controls. Pages are displayed in double-page spreads and users can flick to whichever page they choose. The CD also contains an Exam Café, with fresh revision content that complements and extends the Exam Café in the printed book.

For the Teacher: ActiveTeach CD-ROM

An accompanying ActiveTeach CD-ROM can also be purchased by schools and teachers. As well as containing an electronic version of the book, it provides a host of other features and interactives for classroom teaching. An icon on the electronic book page indicates where an ActiveTeach activity can be accessed. More detail on the ActiveTeach CD-ROM is given on the next page.

Heinemann's OCR Religious Studies B Series

Below is a snapshot of the complete OCR Religious Studies B series. Further detail can be found at www.heinemann.co.uk/gcse

OCR B Philosophy and Applied Ethics Teacher Guide with Resource Browser CD-ROM

ISBN 978-0-435-50152-5

Applied Ethics ActiveTeach CD-ROM

ISBN 978-0-435-50156-3

The **Teacher Guide** has been designed to correspond closely to the Student Book. For every Topic, the Teacher Guide offers four sample lesson plans and worksheets on Christianity, as well as a two page **Grade Studio**. There is careful cross-referencing throughout to help Teachers make the most out of these resources.

In addition, the Teacher Guide contains one sample lesson plan per Topic for Buddhism, Hinduism, Islam, Judaism and Sikhism. Any Teacher covering more than one religion in their course will find this a uniquely valuable resource.

Finally, the Teacher Guide comes with a CD-ROM, which contains the lesson plans along with a fully customisable version of all the worksheets.

The **ActiveTeach CD-ROM** contains an electronic version of the **Applied Ethics Student Book**, along with interactive **Grade Studio** and interactive whiteboard activities for front-of-class teaching. These activities are invaluable in engaging students with the specification content and bringing religious debates and issues to life. Equally valuable are the video and audio clips offered throughout the content. **ActiveTeach** has a special zoom feature, so any part of the book's content can be expanded on the whiteboard, as well as a special **My Resources** feature, where favourite activities, pages or clips can be stored. Finally, **ActiveTeach** includes an electronic Exam Café, which offers fresh revision content, complementing and extending the **Exam Café** in the printed book. A VLE version of **ActiveTeach** is available at no extra cost.

Philosophy Student Book with ActiveBook CD-ROM

ISBN 978-0-435-50150-1

This book provides complete coverage of both units of Philosophy (B601 and B602) and covers all six religions: Buddhism, Christianity, Hinduism, Islam, Judaism and Sikhism. It provides information, activities, and Grade Studio examples for all aspects of the course, as well as an 8-page **Exam Café** for revision. Each book comes with an **ActiveBook CD-ROM. ActiveBook** contains an electronic version of the **Student Book**, as well as an exciting, electronic **Exam Café**, which offers fresh revision content, complementing and extending the Exam Café in the book itself.

For the Teacher, the book is fully supported by the **OCR B Teacher Guide** (see above) and by the **Philosophy ActiveTeach CD-ROM** (see below).

Christian Philosophy & Applied Ethics Student Book

ISBN 978-0-435-50158-7

This book provides complete coverage of both units of Philosophy (B601 and B602) and Applied Ethics (B603 and B604) from the perspective of Christianity. It provides information, activities, and **Grade Studio** examples for all aspects of the course, as well as an 8-page **Exam Café** for revision. Comprehensive support for the Teacher is provided through the corresponding **OCR B Teacher Guide** (see above).

Philosophy ActiveTeach CD-ROM

ISBN 978-0-435-50155-6

The **ActiveTeach CD-ROM** contains an electronic version of the **Philosophy Student Book**, along with interactive **Grade Studio** and interactive whiteboard activities for front-of-class teaching. These activities are invaluable in engaging students with the specification content and bringing religious debates and issues to life. Equally valuable are the video and audio clips offered throughout the content. **ActiveTeach** has a special zoom feature, so any part of the book's content can be expanded on the whiteboard, as well as a special **My Resources** feature, where favourite activities, pages or clips can be stored. Finally, **ActiveTeach** includes an electronic **Exam Café**, which offers fresh revision content, complementing and extending the Exam Café in the printed book. A VLE version of ActiveTeach is available at no extra cost.

Assessment Objectives and Levels of Response

Assessment Objectives, AO1 and AO2

In the new specification, the questions in the examination are designed to test students against two Assessment Objectives: AO1 and AO2. In the specification 50% of the marks will be awarded for AO1 questions and 50% will be awarded for AO2 questions.

AO1 Questions require candidates to 'describe, explain and analyse, using knowledge and understanding'.

AO2 Questions require candidates to 'use evidence and reasoned argument to express and evaluate personal responses, informed insights, and differing viewpoints'.

Each question in the examination is composed of 5 parts, a–e. In more detail:

- Parts **a–c** are worth one, two and three marks respectively and test a candidate's knowledge (AO1 skills).
- Part **d** is worth six marks and tests a candidate's understanding (AO1 skills).
- Part **e** is worth twelve marks and tests a candidate's AO2 skills.

LEVELS OF RESPONSE FOR MARKING AO1 PART (D) QUESTIONS

LEVEL 1
(1–2 marks)

A **weak** attempt to answer the question.

Candidates will demonstrate little understanding of the question.

- A small amount of relevant information may be included.
- Answers may be in the form of a list with little or no description/explanation/analysis.
- There will be little or no use of specialist terms.
- Answers may be ambiguous or disorganised.
- Errors of grammar, punctuation and spelling may be intrusive.

LEVEL 2
(3–4 marks)

A **satisfactory** answer to the question.

Candidates will demonstrate some understanding of the question.

- Information will be relevant but may lack specific detail.
- There will be some description/explanation/analysis although this may not be fully developed.
- The information will be presented for the most part in a structured format.
- Some use of specialist terms, although these may not always be used appropriately.
- There may be errors in spelling, grammar and punctuation.

LEVEL 3
(5–6 marks)

A **good** answer to the question.

Candidates will demonstrate a clear understanding of the question.

- A fairly complete and full description/explanation/analysis.
- A comprehensive account of the range and depth of relevant material.
- The information will be presented in a structured format.
- There will be significant, appropriate and correct use of specialist terms.
- There will be few, if any, errors in spelling, grammar and punctuation.

LEVELS OF RESPONSE FOR MARKING AO2 PART (E) QUESTIONS

LEVEL 0
(0 marks)

No evidence submitted or response does not address the question.

LEVEL 1
(1–3 marks)

A **weak** attempt to answer the question.

Candidates will demonstrate little understanding of the question.
- Answers may be simplistic with little or no relevant information.
- Viewpoints may not be supported or appropriate.
- Answers may be ambiguous or disorganised.
- There will be little or no use of specialist terms.
- Errors of grammar, punctuation and spelling may be intrusive.

LEVEL 2
(4–6 marks)

A **limited** answer to the question.

Candidates will demonstrate some understanding of the question.
- Some information will be relevant, although may lack specific detail.
- Only one view might be offered and developed.
- Viewpoints might be stated and supported with limited argument/discussion.
- The information will show some organisation.
- Reference to the religion studied may be vague.
- Some use of specialist terms, although these may not always be used appropriately.
- There may be errors in spelling, grammar and punctuation.

LEVEL 3
(7–9 marks)

A **competent** answer to the question.

Candidates will demonstrate a sound understanding of the question.
- Selection of relevant material with appropriate development.
- Evidence of appropriate personal response.
- Justified arguments/different points of view supported by some discussion.
- The information will be presented in a structured format.
- Some appropriate reference to the religion studied.
- Specialist terms will be used appropriately and for the most part correctly.
- There may be occasional errors in spelling, grammar and punctuation.

LEVEL 4
(10–12 marks)

A **good** answer to the question.

Candidates will demonstrate a clear understanding of the question.
- Answers will reflect the significance of the issue(s) raised.
- Clear evidence of an appropriate personal response, fully supported.
- A range of points of view supported by justified arguments/discussion.
- The information will be presented in a clear and organised way.
- Clear reference to the religion studied.
- Specialist terms will be used appropriately and correctly.
- Few, if any, errors in spelling, grammar and punctuation.

Topic 1: Religion and human relationships

The Big Picture

In this Topic, you will be addressing religious beliefs and teachings about:

- the roles of men and women in the family
- marriage and marriage ceremonies
- divorce
- sexual relationships and contraception.

What?

You will:

- develop an understanding of the roles of men and women in the family
- find out about teachings on marriage and the ceremony itself, including beliefs about the ethics of divorce, remarriage, sexual relationships and contraception
- explain how these key beliefs and teachings are important to an individual and analyse ethical responses to issues such as contraception
- evaluate different viewpoints to show an informed insight into the different issues involved.

Why?

Because:

- understanding religious beliefs about human relationships will allow you to understand and determine your own values towards the different people in your life
- you will understand a variety of attitudes towards human relationships in different religions and societies
- it will help you to formulate your own priorities towards other humans.

How?

By:

- investigating the key religious beliefs on human relationships, considering different teachings and ethical view points
- making links between the teachings and daily practice in the life of a believer
- relating these teachings to your own ideas about relationships by comparing your own views with those of the religions studied.

Is a woman's place at home cleaning, cooking and looking after the children?

⏰ GET STARTED

'*You can choose your friends but you can't choose your relations!*'

Think about this statement. How important are your friends to you? What responsibilities do you have towards your friends? What responsibilities do you have towards your family?

Make two lists of the three qualities you look for in a friend and the three qualities you expect from your family. Compare your ideas across the class.

Religion and human relationships

Roles of men and women in the family

- Buddhist teaching emphasises mutual respect and faithfulness.
- Some Christians believe God made men and women for different reasons and, although they are equally important, God intended them to have different roles.
- In Hinduism, traditionally men are leaders and women look after the home and family. The god Rama and his wife Sita are seen as role models for men and women in **marriage**.
- Islam teaches that men and women are equal but have different rights and duties.
- In Judaism, it has been traditional for women to look after home and family while men provide for the family and carry out religious duties.
- Sikhs regard men and women as equal, but with different roles.

Roles of men and women in their religious communities

- Buddhists regard men and women as spiritually equal and both may be monks or nuns.
- Some Christians believe only men should become priests, but there are now many women priests and ministers.
- Hindus believe that the **dharma** for a man is different from that of a woman. Women take care of the **puja**, or worship, in the home.
- In Islam, women do not play an active role in public worship.
- Progressive Jews treat men and women equally. In Orthodox Judaism, women sit separately in the synagogue.
- Sikhs follow the teachings of Guru Nanak Dev Ji, who emphasised the **equality** of men and women.

ACTIVITIES

What is your definition of 'family'? What are your first impressions of this family?

Marriage ceremonies and how they reflect and emphasise religious teaching

- Buddhists regard marriage as a civil and social matter and there is no religious ceremony.
- Some Christians believe that marriage is a **sacrament** and a **covenant**. The couple promise that they will stay together and be faithful to each other for life.
- Hindus believe that marriage is given by God. At the ceremony, the participants take seven steps around the **sacred** fire and make promises to each other.
- All Muslims believe that marriage should be for life and that **adultery** is a sin.
- Jews believe that all Jews should marry and may use a shadchan to help suitable marriages happen.

KEY QUESTIONS

KNOWLEDGE AND UNDERSTANDING:
Explain the key features of a wedding ceremony in a religion you have studied.

ANALYSIS AND EVALUATION
How might a religious wedding ceremony help a marriage to work? Do you think it makes no difference? Give reasons for your answers.

Within a Jewish marriage, sex is regulated by **niddah**, and the woman must use a **mikveh** after her period before having sex.

- At a Sikh wedding, the bride follows the groom around the Guru Granth Sahib Ji.

Responses to same-sex marriages

In general, the more orthodox groups in all the major religions do not accept homosexuality. More liberal members of some religions may accept same-sex relationships with one partner for life.

Divorce and beliefs about the ethics of divorce and remarriage

- For Buddhists, the approach to divorce is affected by cultural attitudes. For most Buddhists divorce is allowed to reduce suffering but must be undertaken with care and compassion.
- Protestant and Orthodox Christians allow divorce, but the Roman Catholic Church teaches that marriage is a sacrament that only God can end.
- In Hinduism, divorce is allowed if one of the partners is cruel to the other or if there have been no children after 15 years.
- Muslims allow divorce and remarriage after divorce because it is permitted in the Qur'an.
- In Judaism, divorce is allowed but not approved of.
- For Sikhs, marriage is a sacred bond and therefore for life. However, divorce is permitted.

Beliefs about sexual relationships and contraception

- Buddhists believe **contraception** may be used to prevent (rather than end) suffering.
- Many Christians believe sex is only right between people who are married to each other. Sex outside marriage, same-sex relationships and affairs outside marriage are wrong.
- Some Christians believe that it is sensible for people to use contraception so that they can choose when to have children.
- Hindus believe **kama** is one of the four aims of life and that sex should be enjoyed between people who are married to each other. Same-sex relationships are not talked about. Although Hindu holy books tell couples not to limit the number of children they have, many Hindus do use birth control.
- Muslims believe sex is for pleasure as well as for the creation of children. Sex outside marriage is forbidden. Contraception is not recommended, except under certain circumstances.
- Some Orthodox Jews believe that God intended sex for **procreation** and all contraception except

the rhythm method is wrong. Others believe that women can use contraceptives after they have had at least two children.

- Sikhs believe that contraception should only be used in appropriate circumstances.

KEY WORDS

Aqd Nikah: Muslim marriage contract

adultery: sex between a married person and a person who is not their spouse

Beth Din: the Rabbinical court that decideds on matters of Jewish law

caste system: class divisions in Hindu society based on heredity

commitment: an engagement or obligation

contraception: use of artificial or natural methods to prevent conception

covenant: promise or agreement

divorce: legal dissolution of a marriage

Dharma: religious duty in Hinduism; in Buddhism the same word means universal law or ultimate truth

equality: treating people as equals regardless of gender, race or religious beliefs

iddah: the period when attempts are made to reconcile before a Muslim divorce

lesbianism: same-sex relations between women

Khalsa: literally means the 'Pure Ones' and refers to those Sikhs that have taken initiation and agreed to live by the rules and regulations of the Rehat Maryada

kama: sensual pleasure in Hinduism

mahr: Muslim dowry, or money given by the groom to the bride

marriage: formal, legal union of two people

mikveh: a ritual bath for Jews, which is usually part of the synagogue complex

moral: accepted standards of behaviour

nibbana: in Buddhism, a state free of suffering

niddah: Jewish purity laws

procreation: conceiving and having babies

sacrament: something which cannot be undone

sacred: holy, special

sentient being: a being able to sense pain and pleasure, for example a human being or animal

FOR INTEREST
Did you know that there are now more civil marriage ceremonies than religious ones? In 2006, 66 per cent of ceremonies were civil ones. Can you suggest reasons for this trend?

Buddhism:
Religion and human relationships 1

The next two pages will help you to:

- explain the roles of men and women within a Buddhist family
- explore Buddhist views of marriage, divorce and remarriage.

A Buddhist family praying together.

The roles of men and women

In a Buddhist family

Relationships within a Buddhist family are guided by the idea of the middle path and the five precepts. Relationships should be based on love and compassion, rather than lust. As a result, husband and wife should show respect and consideration for each other. Although the Buddha did not devise a **marriage** ceremony, he did provide some guidance about how husbands and wives should treat each other. He did this in the sigalavada sutta, where he recommended:

- faithfulness from both partners
- a sharing of household responsibilities and authority
- the husband should respect the wife and treat her courteously
- the husband should show his appreciation of the wife with presents

ACTIVITIES

Think/pair/share
Think about the ideal relationship between a man and a woman. With a partner, draw up a list of the ways in which the man and woman should behave. Share your ideas with another pair and pick the five most important to share with the class.

- the wife should work to the best of her ability and manage the household well
- the wife should show respect for her husband's family and take care of the family possessions.

Some of these ideas may seem outdated to some Buddhists today. Many would be happy to amend them, as long as the aim of a harmonious relationship, which allowed both partners to flourish, was maintained.

In the vihara

Some would consider the **bhikkhus** (monks) and **bhikkhunis** (nuns) in a vihara, or monastery to represent a family relationship, since they live together. The rules governing the relationships between the bhikkhus and bhikkhunis are very tightly governed. This is to ensure that the laity do not suspect the bhikkhus and bhikkhunis of having sexual relations, which might lose the monastic community the support of the laity and could be disastrous in some Buddhist communities.

Marriage

Since marriage could be seen to legitimise attachment, the Buddha never introduced a marriage ceremony. In many Buddhists countries, marriage is therefore a civil rather than a religious matter. These ceremonies will vary tremendously and will reflect the cultural norms of the communities in which they occur. In some countries, a bhikkhu will attend a marriage ceremony. They may read a passage from the Buddhist scriptures about the way husbands and wives should treat each other.

In some countries where the Mahayana tradition is practised, a married priesthood has originated and often a religious marriage ceremony has been instituted. Again, the exact details of this ceremony will vary. Often Buddhist teachings about compassion will be used to encourage the husband and wife to show respect for each other.

Divorce and remarriage

There is no single view on **divorce** or remarriage within Buddhism. As with most other issues on these pages, Buddhist views will primarily be influenced by the society in which they are living. In some countries, divorce is less acceptable than in others and may be harder to obtain.

Most Buddhists accept that in some cases divorce is unavoidable. An unhappy marriage causes harm to all those involved, and Buddhists seek to avoid causing harm to others. However, if a divorce is to take place, Buddhists would seek to minimise the harm caused to all involved, in line with the first precept. They would encourage both participants to behave in a fair manner and try to come to an amicable solution as far as possible.

Most Buddhists would support remarriage if it were based on love and compassion. They might encourage Buddhists to consider the likely success of the marriage before remarrying, in order to avoid further harm.

FOR DEBATE

Do you think it is useful to have a set code of moral ethics? How might a general statement such as 'avoid sexual misconduct' be interpreted differently? Does this help Buddhists to live in different societies with different moral codes, or does it make such a code meaningless?

RESEARCH NOTE

Research the details of a marriage ceremony in a Buddhist country. See if you can link the events involved in the ceremony to Buddhist beliefs and practices.

AO2 skills **ACTIVITIES**

Do you think a religion should have a ceremony for all the rites of passage (birth, initiation, marriage, death) in a person's life? Why/why not?

Buddhism:
Religion and human relationships 2

The next two pages will help you to:

- explore Buddhist views on sexual relationships, including same-sex relationships
- investigate Buddhist views on contraception.

Sexual relationships

Buddhists do not have set rules or regulations about sexual relationships. In aiming for **nibbana**, Buddhists should seek to avoid attachment or craving. Any sexual relationship must inevitably involve craving and attachment. Buddhists who are aiming for nibbana in this lifetime should therefore avoid sexual relationships. It is for this reason that bhikkhus and bhikkhunis in the monastic sangha (community) are often celibate.

Marriage is an important teaching for most religions.

However, Buddhism recognises that sex is a natural urge and that for many celibacy (abstinence from sexual relations) is not a realistic option. For lay Buddhists, and in some communities monastic Buddhists, sexual relationships are allowed. The main **moral** code relating to sexual ethics is the third precept. This states that Buddhists should avoid sexual misconduct. It does not, however, specify what sexual misconduct might be. For this reason, Buddhist sexual ethics tend to vary widely. What might be regarded as sexually unacceptable in one country is considered normal in another, and this influences the Buddhist view about whether it constitutes misconduct or not.

Buddhists would also consider the first precept – non-harming – when considering the ethics of a sexual relationship. Most Buddhists would consider short-term relationships as harmful to both participants. When they end they cause distress to both partners and are often based on lust rather than love. Buddhists would encourage sexual relationships based on love and compassion instead, since they are more likely to last and less likely to result in harm to the partners involved.

Same-sex relationships and marriages

Buddhist views on same-sex relationships will generally affect the views of the society in which they are based. Some traditional Buddhist countries will not approve of same-sex relationships, viewing them as a form of sexual misconduct. Other Buddhist countries are

REMEMBER THIS

The main moral code for lay Buddhists is the five precepts:

- not to harm living beings
- to avoid false or harmful speech
- to avoid sexual misconduct
- to avoid taking that which is not given
- to avoid intoxicants.

AO1 skills ACTIVITIES

In small groups, discuss the advantages of long-term relationships over short-term ones.

Create a pyramid, and place the most important advantage of a long-term relationship at the top of the pyramid, the next most important on the second row, and so on. Be prepared to explain your choices to your teacher.

more accepting of same-sex relationships, viewing them as no more or less harmful than heterosexual ones.

Where same-sex relationships are accepted, Buddhists would encourage them, as with heterosexual relationships, to be based on a foundation of love and compassion, rather then lust. As a result, some Buddhists are in favour of Civil Partnerships, since they provide a more solid and loving foundation than short-term relationships.

Contraception

Buddhist views on **contraception** vary, often reflecting the norms of the surrounding community. The main principle affecting Buddhist views on contraception is the first precept – ahimsa, or non-harming. Although contraception prevents a **sentient being** from being reborn, some Buddhists would say that bringing an unwanted child into the world would cause harm both to the child and to the parents. Also, it will only prevent a sentient being from being reborn at that particular time and place – the being will simply be reborn in other circumstances. So, in many cases, contraception is accepted.

For some Buddhists, the method of contraception used is important. Barrier methods of contraception (which prevent conception taking place, e.g. a condom or diaphragm) would usually be acceptable. Chemical means of preventing conception such as the contraceptive pill would also generally be acceptable.

More controversial would be IUDs, which may prevent a fertilised egg implanting in the womb. Similarly the 'morning after pill', which may act to expel a fertilised egg, would also be less widely accepted. Some Buddhists feel that the fertilised egg is a sentient being, so these methods cause harm to a sentient being, breaking the first precept. However, other Buddhists would regard the harm to a newly fertilised egg as being less than that to an unwanted child, and distressed parents, so they would still be prepared to accept these methods.

AO1 skills **ACTIVITIES**

Design a leaflet about contraception for Buddhist teenagers. Try to explain which methods of contraception would be preferred. Make sure you include the Buddhist beliefs and guidelines upon which these views are based.

AO2 skills **ACTIVITIES**

Does it matter that Buddhists in different countries and from different traditions have different views on sexual ethics?

GradeStudio

AO1

QUESTION

Explain Buddhist beliefs about marriage **[6 marks]**

You can build your answer like this:

Level 1
You might begin by saying that Buddhist marriages do not have to have any religious involvement, but often have a blessing from a Buddhist bhikkhu.

Level 2
Continue by explaining that Buddhist teaching is that giving alms helps a couple to start their marriage with a positive attitude and good kamma. After many Buddhist marriage ceremonies, alms might be given to the bhikkhus.

Level 3
Finally, you might also mention that Buddhist couples often include a reference to the five precepts, especially the third, within the ceremony.

Christianity:
Religion and human relationships 1

The role of men and women in the family

Roles in a Christian family

Christians have a variety of views about the roles that men and women should have in family life. Many base their opinions on one of the creation stories in Genesis, which describes how Adam was made first and Eve was made later, to be his helper. Later in Genesis, the account of the temptation of Eve has led some Christians to believe that women are weaker than men, as Eve gave in to temptation before Adam.

> **1 Peter 3:1a, 7a**
> *Wives, in the same way be submissive to your husbands… Husbands, in the same way be considerate as you live with your wives, and treat them with respect as the weaker partner…*

Women may be seen to be the homemakers, taking care of the children and supporting the man in his work to provide for the family.

However, other Christians feel these views belong in the past. They feel that men and women are equal as they were both made 'in the image of God', so work outside the home, childcare and other jobs should be shared, depending on the strengths of the couple. They may also back up this view with this quotation:

> **Galatians 3:28**
> *There is neither… male nor female… for you are all one in Christ Jesus.*

Marriage

A Christian **marriage** is a civil contract as well as a **covenant** between the couple and God to:

- provide each other with help and support in good and bad times
- enjoy a sexual relationship
- have children and bring up a family.

The next two pages will help you to:

- identify Christian ideas about different roles in the family and in Church families
- explain how Christians understand and celebrate marriage
- evaluate Christian responses to Civil Partnerships.

 **ACTIVITIES**

Have a class vote on these statements. Ask for people to explain their opinions and see if their arguments make you change your mind.

- Men and women are equal in all things.
- It doesn't matter who goes out to work as long as a family is happy.
- Some jobs in the home are more suitable for a man/woman.

AO1 skills **ACTIVITIES**

Make a spider diagram to show the different roles of men and women. Use one colour to show a traditional view and another to show a more modern attitude.

AO1 skills **ACTIVITIES**

Make an advert for your ideal partner. Include at least eight characteristics, but no more than two should be to do with looks!

Roles in the family of the Church

Roman Catholic and Orthodox Church	Church of England	Other Churches
Jesus did not have any women disciples, so obviously he did not want any women as leaders	Jesus treated women in a positive way and gave them more notice than was usual in his time	Methodist and most others support the equality of the sexes
St Paul said that women must obey men and be silent in church	Galatians 3:28 says that men and women are equal God created both men and women 'in his likeness'	Quakers feel that everyone can understand the will of God and can teach it to others
The priest represents Christ during Holy Communion. Women should not celebrate the Eucharist, so they cannot become priests	Women feel called to be priests just like men and should be allowed to follow their faith	
An all-male priesthood is a tradition that goes back to Jesus. It should not be broken	In the Early Church there seem to have been women in authority The Church Of England has allowed women to become vicars since 1994. Discussion is still going on concerning women bishops	Most of the Free Churches accept women ministers

What happens in a marriage ceremony?

In a Christian marriage, the couple make vows (promises) to each other in front of everyone and before God.

❝I _____, take you _____, to have and to hold, from this day forward: for better for worse, for richer, for poorer, in sickness and in health, to love and to cherish, til death do us part, according to God's holy law, in the presence of God I make this vow. ❞

(Christian Marriage Ceremony)

Rings are exchanged, the circle symbolising that marriage is never-ending.

What are Christian views about Civil Partnerships?

Some denominations, such as the Quakers, think that same-sex unions are acceptable and should be welcomed. The Methodist Church may officially bless same-sex couples – they encourage their members to be 'welcoming and inclusive' – but the union is not seen as a marriage. Some Church of England members have similar views and may bless couples.

The Roman Catholic Church does not accept any union between same-sex couples. They might encourage people who are attracted to the same sex to remain within the church, but not to have any active sexual relationships.

At a Christian marriage, the ring symbolises that the marriage will be forever.

ACTIVITIES

Think/pair/share
Why it is important for Christians to make promises when they marry? Discuss, then share with another pair, and decide on three statements you all agree on.

1 Corinthians 6:9
Do you not know that the wicked will not inherit the kingdom of God? Neither the sexually immoral... nor homosexual offenders...

Christianity:
Religion and human relationships 2

The next two pages will help you to:

- identify differing Christian beliefs about divorce and remarriage
- explain Christian beliefs about sexual relationships and contraception.

Christian attitudes to divorce and remarriage

In the vows made during a Christian **marriage** ceremony, the couple promise to stay together 'til death do us part'. It is clear from this that, in an ideal situation, **divorce** would not happen. But most people understand that life is not always ideal and sometimes a couple are no longer able to stay together.

However, Christians have different ideas about what should be done if this is the case.

- The Roman Catholic Church accepts that a couple may choose to live apart, but they may not divorce and then marry someone else in a religious ceremony. They believe that a marriage was made before God and is a **sacrament** – it cannot be undone. Sometimes an annulment is allowed, but the rules for this are strict.
- An annulment might be granted if a couple were under age when they married. It might also be granted if one or both of the couple were unaware of their actions due to diminished responsibility, or if one of the couple were pressurised or even forced into marriage. Finally, annulments may be granted due to non-consummation (that is, no sexual relationship took place after the marriage).
- In some cases, the Church of England will accept divorce and may agree to a divorced person remarrying. It is up to the vicar of a particular church, who may agree to perform a marriage ceremony or a blessing for the couple.
- Other denominations accept that a marriage is ended, not by the death of a partner, but by the death of the love between a couple. They will generally allow remarriage because they wish to encourage a couple to start a new relationship within the faith.
- All Christians will try to support a couple if they are having difficulties within their marriage and do all that they can to help them maintain a happy marriage.

Christian beliefs about sexual relationships and contraception

Sexual relationships

All Christian denominations agree that a sexual relationship is a unique and special one, as it is an expression of love between two people that has been blessed by God. In Genesis 1, sex is linked to reproduction, so many Christians would think that sex should be solely between a man

ACTIVITIES

In pairs, arrange the factors below into a diamond 9 to show which you think are most likely to lead to a marriage breaking down. Add in one factor of your own.

Money problems
Unfaithfulness
Serious illness
Lots of arguments
Pressure from family
Different interests
Children/no children
Work commitments

RESEARCH NOTE

Find out what Jesus had to say about divorce. Look at Matthew 5:31–32 and Mark 10:6–12.

and a woman. As sex is so special, it should only take place within a loving relationship. Some Christians believe that this may mean a long-term relationship without marriage. All Churches disagree with casual sex and with adultery (sex between a married person and a person who is not their spouse).

1 Corinthians 6:19a, 20b
Do you not know that your body is a temple of the Holy Spirit… Therefore honour God with your body.

AO1 skills ACTIVITIES

Summarise Christian beliefs and attitudes about sexual relationships and contraception, explaining different viewpoints.

Contraception

One of the main purposes of marriage is to bring up a family, so some Christians disagree with artificial forms of **contraception**. Roman Catholics follow the guidance from Pope Paul VI in *Humanae Vitae*, in which he explained that God made sex so that children could be born. He said that a couple should not try to prevent this by anything other than natural methods.

Other Christians feel that it is better to have families responsibly, and that fewer children who can be cared for adequately is better than large families without enough resources to care for them. They feel it is sensible for a couple to use contraception.

All agree that every child should be loved and wanted by its parents.

Members of the Silver Ring Thing promise to abstain from sex before marriage.

GradeStudio

AO1

QUESTION
Explain Christian attitudes towards divorce. **[6 marks]**

Level 1
First, let the examiner know that you know what the question is about. For example, Christians think that marriage is a sacrament and that when people marry in church they are marrying for life.

Level 2
Next, go on to explain in more detail about how Christians think of marriage and the particular vows that are made. You should also mention that they are made before God.

Level 3
Finally, explain how this belief about marriage can cause problems. All Christians believe in the sanctity of marriage and that it should last a lifetime. No Christian denomination approves of divorce, but most realise that sometimes it is inevitable. Some churches will allow people to remarry in church, but the Roman Catholic Church will only allow this if the couple have received an annulment.

Hinduism:
Religion and human relationships 1

The next two pages will help you to:

- explain the attitudes Hindus have to marriage
- explore the roles of men and women in Hindu families
- evaluate how Hindu beliefs influence their actions in this area.

A Hindu wedding ceremony marks the coming together not just of a couple, but of two families.

Getting married?

To Hindus, **marriage** is not just about the man and the woman involved but the families that are brought together by the union. As community is seen as so important, Hindu parents often help to arrange a marriage, by getting in contact with families they feel might have suitable children to marry their sons or daughters. It reflects the **varnashramadharma**, their duty to their varna. To make a good choice will help to reward their family with good **karma** during the stage of life which is called the grihasta (householder).

There are many different customs in connection with Hindu marriages in the UK, which reflect the different parts of India. The ceremony usually takes place in the bride's home, where there has been a great deal of preparation for many weeks. The time for the ceremony will have been chosen after consulting the couple's horoscopes, to make sure that it happens at the most blessed time.

AO1+AO2 skills ACTIVITIES

What qualities do people need to make good relationships like a friendship or a marriage? Working with a partner, write a list of the qualities that a person needs and then try to grade them, from the most important to the least important.

At the start of the ceremony, the bride waits in the entrance of the house for the groom and his family to arrive. A priest sings blessings to the couple, then the parents join the hands of the couple. The priest lights a sacred fire to the god Agni. The groom asks that the marriage will be blessed with children. The bride's sari is then tied to the groom's scarf, as a sign that they are joined together.

In some ceremonies, the couple takes seven steps around the fire and asks for these blessings:

- to have food
- to be given strength
- to have wealth
- to have wisdom and happiness
- to be blessed with children
- for good health
- for true friendship with each other.

Celibacy

Some Hindus believe that celibacy is a good ideal to work towards, renouncing their family life and going to live in a forest as a way of giving up tamas, the destructive potency that can govern life. Mahatma Gandhi followed this path, believing that the sexual urge could sap a person's willingness to serve God.

Roles in a Hindu family

Hinduism teaches that men and women have very distinctive roles in family life. Each has a particular **dharma** (religious duty) that they need to follow.

A woman is normally supported by her father until she is married, when the responsibility is then taken over by her husband. As this is often quite a burden financially to a family, Hindu society has often welcomed the birth of boys more than girls. Quite often, girls have been given less education as it was felt that the boy needed to get the best job in order to bring in a wage to support the family, rather than the woman.

Many married Hindu women are expected to look after their mothers-in-law. They also have to be in charge of caring for the children on a daily basis. The woman has the responsibility for making **puja** (worship) happen in the home, and is expected to make sure that the house is well managed, clean and comfortable.

Men should be faithful to their wives and should work as hard as they can to support family members. If a man chooses to do a household chore, that is his choice – he does not have to do them. A son has particular roles and duties to carry out at his father's funeral.

Many Hindus look at the story of the god Rama and his consort Sita as an ultimate example of the way married couples should be. Sita gave up her life of comfort in a palace to live with Rama in the forest. She was a modest person and loyal to her husband. Rama too was a good role model, as he was brave and protected Sita when they had difficulties.

FOR DEBATE

What do you think about the list of items Hindus want to be blessed in a marriage? Are there other things that you think should be on the list? Do you think some items should not be there?

FOR DEBATE

How should men and women behave in a family?

RESEARCH NOTE

Find out more about the story of Rama and Sita.

ACTIVITIES

- 'Arranged marriages are totally wrong in the 21st century.' How might a religious Hindu answer this? What do you think? Remember to show that you have thought about the idea from more than one angle.
- Hindus believe that marriages should be for life. Do you think that this is realistic? Explain why you have come to your conclusion.

Hinduism:
Religion and human relationships 2

The next two pages will help you to:

- explain the attitudes Hindus have towards sex, contraception, divorce and Civil Partnerships
- evaluate how Hindu beliefs influence their actions in these areas.

For the vast majority of Hindus, sex is seen as both a pleasure and a responsibility.

What is sex for?

'What is sex for?' might sound like a silly question, but sex has an important role within Hinduism. Sensual pleasure is called **kama** and is one of the four purushartas – the basics of life. However, this needs to be balanced with a spirit of self-control. For the vast majority of Hindus, sex should only take place in the context of marriage. The Hindu book the *Kama Sutra* explains in detail how relationships should develop. This book is still read today, by Hindus and non-Hindus alike.

Most Hindus try to discourage sex before marriage. Traditionally, young people were supposed to be students, so did not marry so that they could concentrate on that role. Parents will try to supervise their children so that they behave in a way that does not dishonour their family. It is especially important that girls behave in a restrained way; if they do not, they may risk not being married, which is seen by many Hindus as their ultimate calling.

AO1+AO2 skills **ACTIVITIES**

What issues would a couple have to think through before planning to have a child?

Working in a pair, try to think of five issues that would need to be thought about and then try to grade them in the order of importance.

Civil Partnerships

Many Hindus accept that some people are attracted to members of the same sex. However, rather than condemning these relationships, they are not discussed within Hinduism. Hindu literature does not refer to homosexuality. Civil Partnerships are not welcomed, especially because their families will not see a new generation of children being born to keep their name alive.

When is it right to have children?

Contraception has only been a possibility in the last few decades. Many Hindu **sacred** texts encourage families to be as large as possible and not to limit the family in any way. Being childless is much more worrying for many Hindus than having too many children.

However, as access to methods of contraception has increased, many Hindus have begun to think through the issue. A large family was necessary when there was not a health service to care for you, but now, with much better care available, the need for having a large family has diminished.

India has a rapidly growing population. Since the 1970s, its governments have tried to encourage contraception, hoping that people would limit their families to two or three children. However, it is difficult to influence those who, while desperate to have a son, find themselves with only daughters.

What if a marriage seems to die?

Marriages can be tough. Hindu marriages, which tend to be arranged, accept that there will be times when the husband and wife find things difficult. As many couples have not really got to know each other until after they have married, they expect there to be problems – this contrasts with marriages in the West, where people might have lived with each other or known each other for a long period before actually getting married.

If the couple feel that the marriage should end, it will affect two families. Although the joining of hands at the ceremony should be a sign that they can never be parted, in reality **divorce** and separation do happen. There is a large social disgrace in divorce, so many couples will stay together even if their relationship is very bad. Lower caste Hindus may find that they are able to get divorces with greater ease than higher caste Hindus.

Many methods of contraception are now available.

FOR DEBATE

'You have a duty to limit the number of children you have to make sure that everyone can be fed.' What do you think?

AO1+AO2 skills ACTIVITIES

- 'Hindu society is wrong to try to dissuade people from divorce.' What do you think? Give reasons for your answers, showing that you have thought about it from more than one point of view. Make sure that you refer to Hindu teaching in your answers.

- Do you think that the Indian government should have tried to encourage contraception?

- Do you think that married couples with young children should stay together until their children are young adults? Give reasons for your answer.

Islam:
Religion and human relationships 1

Roles of men and women

According to Muslim teaching, men and women are created equal and Allah will judge them according to the way in which they have lived. However, in a traditional family, the man goes out to work and the woman's role is to care for the home and the children.

Islam teaches that men should respect and value women as people, not for their bodies, so many Muslim women keep themselves covered in public.

Some Muslim men and women may be shocked by the way in which girls and women in particular dress in Western society. Islam often sees this as the exploitation of women by men and the media. However, some Muslims would be equally shocked by the clothing of some Muslims in Muslim dominated countries.

At the time of Muhammad ﷺ, women, particularly widows, were often treated badly. He changed this so that now women have the right to own property, study, **divorce**, inherit wealth (although only half of what a male relative can inherit), run a business and take part in politics, and are not responsible for their male relatives.

Sexual relationships

Muslims have strict rules about sexual relationships, which are found in the Qur'an and the Sunnah/Hadith. All sexual relationships are to take place within family life.

The Qur'an states what Allah expects within **marriage**.

> **Surah 30:20–21**
>
> *And among His Signs is this, that He created for you mates from among yourselves, that ye may dwell in tranquillity with them, and He has put love and mercy between your (hearts): verily in that are Signs for those who reflect.*

> **Surah 2:187**
>
> *Permitted to you, on the night of the fasts, is the approach to your wives. They are your garments and ye are their garments.*

The second quote is from the rules concerning the fast of Sawm during Ramadan.

The next two pages will help you to:

- develop your understanding of Muslim teachings about the roles of men and women
- explore Muslim attitudes towards sexual relationships
- investigate Muslim ideas about Civil Partnerships.

AO1 skills **ACTIVITIES**

Think/pair/share
What are the conventional ideas about how a man and woman should behave in a relationship? List as many as you can.

> **Surah 33:59**
>
> *O Prophet! Tell thy wives and daughters, and the believing women, that they should cast their outer garments over their persons (when abroad): that is most convenient, that they should be known (as such) and not molested. And Allah is Oft-Forgiving, Most Merciful.*

Muhammad's ﷺ teachings mean that Muslim women can now be involved in business.

As in many religions, Islamic society is based on the family.

Many Muslims live in extended families.

Arranged marriages are allowed within Islam; forced marriage is not.

Men are warned that they should be very careful about the woman they decide to marry.

In Islam, marriage is the joining of two families as well as of bride and groom. Many Muslims live in extended families with other relatives, so it is common for the bride to move into the home of the groom's family.

Sexual intercourse is seen as an act of worship. It is a means of having children, as well as fulfilling the emotional and physical needs of both husband and wife. Within a marriage, the husband and wife are responsible for fulfilling the sexual needs of each other.

Hadith

A woman is taken in marriage for three reasons; for her beauty, for family connections or the lure of wealth. Choose the one with faith and you will have success.

Islam realises that both men and women can be tempted to have sexual relationships outside of a marriage, so men are not allowed to be alone with women except their wives and those to whom they cannot get married.

Hadith

Let no man be in privacy with a woman who he is not married to, or Satan will be the third.

In Islam, adultery is a serious crime, and has a specific punishment.

Surah 24:2

The woman and the man guilty of adultery or fornication – flog each of them with a hundred stripes: let not compassion move you in their case, in a matter prescribed by Allah, if ye believe in Allah and the Last Day: and let a party of the Believers witness their punishment.

AO2 skills **ACTIVITIES**

- Do you think it is right for a religion to have rules about how people should behave sexually?
- Consider the Muslim attitude towards Civil Partnerships. How many different supported opinions can you think of in favour of and against Civil Partnerships?

Civil Partnerships

Civil Partnerships are a relatively new way in which same-sex couples can publicly acknowledge their relationship and get protection from the law, with the same status as the civil ceremonies heterosexual couples have.

All homosexual relationships are forbidden in Islam because they are seen as unnatural. In practice, this prohibition is often ignored, though some Muslim lawyers have argued that these activities should incur the death penalty because they are impure.

Surah 26:165–166

Of all the creatures in the world, will ye approach males, And leave those whom Allah has created for you to be your mates? Nay, ye are a people transgressing (all limits)!

Islam:
Religion and human relationships 2

The next two pages will help you to:

- understand Muslim attitudes towards marriage and divorce
- analyse the importance of the Muslim marriage ceremony.

Marriage

Muslim couples are not allowed to 'go out' together; often the couple are only allowed to meet when members of their families are present. Although these marriages are sometimes 'arranged' by families, a forced marriage would be completely invalid; the couple must voluntarily agree to the marriage.

The Qur'an permits Muslims to have up to four wives, but the man must ensure that each wife is treated equally. Although Muhammad ﷺ had many wives, many Muslims today have only one wife because of the laws of the country in which they live, or because they choose to do so.

A Muslim man is permitted to marry a Jew or a Christian, but a Muslim woman may only marry a Muslim man.

At Muslim weddings it is traditional for the bride to wear red.

The Muslim marriage ceremony

A Muslim marriage ceremony can take place at home or in the mosque. The couple agree to the marriage in the presence of two witnesses. There is a declaration made to the witnesses that the couple are marrying of their own free will.

Although there are few formal parts to a Muslim marriage ceremony, the couple may make promises that they see their marriage as an act of submission to the will of Allah.

The imam and the guests say prayers for the couple. The **Aqd Nikah** or marriage contract is read out, and the couple sign three copies. The contract shows their agreement to the marriage and also the **mahr** (dowry) that the groom gives to the bride, which remains hers for life. The wedding may conclude with a feast called a walimah.

Sometimes the bride does not attend the ceremony and is represented by an agent and witnesses who have heard her agree to the marriage three times.

Wedding reading from the Qur'an

Surah 4:1

'O mankind! Reverence your Guardian-Lord, who created you from a single Person, created, of like nature, his mate, and from them twain scattered (like seeds) countless men and women – reverence Allah, through Whom ye demand your mutual (rights), and (reverence) the wombs (that bore you): for Allah ever watches over you.'

AO1+AO2 skills ACTIVITIES

Explain the possible advantages and disadvantages of a formal marriage contract.

Divorce

As in all religions, Muslim marriage is intended to be permanent and divorce is never welcomed. However, Muslims realise that sometimes marriages break down and the marriage contract can be ended, particularly if continuing would bring misery to the couple and their children.

The signing of the Aqd Nikah.

> ### Surah 4:128
>
> *If a wife fears cruelty or desertion on her husband's part, there is no blame on them if they arrange an amicable settlement between themselves; and such settlement is best; even though men's souls are swayed by greed. But if ye do good and practise self-restraint, Allah is well-acquainted with all that ye do.*

Before divorcing a wife, a man must ensure that she is not pregnant. There is a three-month period called **iddah** when reconciliation attempts are made and which ensures that the women is not pregnant. After this time the divorce can take place. Men and women can remarry each other twice but, if they divorce a third time, they can only remarry if the woman has been married and divorced from someone else in the meantime.

A woman can end her relationship with her husband by returning her mahr (dowry). She can divorce her husband because of the way she has been treated or by reaching an agreement (khul) with him.

AO1+AO2 skills   ACTIVITIES

'Before any divorce, it is essential to know whether the wife is pregnant.' Discuss. Remember to support your opinion with arguments.

Contraception

According to Islam, Allah created the world and everything it contains, so all life is a special gift. The birth of a child does not happen by mistake, as it is a gift of life from Allah.

Given this teaching, it is not surprising that **contraception** is not a popular choice in Islam. However, in 1971 the Conference on Islam and Family Planning said that safe and legal contraception could be permitted where:

- there was a threat to the mother's health
- the use of contraception would help a woman who already had children
- there was a chance of the child being born with mental or physical deformities
- the family did not have the money to raise a child.

> ### Surah 42:49–50
>
> *To Allah belongs the dominion of the heavens and the earth. He creates what He wills (and plans). He bestows (children) male or female according to His Will (and Plan),*
> *Or He bestows both males and females, and He leaves barren whom He will: for He is full of Knowledge and Power.*

The preferred method of contraception is the 'rhythm method', where intercourse only takes place when the woman is least fertile. However, artificial methods such as condoms can also be used. Permanent treatments such as sterilisation are generally not permitted.

AO1+AO2 skills   ACTIVITIES

- 'Contraception is always wrong because it interferes with the plans of Allah.' Discuss. Remember to give your own opinion as well as Muslim views.
- Prepare a guide for a young Muslim woman, explaining what is expected of her within a marriage.

Judaism:
Religion and human relationships 1

The next two pages will help you to:

- explain the roles of men and women within a Jewish family
- explore Jewish views on sexual relationships including same-sex relationships.

Sexual relationships

For sexual relationships, Jews have strict rules and regulations, which are found in the Torah and Talmud.

However, Judaism does have a natural and open approach to matters of sexuality. It recognises that sex plays an important part in human relationships and the strength of sexual desires between people. It believes that these desires must be carefully controlled and can only properly be expressed within a **marriage**.

Unlike some other religions, Judaism does not believe that **procreation** is the only purpose of sexual activity: it is a means by which people can show their love to one another, even when they are too old to have children.

Adultery

Adultery is forbidden by the seventh commandment – 'You shall not commit adultery' (Exodus 20:13) – which is strictly observed within Judaism. Although some of the early Jewish leaders in the Bible had more than one wife, this is no longer permitted.

The Jewish view of the importance of marriage is reflected in the fact that there is no teaching of celibacy (living without sex) in Judaism. Jews believe that G-d intended men and women to live together and take part in sexual activity, both to create children and for enjoyment – so choosing to be celibate would be viewed as abnormal.

Purity laws

Within a Jewish marriage, sex is regulated by the laws of **niddah**, or purity laws. These mean that, during a woman's monthly menstruation, she is not permitted to have any sexual contact with her husband. In some families, this is extended to no physical contact at all.

> **Leviticus 18:19**
>
> *Do not come near a woman during her period of uncleanness to uncover her nakedness.*

AO1+AO2 skills ACTIVITIES

Think/pair/share
Think about the ideal relationship between a man and a woman. With a partner, draw up a list of the ways in which the man and woman should behave – should these be different? Share your ideas with another pair, and pick the five most important to share with the class.

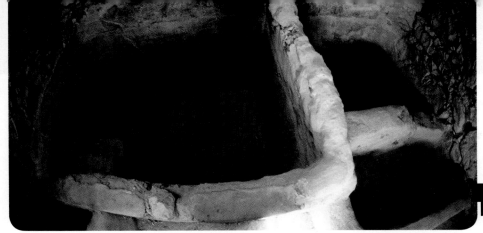

After the menstrual period is over, the women goes to a **mikveh**. The mikveh is a pool of water, part of which must be fresh, i.e. not tap water. Before the bath, the woman bathes or showers normally and removes all make-up, nail polish and hair preparations. She then walks through to the mikveh where, naked, she immerses herself three times in the pool, each time saying this blessing:

> *Blessed are you, Lord our G-d, King of the Universe, who commands us concerning the use of the mikveh.*

After this, she can return to normal sexual relationships with her husband until the beginning of her next period.

> **Talmud**
> *A wife returning from the mikveh is as fresh to her husband as on their wedding day.*

The rules of niddah are followed by most Orthodox Jews, but some progressive Jews feel that they are now out of date.

Civil Partnerships

Civil Partnerships are a relatively new way in which same-sex couples, whether male or female, can publicly acknowledge their relationship and give it legal status. Although they have been described as 'gay weddings', Civil Partnerships have the same status as the civil ceremonies that heterosexual couples have.

Male homosexual activity is forbidden within Orthodox Jewish tradition. There is no mention of **lesbianism** in the Torah, but the Talmud forbids it. Many Jews believe that homosexuality is a condition brought about by circumstances and that people can be helped out of it. However, in recent years, many progressive Jewish communities have welcomed homosexuals and homosexual couples, and there are a number of gay Rabbis, particularly in the USA.

> **Leviticus 18:22**
> *Do not lie with a male as one lies with a woman; it is an abhorrence.*

 **ACTIVITIES**

In small groups, think about the idea of using the mikveh. Do you think that this is a positive or negative way to approach women? Imagine how a married Jewish woman might think that this is an important aspect of her religious life.

 FOR DEBATE

- Do you think it is right for religions to have rules about how people should behave sexually?
- Does the fact that Jews belonging to different communities interpret these rules differently mean that they are wrong or that the laws are wrong?

Judaism:
Religion and human relationships 2
Jewish marriage

The next two pages will help you to:

- explore Jewish views on marriage, divorce and remarriage
- investigate Jewish views on contraception.

Talmud

A man without a woman is doomed to an existence without joy, without blessing, without experiencing life's true goodness, without Torah, without protection and without peace.

Ideas about Jewish **marriage** and its importance are found at the beginning of the Torah.

Genesis 2:24

Hence a man leaves his father and mother and clings to his wife, so that they become one flesh.

This is later explained in the Midrash.

G-d created the first human being half male, half female. He then separated the two parts to form a man and a woman.

Maimonides, a great Jewish teacher, said:

66 *Through the sanctification of marriage, a husband and wife become the closest of relatives.* **99**

In the past, many Jewish marriages were arranged and the couple were introduced by a shadchan or matchmaker. Today, this practice has stopped and young Jews meet each other in the same way as most other people. The only problem is that many Jews fall in love with non-Jews, which can lead to the idea of 'marrying out' – something many Jews are opposed to.

Deeply Orthodox Jews may disown their child if they marry out and may say the Kaddish (the prayer said at funerals), showing that to them that child is dead:

Deuteronomy 7:3–4

You shall not intermarry with them: do not give your daughters to their sons or take their daughters for your sons. For they will turn your children away from Me to worship other gods, and the Lord's anger will blaze forth against you and He will promptly wipe you out.

 **ACTIVITIES**

Look at the sacred text. What do you feel about this idea of human relationships? Discuss in pairs, then as a class.

 **RESEARCH NOTE**

Who was Maimonides and why is he important?

 FOR DEBATE

A Jewish proverb states that love comes after marriage not before. How far do you agree with that statement?

The wedding ceremony

A Jewish wedding may take place anywhere provided that the bride and groom stand under a huppah (wedding canopy), which represents their new home together.

The ketubah, or wedding contract, is an important part of the ceremony, in which the groom promises to look after his wife. The ketubah is often a beautifully decorated document, which is hung over the bed in the new couple's home. In progressive communities, the ketubah is signed by both the bride and the groom.

The actual wedding ceremony is very short. The man makes a vow to the woman as he gives her a ring, saying: 'Behold, you are consecrated to me by means of this ring, according to the rituals of Moses and Israel.' After this, the Sheva Berachos (Seven Blessings) are said over a glass of wine.

At the end of the ceremony the groom smashes a glass under his foot. No one knows why this is done: some say that it shows that marriage can be fragile, while others believe that it represents the destruction of the Jerusalem Temple in 70 CE, and reminds people that life is not perfect.

Divorce for Jews

Jews believe that marriage is intended to be for life. However, they do accept that **divorce** is sometimes inevitable. If this is the case, the man must issue his wife with a 'get' – a divorce document from a **Beth Din** (Rabbinical Court).

> **Deuteronomy 24:1**
>
> *A man takes a wife and possesses her. She fails to please him because he finds something obnoxious about her, and he writes her a bill of divorcement, hands it to her, and sends her away from his house.*

The divorce cannot take place for three months to ensure that the woman is not pregnant.

If a get is not issued, neither the man nor the woman can remarry in a synagogue. Because a man can refuse to give his wife a get, some progressive communities now allow the woman to issue one.

Contraception

Within a Jewish marriage, sexual relationships are seen as a husband's duty and a woman's right. In Genesis, Jews are told: 'Be fertile and increase, fill the earth' (Genesis 1:28). Later this idea is found in the book of Isaiah.

Because of these teachings, the use of **contraception** is not encouraged within Judaism. Contraception is not allowed when people are single or when they simply do not want a child – this would be seen as interfering with G-d's plan. However, any restriction on their use is lifted if a woman's life is seen as being at risk, either physically or psychologically, if she were to become pregnant.

If contraceptives are used, women should take them so that intercourse remains as natural as possible. Sterilisation and vasectomies are not permitted because they are seen as mutilating the body that G-d created.

AO1 skills **ACTIVITIES**

Look up the Sheva Berachos and try to explain each one in your own words. What are they about?

A man applying to a Beth Din for a get.

> **Isaiah 45:18**
>
> *For thus said the Lord,*
> *The Creator of heaven who alone is G-d,*
> *Who formed the earth and made it,*
> *Who alone established it.*
> *He did not create it a waste,*
> *But formed it for habitation:*
> *I am the Lord, and there is none else.*

AO2 skills **ACTIVITIES**

Do you think a religion has the right to say how men and women should live their lives in their own home? Consider both sides of the argument.

Sikhism:
Religion and human relationships 1

Are men and women equal?

The next two pages will help you to:

- develop your knowledge and understanding of Sikh teachings about the roles of men and women
- develop your understanding of the Sikh attitude to sexual relationships and contraception.

In many families traditional roles for men and women have changed.

AO1+AO2 skills ACTIVITIES

- What do you understand by the term 'equality'?
- Who do you think has responsibility for housework – men or women? Explain your answer.

Gender **equality** refers to the opinion that both men and women have equal responsibilities. This also means that the traditional image of a male being the main earner, while the woman stays at home, is challenged in modern-day society.

As in any other modern society, Sikh women are career-minded and go to work. The stage of a householder and having children is emphasised greatly in Sikh teachings; many Sikh women do have children, but these days many pursue a career too. They may look for outside childcare such as babysitters and nurseries; alternatively, as many Sikhs live in extended families, where grandparents, uncles and aunts live together, they may have the advantage of relatives who can help out with such matters.

AO1+AO2 skills ACTIVITIES

Traditionally, a mother's nurturing of a baby is seen as vital for it to develop particular skills. In pairs, list the advantages and disadvantages for a mother returning to work shortly after having a baby.

The Sikh Gurus actively encouraged the education of girls – something that Sikh parents continue to the present day. Very few Sikh girls will leave school without any qualifications, and many go on to studying at college and university.

> **Guru Granth Sahib Ji, page 473**
>
> *From a woman, a woman is born. Without a woman, there can be none.*
> *Nanak, only the one True Lord, is without a woman.*
> *The mouth which ever praises the Lord, is fortunate, rosy and beautiful.*
> *Nanak, those faces shall be bright in the court of that True Lord.*

Sikh women in the gurdwara

In promoting gender equality, there are no teachings in Sikhism that deny women the right to be fully in charge of services in the gurdwara (the Sikh place of worship). However, it is generally men who tend to be in charge of the service, while women take on responsibility for the food. Food plays a very important part in Sikh worship, so lots of work constantly needs to be done in the kitchen and food hall of the gurdwara.

Importantly, there is no priesthood in Sikhism: any person (male or female) who is learned in the scriptures can lead the service. Since the stage of householder is an important aspect of Sikh life, the role of the mother is seen as very important indeed.

Sexual relationships and contraception in Sikhism

Sex other than with one's spouse is strictly forbidden in Sikhism. There is no insistence on celibacy since the creation of children and living the life of a householder are encouraged. Sex is seen as a part of a happy married life between husband and wife. Homosexual sex is not discussed in the Sikh scriptures.

There are different views on **contraception** amongst Sikhs. No holy scripture deals with it, nor does the Rehat Maryada. Although children within a **marriage** are encouraged, offering the children a decent lifestyle is also valued – the couple should be able to provide both financially and socially for their offspring. In practice, most Sikh couples have no objection to using contraception such as the pill or condoms.

ACTIVITIES

Think/pair/share
Guru Nanak was revolutionary for his time and taught that men and women are equal in all respects, both socially and religiously. In the text, what do you think Guru Nanak Dev Ji is indicating about the position of women in society? Share your answers with a partner. Now share your responses with the rest of the class.

RESEARCH NOTE

The role and limitations on menstruating women provide interesting insights into the role of women on a practical level. Research the works of Dr Nikky-Guninder Kaur Singh and Dr Opinderjit Kaur Takhar to get an insight into the role of women on a practical level in Sikhism.

ACTIVITIES

Produce an informative pamphlet for couples visiting the local family planning centre. Draw out the risks of promiscuity and the advantages of sex within a marriage or stable relationship. Make sure you give readers an ample amount of information to make their choices about contraception and which methods to use.

Sikhism:
Religion and human relationships 2

The next two pages will help you to:

- develop your understanding of Sikh attitudes towards marriage
- examine the Sikh marriage ceremony
- analyse the Sikh view of divorce.

The bride and groom at a Sikh wedding standing in front of the Guru Granth Sahib Ji.

Is marriage important for Sikhs?

Marriage is regarded as a very important stage of life in Sikhism – Guru Nanak Dev Ji strongly rejected celibacy. All Sikhs are encouraged to marry, and it would be quite unusual to hear of an unmarried elderly male or female.

Marriages in Sikhism are to be performed endogamously – people marry another member of the same group. Sikhs have a **caste** system in which people are born into the caste of their ancestors. Traditionally the marriage will be arranged between two people of the same caste, but with different surnames.

There are no forced marriages in Sikhism. In modern society, men and women are introduced to each other and given a choice as to whether they wish to meet again. Perhaps the term 'assisted marriage'

AO2 skills ACTIVITIES

'Marriage is old-fashioned and out of date.' Have a class debate on the statement, in two groups: one agreeing with the statement, one disagreeing. One member of the class needs to be the judge and make notes on the board under these headings:

- Marriage is old-fashioned and out of date.
- Marriage is a special bond and is still very cool.

The group with the strongest argument wins. Copy the notes from the board into your book.

is more appropriate than 'arranged marriage'. Many Sikhs also find their own partners and are free to marry as long as they belong to the same caste.

Child marriages are strictly forbidden in Sikhism.

The marriage ceremony

Most Sikhs follow the Anand Karaj ceremony or 'ceremony of bliss', passed in 1909 CE (before this, Sikhs got married according to Hindu marriage ceremonies). In the ceremony, the couple walk clockwise around the Guru Granth Sahib Ji four times, in time with the four stanzas of the lavan hymn composed by Guru Ram Das Ji (the fourth Sikh Guru) for his own daughter's wedding. The Sikh wedding service emphasises the union of two souls, intended to be a lifelong, happy union in which the creation of offspring is encouraged.

There are no overt teachings about same-sex marriages in Sikhism, and there is no Sikh ceremony at present to cater for homosexual marriages. Though traditionally Sikhs are not comfortable with the issue of homosexuality, the attitudes of the younger generation can be quite different to those of their parents of grandparents. This is largely due to Western education and the principle of freedom of speech.

Does divorce devalue the sanctity of a Sikh marriage?

Although marriage is intended to be a lifelong **commitment**, **divorce** is allowed where the couple cannot settle their disagreements (note, however, that the Sikh Guide for Khalsa Sikhs, the Rehat Maryada, does not approve of divorce). The divorcee is allowed to remarry in the gurdwara. The Sikh Gurus were also in favour of widow remarriage.

The influence of Western society means that divorce is now readily acceptable in Sikhism. This is in sharp contrast to traditional attitudes, where the preservation of the family's honour (izzat) was a main consideration and divorce was largely frowned upon.

 **ACTIVITIES**

What is your view of two people of different faiths getting married? Explain your answer. How would the couple resolve on which religious ceremony they would have?

 **ACTIVITIES**

Bearing in mind the special union of two souls during a Sikh marriage, why do you think that traditionally divorce is frowned upon in Sikhism?

 **ACTIVITIES**

In pairs, research and produce a report to be submitted to the Gender Equality Council about the equality of men and women in Sikhism. The only published material you can use is the *Guru Granth Sahib Ji*. How are you going to conduct your research sensitively, without causing offence to any member of the community? How will you know that the information you are receiving is an accurate representation of the community as a whole?

 GradeStudio

AO1

QUESTION

Explain how a Sikh marriage service might guide a couple in their married life. **[6 marks]**

You could build an answer like this:

Level 1

First, let the examiner know that you are aware of what the question is about. For example, 'Marriage is a very important institution in Sikhism. The Anand Karaj ceremony lays out very clearly the expectations from the couple.'

Level 2

Next, look at in detail each of the four stanzas of the lavan hymn and outline the duties of the couple as husband and wife. You could also highlight the implications that Anand Karaj is translated as the 'Ceremony of Bliss', and is therefore a guide to a harmonious relationship.

Level 3

Finally, your answer could look at the meaning behind other parts of the marriage service such as the emotional pala ceremony and the milni ceremony as promoting the union of two families and the traditional binding of man and wife. You could also look at the importance of children.

Welcome to the Grade Studio

Grade Studio is here to help you improve your grades by working through typical questions you might find on an examination paper. You will see different answers to the questions, showing you how you can improve each answer to get a better grade.

How the grades work: OCR questions in Spec B always consist of five parts, **a–e**. Parts **a–c** test factual recall only (AO1 skill). Part **d** is always a six-mark question testing understanding (AO1), and part **e** is always a 12-mark question testing evaluation and personal response (AO2 skills).

For parts **a–c**, you just need to revise the material for the Topic and make sure that you know it thoroughly – Grade Studio cannot help you with this!

However, for parts **d** and **e** you need to structure your answers to show your skills – and this is where you can use the Grade Studio to help you improve your answers.

Examiners use levels to measure the responses (these are marked in the answers below). You can find a full description of the levels examiners will use to mark your answers on pages x and xi.

> **AO1 Skills**
> Describe, explain and analyse, using knowledge and understanding of the specification content.
>
> **AO2 Skills**
> Use evidence and reasoned argument to express and evaluate personal responses, informed insights and differing viewpoints.

AO1

Question

Explain how Christian beliefs are reflected in a Christian marriage ceremony. **[6 marks]**

Student's answer

A Christian wedding ceremony reflects belief because the bride wears white, which shows that she is still a virgin. People also make vows to each other to say that they will always stay together and look after each other. If someone broke these vows, they might get divorced.

Examiner's comment

The candidate has given a satisfactory answer to the question. There are two relevant points but only one of them, the vows, has any explanation. The answer needs to give more information and examples in order to reach Level 3. The candidate could also use more technical terms from the specification to show the breadth of their knowledge and understanding.

Student's improved answer

A Christian wedding ceremony reflects belief because the bride wears white, which shows that she is still a virgin. People also make vows to each other to say that they will always stay together and look after each other. If someone broke these vows they might get divorced. The major importance of the vows is that they are made before God, so if people break them, they are breaking a promise to God.

Examiner's comment

This is now a good answer to the question. The candidate has shown a clear understanding of the question. There is good description and explanation of a variety of different ways in which the service reflects Christian beliefs. The candidate has shown some analysis in dealing with the vows. The information is presented clearly and there is good use of technical terms.

Student's improved answer (cont.)

The ring is also an important part of the service because it symbolises the unity of the two people being married and also the unity of God and God's love. It is also important that in the service the priest or minister says that one of the purposes of marriage is for the couple to have children and bring them up as Christians.

AO2

Question

'Divorce is wrong.' Discuss this statement. You should include different, supported points of view and a personal viewpoint. You must refer to Christianity in your answer.   [12 marks]

Student's answer

Divorce is always wrong for Christians because they promise to stay together until 'death do us part'. Some Christians might also say that if people do get divorced, they are breaking a promise they made to God as well as to each other.

Examiner's comment

The candidate has given a limited answer to the question. There are two relevant points but they both address the same issue and neither is expanded very far. In order to reach Level 4, the candidate needs to give alternative viewpoints and to include a personal response.

Student's improved answer

Divorce is always wrong for Christians because they promise to stay together until 'death do us part'. Some Christians might also say that if people do get divorced, they are breaking a promise they made to God as well as to each other.

On the other hand, some Christians may believe that, if a husband and wife are very unhappy together, they should consider a divorce rather than staying together and being miserable. This can also possibly have a bad effect on their children. Christians will always try to help a couple to stay together, but there are circumstances in which this is not possible.

My personal opinion is that sometimes people are just not suited to one another and that they are better off getting a divorce and having the opportunity to start their life again. However, I do think that it is important that the needs of any children are taken into account when a divorce takes place.

Examiner's comment

This is now a good answer to the question. The candidate has shown a clear understanding of the question and has presented a range of views supported by evidence and argument. The answer explains Christian views, amongst others, and includes a personal viewpoint, which is also supported.

These specimen answers provide an outline of how you could construct your response. Space does not allow us to give a full response. The examiner will be looking for more detail in your actual exam responses.

These examples only use Christianity but you could use the Grade Studio to apply to any of the religions you are studying and the structure of the answers would work in the same way.

Topic 2: Religion and medical ethics

The Big Picture

In this Topic, you will be addressing religious beliefs and teachings about:

- attitudes to abortion
- attitudes to fertility treatment
- attitudes to euthanasia and suicide
- using animals in medical research.

What?

You will:

- develop your knowledge of religious beliefs and teachings about abortion, fertility treatment, euthanasia, suicide and using animals in medical research
- explain the beliefs and different attitudes in light of religious teachings and analyse the reasons for these attitudes
- evaluate how these beliefs and teachings affect a religious person by using evidence and create informed insights into how religions approach medical ethics.

Why?

Because:

- you will have a better insight into how you and people with different beliefs view human life
- this will impact on how you approach and make decisions about medical ethics in your own life
- you will be able to assess how you think animals should be used to benefit humans.

How?

By:

- interpreting the key teachings involved in order to understand the different attitudes towards medical ethics
- examining these teachings and beliefs in order to understand the decisions a believer may have to make throughout their life
- relating these religious teachings to your own beliefs about the value of life, recognising similarities and differences between your own experiences and those of the religions studied.

Blessed Mother Teresa of Calcutta with a young baby.

GET STARTED

WANTED

The Sunflower Hospice is looking for a volunteer to visit and to help to support patients.

Do you have the qualities to help?

If so, we would like to hear from you.

What kind of person would you need to be to work at the Sunflower Hospice?

Could you do it? If not, why not?

Religion and medical ethics

Medical ethics is about making decisions regarding what is right and wrong in matters of health care and medicine more broadly. People from all religious backgrounds have strong views about medical ethics based on their beliefs. Most religions teach that life is given by God and is **sacred**, or holy.

Attitudes to abortion and the reasons for them

- Some Buddhists believe **abortion** is not acceptable, especially as they believe in preventing **dukkha**, but others think it depends on individual circumstances and that compassion should be shown.
- Christians have different views about abortion. The Roman Catholic Church forbids it under any circumstances, except for the occasion known as 'double effect' – where it would be a foreseen side-effect of doing something morally good. Christians from other churches may support this view using the Bible as evidence, but others believe abortion is permissible under certain circumstances.
- Many Hindus do not agree with abortion because it contradicts teaching about **ahimsa** and stops the **atman** (soul) from being reborn into a new life.
- Islam does not permit abortion except where doctors consider the pregnancy will result in the mother's death.
- Jews believe that the foetus does not become a person until the moment of birth, so abortion is not murder. It is permitted if the mother's life is at risk or the pregnancy is the result of rape.
- Sikhs forbid abortion because they believe it interferes with the creative work of God, who is present in every being.

Responses to issues raised by fertility treatment and cloning

- Buddhists believe that **sila** should be based on doing good rather than harm, so treatment that helps people to have children is acceptable.

Are humans playing at 'being God' when they intervene in matters of life and death?

- Christians have different views about fertility treatment. Some believe that helping people to start a new life is a good and loving way to act; others think it is going against the will of God.
- Hindus believe that having children is very important. Most Hindus agree with fertility treatment because it enables people to have children.
- Some Muslims think people should accept that it is the will of Allah if they cannot have children. Others think some fertility treatments such as **IVF** are acceptable.
- Jews see children as a great blessing from G-d and believe that some fertility treatments are acceptable: **AIH** is always acceptable, while **AID** is sometimes permitted.
- For Sikhs, the family is very important and some fertility treatments are approved.

KNOWLEDGE AND UNDERSTANDING
Explain the belief that all life is sacred. How does this belief influence the views of Christians and followers of any other religion you have studied when they have to make decisions about abortion and euthanasia?

ANALYSIS AND EVALUATION
What factors do you believe should govern decisions about rights to life?

Attitudes to euthanasia and suicide and reasons for them

- Buddhists have no shared view on these issues, however, all Buddhists will try and cause the minimum amount of suffering for all involved.
- Many Christian **denominations** think **euthanasia** and **suicide** are wrong because they believe that God gave the gift of life, so only God can take it away.
- Hindus may disagree with euthanasia because they believe it is always wrong to take a life. They do not agree with suicide unless the person is sacrificing their life for others.
- Muslims do not agree with euthanasia or suicide because only Allah can decide when someone should die. Euthanasia and suicide are **zalim**.
- Jews believe all life is sacred, so suicide is a sin. They do not agree with euthanasia because only G-d can decide when someone should die.
- Sikhs have great respect for life as a gift from God. Sikhs believe the timing of birth and death should be left to God and most are against euthanasia and suicide.

Beliefs about use of animals in medical research

- Some Buddhists would object to all use of animals in medical research, however, other Buddhists might allow the use of animals in medical research if such use will reduce dukkha (suffering).
- Many Christians support the humane use of animals in medical research because it can help prevent human suffering.
- Most Hindus believe animals are as important as humans. Hurting or destroying animals is against ahimsa, bringing bad **karma** in the next life. Some Hindus support animal testing for medical research only if there is no alternative.
- Muslims believe all life belongs to Allah, but humans are more important than animals and experiments on animals can be done to help humans. Muhammad ﷺ showed respect for animals. Shari'ah gives legal rights to animals.
- Jews believe G-d gave humans power over all animals. Animals must be treated with respect and without cruelty. Animals may be used for necessary scientific experiments as long as they suffer as little as possible.
- Sikhs believe in living in harmony with all creation and are divided about this question.

FOR INTEREST Find out about the case of conjoined twins Jodie and Mary at the BBC website. What religious arguments were put forward to support and oppose their separation? What do you think? Consider how a Buddhist might have responded to this case.

Buddhism:
Religion and medical ethics 1

The next two pages will help you to:

- explore Buddhist attitudes to abortion
- explore Buddhist attitudes to euthanasia and suicide.

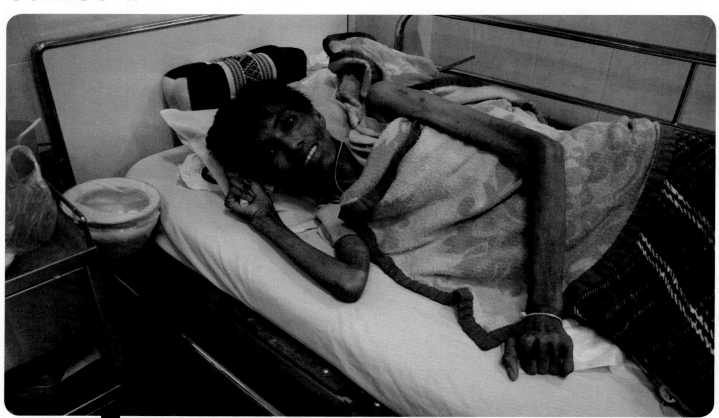

How far should we go to prevent suffering like this?

Preventing dukkha

One of the primary aims of Buddhism is to prevent **dukkha**, loosely translated as suffering or unsatisfactoriness. This aim of preventing dukkha can be seen in the first precept, which is to prevent harm to others.

The problem we have applying this teaching to issues such as **abortion**, **euthanasia**, **cloning** and medical research is that often there is no option available that completely eliminates harm. Buddhists are then forced to assess and judge which action causes the most harm, or the worst type of harm. There are no agreed ways in which to assess these harms, so Buddhists have reached different conclusions about how to respond.

ACTIVITIES

Think/pair/share
Look at the image and think about what action you would be prepared to take to prevent suffering like this.

With a partner, discuss whether your views are similar or different and why. Consider whether other people might have other views.

Be prepared to explain to the class why you think people have different views about what we can or should do to prevent suffering.

Buddhist attitudes to abortion

Buddhist attitudes to abortion are often influenced by the culture in which they originate. As a result, some Buddhists are less accepting of abortion than others. Buddhists see abortion as a serious act which becomes more serious with the age of the embryo. This is based on the Buddhist ideal that destroying a more developed being generates greater consequences. Some Buddhists claim that any abortion breaks the first precept since it harms the unborn foetus. They therefore feel that abortion is not acceptable. Other Buddhists agree that abortion breaks the first precept, but feel that, in some circumstances, continuing an unwanted pregnancy may cause even greater harm. Buddhist authorities have not usually outlined what these circumstances might be, so it is left to individual Buddhists to make the final decision about when abortion may be acceptable as the least worst option.

Euthanasia and suicide

As with abortion, Buddhist attitudes to euthanasia and suicide are often influenced by the culture in which they originate. Again, the first precept is the guiding influence for Buddhists when deciding whether euthanasia and suicide are acceptable or not. All Buddhists would regard involuntary euthanasia as unacceptable, regarding it as murder.

Some Buddhists believe that any hastening of death is harming the body, which breaks the first precept. Some also feel that carrying out active forms of euthanasia or committing suicide will not relieve any dukkha being experienced in the long term.

Most dukkha in Buddhism is seen as the result of **kamma**. Trying to evade the dukkha by ending this life does not remove the consequence and, since Buddhists believe in **rebirth**, this consequence will still be experienced in the next life. These Buddhists might encourage the use of **meditation** to minimise pain, or to encourage detachment from the pain being experienced.

Some Buddhists may see passive euthanasia as acceptable, since medical treatment that extends the period of time a person is in pain might be regarded as breaking the first precept.

In some Buddhist cultures, suicide has been used as a form of protest by Buddhist **bhikkhus** (monks). Buddhists might argue that, if rebirth takes place, then this life is not final. As a result, if a sacrifice serves a greater purpose, it may be regarded as acceptable. Thus some bhikkus who have overcome attachment to their bodies may feel able to carry out suicide to highlight issues affecting the Buddhist community. Such actions are still rare within Buddhism and would generally only be carried out by bhikkhus.

ACTIVITIES

- Research the main reasons given for abortion in the UK. In which of these circumstances might a Buddhist feel that continuing the pregnancy is more harmful than having an abortion?
- Is it easy to decide whether a Buddhist might allow abortion or not? Why/Why not?

REMEMBER THIS

Kamma is the Buddhist concept of cause and effect. Buddhists believe that every intentional action has a consequence. Positive actions will have positive effects. Negative actions will have negative effects.

ACTIVITIES

Write a newspaper article explaining different Buddhist views on abortion. Remember to include why Buddhists do not all agree, and the key religious teachings affecting their views.

Create a grid showing the different types of euthanasia. For each, explain how Buddhist teachings might affect the view of a Buddhist.

	Voluntary	Non-voluntary	Involuntary
Active			
Passive			

Buddhism:
Religion and medical ethics 2

Do Buddhists object to fertility treatment?

There is no one Buddhist view here. In general, Buddhists regard a human rebirth as the most fortunate. It is the realm with the best mix of dukkha and sukkha (happiness) to encourage people to search for a cure to dukkha, and begin the path to **nibbana**. Therefore, for Buddhists, processes which increase the number of human births might generally be regarded favourably. This will, however, be influenced by cultural expectations in different countries.

For some Buddhists, fertility processes that use donor eggs or sperm might be regarded as breaking the third precept. Using eggs and sperm from another person might be seen as tantamount to unfaithfulness, and considered sexual misconduct. This view is not universal, and some Buddhists do not regard such medical interventions as sexual in nature, so accept such processes.

Buddhist views about who should be able to access fertility treatment will be largely determined by culture. In some cultures, married couples will be considered the only suitable candidates for fertility treatment, as they represent the traditional family unit. In cultures where sex outside marriage is more widely accepted, Buddhists are more likely to accept non-married couples in long-term relationships as suitable candidates for treatment. This might also be applied to same-sex couples in cultures where homosexuality is widely accepted. Some Buddhists will accept a single parent seeking fertility treatment, providing it was done in the interest of the child, and not a selfish need of the parent.

When determining who should be able to access fertility treatment, a Buddhist will usually consider the wellbeing of the potential child to be of prime importance. Bringing a child into the world in a situation where they are likely to be harmed – for example, by the failure of the parents' relationship – could be seen as breaking the first precept. The overriding factor will be how well the parent could care for the child.

Buddhist views on cloning

While there is no Buddhist position on **cloning**, most Buddhists who have expressed opinions on the matter have concerns about it, questioning whether cloning is serving the best interest of the life being created.

The next two pages will help you to:

- investigate Buddhist responses to the issues raised by fertility treatment and cloning
- evaluate Buddhist beliefs about the use of animals in medical research.

How far should we go to create human life?

ACTIVITIES

Look at the picture. Think of all the reasons why people might want a baby. Are all of these reasons positive? Are there any circumstances in which people should not be allowed to have a baby?

REMEMBER THIS

Nibbana means the blowing out of the fires of greed, hatred and ignorance. It is a state free of suffering...

FOR DEBATE

Who should decide who is entitled to fertility treatment? On what basis should this decision be made? Should the NHS pay for fertility treatment?

At present, most cloning is carried out on animals, to create animals that serve us better. Many clones are disabled or die earlier than would be expected. This leads to concerns that the first precept is being broken. Some limited human cloning has recently been allowed in the UK. This will allow the creation of early stage embryos, which will be used for research purposes and then destroyed. This may lead to advances in medical research. Buddhists will have mixed views on this, but most would be concerned at the creation of a sentient being purely for medical research. This creation serves no purpose for the being created, and would almost certainly be regarded as breaking the first precept.

The use of animals in medical research

Buddhists have come to different conclusions about whether the use of animals in medical research is acceptable. For some, any use of animals for purposes that do not directly benefit them is breaking the first precept. Buddhists may also consider that any animal could potentially be or have been a relation of theirs in a future or past rebirth. They might then consider if they would wish such experimentation on a member of their family.

On the other hand, the Buddha did say that Buddhists had a responsibility to care for their bodies. To this end, meat may be eaten if necessary for a Buddhist's health. Some Buddhists transfer this teaching to the use of animals for medical research. If the use of animals could reduce the suffering of many humans, then perhaps it can be justified.

All Buddhists would agree that animal research should be as limited as possible, should minimise the suffering of the animals involved, and should only be used where no other alternative is possible.

 **ACTIVITIES**

- Create a leaflet explaining Buddhist views on fertility treatment. Would it be more helpful for Buddhists if there were one Buddhist teaching telling them whether fertility treatment was right or wrong? Why/why not?
- Explain in 50 words why Buddhists might have concerns about cloning. Are Buddhist concerns valid?

 **ACTIVITIES**

Write a letter to a local newspaper explaining Buddhist views on the use of animals for medical research.

GradeStudio

AO2

QUESTION

'Every woman has the right to have a baby.' Discuss this statement. You should include different supported points of view and a personal viewpoint. You must refer to Buddhism in your answer. **[12 marks]**

Level 1
First, show you understand the question, and state an opinion. For example, you might say that Buddhists do encourage families to have children and so might be supportive of women having children.

Level 2
Next, justify this view by referring to a religious teaching. You might say that in Buddhism the concept of ahimsa is very important.

Level 3
Next, offer a deeper explanation. If a woman having a child might cause harm to that child – for example a drug addict who might have a baby born addicted to drugs – Buddhists might argue that this would not be in accord with Buddhist teachings. You must also give a personal opinion.

Level 4
Finally, offer a deeper explanation and give your own opinion and support it with evidence and argument.

Christianity:
Religion and medical ethics 1

The next two pages will help you to:
- explain the views Christians have on life and abortion, and why there are differences
- examine and analyse Christian responses to fertility treatment and cloning.

Christian ideas about the sanctity of life and abortion

Christians believe that all life has **sanctity**. All life is a special gift from God and all life is valuable. God, as the creator, has made everyone as individuals. People are all unique, and should be treated with respect. This means that every human being has a right to live regardless of age, health or ability.

When it comes to **abortion**, Christians base their views on the sanctity of life. However, this is not always as simple as it might seem. Opinion is divided, as there is no direct teaching in the New Testament, although there are references to the importance of the unborn child elsewhere in the Bible.

The Roman Catholic Church says that abortion is never acceptable. The unborn child (foetus) is considered to have the potential to become a human being from the moment of conception, so to have an abortion would be to kill a child. This would be against the sixth of the Ten Commandments: 'You shall not murder' (Exodus 20:13). The only time it might be acceptable to have an abortion would be if the mother's life was in danger.

> **Psalm 139:13**
> *For you created my inmost being: you knit me together in my mother's womb.*

> **Jeremiah 1:5a**
> *Before I formed you in the womb, I knew you.*

Most other Christian **denominations** would agree that abortion should be avoided if at all possible. They do think that there may be some circumstances when it can be justified: for example, if the pregnancy might lead to the mother's death, or if the unborn child is severely disabled. Some would also include a pregnancy that is a result of rape.

In all cases, a Christian will consider what is morally acceptable and may refer to the Golden Rule in Matthew 7:12a: 'Do to others what you would have them do to you.' They might try to put the Christian principle of agape (unconditional love) into practice, and work out what the most loving course of action would be.

Is a foetus a human being?

AO1+AO2 skills ACTIVITIES

As a group, brainstorm all the different ways humans are 'special'. Make a mind map on a board, giving everyone in the group the chance to add their ideas.

AO1 skills ACTIVITIES

Think of a line, with 'Most valuable' at one end, and 'least valuable' at the other. Rank the following people along the line: a doctor, a terminally ill person, someone in a wheelchair, a businessman, an unborn child, yourself, a serial killer.
Consider the Christian ideas about the Sanctity of Life. How would a Christian rank these people? Why?

RESEARCH NOTE

Go to the BBC website to find out more about the issue of abortion.

Fertility treatment and genetic engineering

Many couples wish to have a family but are unable to conceive. Fertility treatment can provide medical assistance in a variety of ways to allow conception to take place. In certain circumstances, some Christians might agree that treatment is acceptable – for example, if sperm from the husband is used (**AIH**). However, if there is a donor other than the husband (**AID**) this may be seen as unacceptable.

A third form of treatment is **IVF**, when a baby is conceived outside of the mother's womb, using an egg and sperm from the couple. This might be considered in a positive way, although some people might feel that any treatment goes against God's plan. In the book of Samuel, Hannah has no children because 'the Lord had closed her womb' (1 Samuel 1:5).

Roman Catholics believe that any treatment that allows a third party into the relationship (as a donor) is wrong, as only a husband and wife should be a part of a marriage. A childless couple might seek to adopt a child and bring it up in a loving family as an alternative to seeking medical treatment.

It is important to understand that there is no specific teaching in the Bible about this, but there are quotations that might help a Christian to decide on this issue.

Cloning

Other issues that may be considered include the uses of 'spare' embryos. These may have been stored as a part of fertility treatment. Christians may be concerned that the embryos could be used for medical research. Many would think this is unacceptable, as they believe that each embryo is a potential human being and is therefore **sacred** or **holy**. They may be concerned that scientists are trying to take over God's role as Creator, and this might lead to lives being created to provide 'spare parts' or to cure existing diseases, rather than for themselves.

There are also concerns about **cloning** (where an exact replica of an animal is created), as once again this might lead to people trying to create the perfect human, rather than relying on God's gift of life.

AO2 skills **ACTIVITIES**

Decide whether you are in favour of or against genetic engineering. Write an article for a magazine to convince other people of your opinions.

Dolly the sheep (1996–2003) was the first mammal to be cloned successfully.

AO1+AO2 skills **ACTIVITIES**

Case Study

We had been married for eight years and I had suffered two miscarriages. As time went by and I did not conceive, we began to think that we would never have a family of our own. Eventually we were referred to a clinic and I underwent fertility treatment. Soon the unbelievable happened! I was pregnant and gave birth to a beautiful baby girl. Three years later we repeated the process and had a son. Now in their teens, we still marvel that we have been given two special children who are a gift from God as well as a miracle of modern science.

a In your view what are the benefits of fertility treatment for this couple?

b Write a letter to the couple from a Christian who might have some advice for them about undergoing fertility treatment.

Christianity:
Religion and medical ethics 2

The next two pages will help you to:

- demonstrate an understanding of Christian responses to euthanasia and suicide
- investigate and evaluate Christian attitudes to the testing of animals for medical research.

Beliefs that Christians have about life are important not only in decisions about when life begins, but also when it ends.

Medical advances have meant that it is possible to prolong life with a greatly reduced quality – perhaps with serious physical disability or with very little conscious life at all. Someone in a PVS (persistent vegetative state) may be able to breathe for themselves, but have no awareness of their identity or situation. It is rare for them to recover, although this is not completely impossible.

Christian teachings about euthanasia

Most Christians believe that God gives life and only God can decide when a life should be ended.

Some Christians say that as humans have free will, they have a choice between life and death, but that to choose death would be a sin.

The Roman Catholic Church and the Church of England teach that **euthanasia** is wrong, as it goes against the sixth commandment. However, Roman Catholics do accept the doctrine of 'double effect', where a patient who is dying in a lot of pain can be given a painkiller that might make death occur more quickly.

Some Christians accept passive euthanasia, while others might say that sometimes it is kinder to allow a person to die if they are in great pain. Many Christians would prefer that a terminally ill person has palliative care – when special care is given to ensure that a person's last illness is as painless as possible, and they and their family can come to terms with death. This usually takes place in a hospice.

Christian teachings about suicide

Suicide is not illegal in Britain, but the majority of Christians would agree that it is not what God would want for a person. They would say that God has fixed an indiviual's life span and suicide goes against God's plan – a belief supported by Acts 17:26:

> From one man he made every nation of men, that they should inhabit the whole earth; and he determined the times set for them and the exact places where they should live.

Generally, Christians would aim to give support and care to those who contemplate suicide. Many support the work of the Samaritans.

 REMEMBER THIS

Look back at Christian ideas about the sanctity of life. The same principles apply to the issue of euthanasia.

Ecclesiastes 3:1–2
There is a time for everything, and a season for every activity under heaven: a time to be born and a time to die, a time to plant and a time to uproot.

 RESEARCH NOTE

Use the internet to investigate the case of Diane Pretty. Explain what she tried to do and say how this relates to Christian teachings.

Quakers believe that everything in life offers new opportunities, and a person should learn from whatever happens to them, rather than seek to end their life.

The use of animals in medical research

Christians believe that God created animals before humans, and it is the responsibility of humans to take care of other living things. However, humans are seen as the most important thing that God made and are the only part of God's creation to have a soul.

Whilst animals deserve respect and should be treated without cruelty, they can be used for the good of humans, so most Christians will eat meat and keep animals as pets as long as they are well treated.

Roman Catholics believe that as long as there are people in the world who are suffering from disease or starvation, it is wrong to make a lot of fuss over pets and to spend vast amounts of money on them unnecessarily. Resources should be given to humans before animals.

In the same way, it is often argued that animals can be used for medical research as long as the result is for the benefit of humans. However, the animals should not be treated with cruelty.

The Samaritans, which takes its name from the Bible story, offers sympathy and support to those feeling suicidal or depressed.

GradeStudio

AO2

QUESTION

'Abortion is murder.'

Discuss this statement. You should include different, supported points of view and a personal viewpoint. You must refer to Christianity in your answer.

[12 marks]

Level 1

First, show you understand the question, and state an opinion. For example, Christians believe all life comes from God, so an abortion is murdering a human being and is against God's will.

Level 2

Next, justify this view by referring to a religious teaching, such as the Commandment 'You shall not commit murder'.

Level 3

Next, offer an *explanation*. For example, Roman Catholics believe that abortion is playing God because only God can take life away. Some Christians believe that the foetus is not yet a human being so an abortion ends the life of the foetus, but is not murder. Give a personal opinion.

Level 4

Finally, offer a *deeper explanation*. For example, many Christians believe there are cases where abortion is acceptable, such as after rape. I believe the foetus is not a human being until it is born. Abortion is never good, but it is the mother's right to choose. You must give a personal opinion and support it.

AO2 skills ACTIVITIES

- In your view, when is euthanasia acceptable? Discuss your views with a partner.

- Imagine you are either a scientist conducting whose research involves experimenting on animals or a campaigner opposed to such research. Write a letter to the other person expressing your views.

Hinduism:
Religion and medical ethics 1

The next two pages will help you to:

- learn about the Hindu attitudes to abortion, fertility treatment and euthanasia
- reflect on and be able to explain how these views affect Hindu actions.

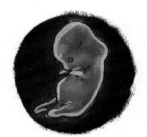

Here is a foetus at 4, 10 and 24 weeks.

When does life begin?

The issue of **abortion** comes down to when a human life begins. In the UK, the law says that, except in exceptional cases, no abortion should be carried out after 24 weeks.

In India, abortion is legal and is accepted by many Hindus as a method of ending an unwanted pregnancy. In many Hindu **sacred** texts, abortion is seen as wrong as it goes against the idea of **ahimsa** – doing no harm to any living thing. Some Hindus believe that abortion prevents the rebirth of a foetus, thus denying the opportunity to have a human life from which to remove bad **karma**.

Some Hindus argue that legal abortion means that children do not have to be born into poverty. Others believe that, if the mother's life is in danger or if the child would be born severely handicapped, it is permissible.

As it is possible to tell the gender of a child from a scan, some Hindus may find it acceptable to have an abortion based on gender, often preferring to allow a son to be born but not a daughter. Even though this is against Hindu teaching, it happens often. As a result, many hospitals in India refuse to tell a couple what gender their baby is.

Is fertility treatment acceptable?

An obligation in **marriage** for Hindus is to produce children; it is part of their **dharma** or duty. Therefore, it is important that they try to conceive, and reproductive technology can be used. However, many Hindus prefer to avoid techniques where 'spare' embryos are destroyed if they have not been successfully implanted. This raises concerns about ahimsa – respect for life.

ACTIVITIES

- Look at the photos of a foetus at various stages. Up to when do you think that abortion should be allowed?
- Who matters most – the mother or the potential life she carries?

FOR DEBATE

What are acceptable reasons for abortion? What are unacceptable reasons?

RESEARCH NOTE

Make your own notes on the UK abortion laws.

Fertility treatments are often so expensive that only the rich can afford them. There is a concern that a lower **caste** woman's cells might be used to enable a higher caste Hindu conceive, against the natural order.

When should life end?

A 22-year-old man called Daniel James took his life when he was faced with a lifetime of disability following a sporting accident. His parents, who travelled to a Swiss assisted-suicide clinic, have said their son could not face the pain of knowing that his life would be severely restricted due to the tragedy.

Many Hindus believe that no one should choose when to die. They believe that life is sacred, so only the gods can give or take it. If someone is suffering to the point of death, this should be seen as a product of their karma; the way they deal with this situation gives them the opportunity to help improve their state in their next life. If a Hindu is a doctor or a nurse, they should do all that they can to bring dignity to the person facing death, in order to improve their karma.

Many Hindus may take the decision that they are near to death and stop eating and drinking to accelerate their own death. They believe that renouncing the world like this is a way to blessing. Many Hindus see such actions as noble, as long as only the person is involved in the action. To die in this view is seen as moving the atman forward to a new existence as the cycle of samsara starts again.

Suicide is seen as inappropriate if depression or despair are the cause. If it is due to an act of self-sacrifice or because they cannot bear to be parted from a person who has already died, this will be seen as acceptable. In the past, Hinduism supported suttee – the ritual suicide of a widow by leaping on to their husband's own funeral pyre – but this was outlawed in 1829.

FOR DEBATE

When might it be appropriate to allow a life to be ended?

AO1+AO2 skills **ACTIVITIES**

- Give a postcard-length explanation (100 words) of the key ideas that influence Hindu ideas about abortion and euthanasia.
- 'Life is always sacred.' What do Hindus think? What do you believe? Make sure that your answer includes more than one opinion.

GradeStudio

AO1

QUESTION

'Explain what Hindus believe about abortion.' **[6 marks]**

Level 1

First let the examiner know that you know what the question is about. For example, 'Hindus believe that abortion (the medical termination of a pregnancy) has to be considered before continuing.'

Level 2

Next, go on to to explain in more detail how Hindus have differing opinions that influence their attitude to abortion, and explain a couple of ideas that shape their thinking.

Level 3

Finally, explain that this is a difficult issue to resolve. Hindus believe that there are many different factors that influence whether a woman should have an abortion. Their religious teachings encourage them to think about the value of human life (ahimsa), but they also have to balance this against a sense of duty (dharma).

Hinduism:
Religion and medical ethics 2

The next two pages will help you to:

- explain the attitudes Hindus have to animals
- evaluate how Hindu beliefs influence their views about animal testing.

Krishna, an avator of Vishnu, was a cowherd, one of the reasons why cows have become holy to Hindus.

AO1+AO2 skills **ACTIVITIES**

- Working with a partner, list the ways in which animals have been used by human beings. Which do you think are acceptable? Which do you think are unacceptable?
- Why have you come to the conclusions you have?

Cute and cuddly?

Animals are often presented as cute and cuddly. Think about the toys that you had when you were a small child. How many of them were animals, like teddy bears? When we first learn to read or watch videos, many of the stories we hear are about animals.

Yet animals are not like that in reality. They can be violent and will use their instincts to attack. They are not open to reason.

Animals in Hinduism

Animals have often played an important part in the Hindu faith. In some of the stories of the gods, animals such as tigers, eagles and swans have been used as vahanas – they have transported the gods and as a consequence have become holy themselves in Hindu understanding. The cow has been given a high status in Hindu thought because the god Vishnu was once in charge of cows in one of his human forms. Also, the power of creation from Lord Brahman has meant that animals are seen as his creations and should be treated with respect.

The principle of ahimsa, doing no harm to any living thing, has also become important for many Hindus. This has led many to become vegetarian and to avoid not just eating meat but also using products from animals, such as leather.

 **RESEARCH NOTE**

Find out more about the role of animals in one of the key stories about the gods.

Hindus do not necessarily believe that human life is more important than animal life. Deliberately hurting or killing animals will create bad karma. People who do such things in this life might find themselves the hunted in a life to come, unless they show respect to other creatures.

Should you experiment on animals?

The ideas above are important to consider when thinking about Hindu views on when it might be acceptable use an animal in experimentation.

Most Hindus reject the idea of testing perfumes or shampoos, for example. However, when it comes to medical research on animals, there is much discussion within Hinduism.

Some Hindus accept that some experiments are essential to human wellbeing and are therefore permissible. India does allow animal testing but it is on a much more limited scale than in Western countries like the UK and the USA.

Hindus opposed to animal testing might not only be concerned at the cruelty that might have to be inflicted on the animal, but might also suggest that you cannot rely on getting the right results from such research. For example, penicillin can kill some animals but is a great lifesaver to human beings. Even apes, which can be as little as one per cent genetically different to human beings, can produce significantly different results to human beings.

They might suggest that long-term studies of human behaviour can reduce the need for animal testing – for example, tracking the health of smokers found a link between lung cancer and smoking more effectively than animal experiments. It is also possible to use computer models, and work on cells can produce important results.

Gandhi's views on animals

The Hindu leader Mahatma Gandhi called vivisection (experimentation on live animals) 'the blackest of black crimes that [humanity] is at present committing against God and [God's] fair creation'. Many Hindus believe that, as animals cannot speak back, we cannot truly know the suffering that they go through and that we risk creating bad karma for ourselves if we are involved in this type of research.

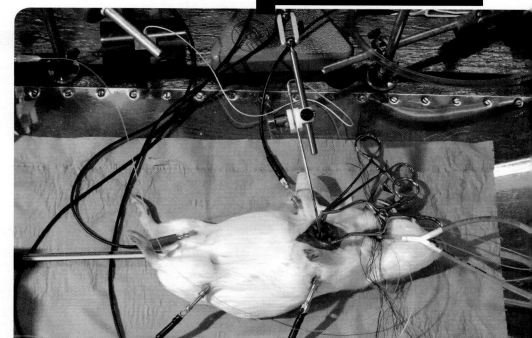

Is it acceptable to experiment on an animal like this?

FOR DEBATE

When do you think it might be right to carry out scientific research using animals?

AO1+AO2 skills ACTIVITIES

- 'Hindus should be totally opposed to animal experimentation.' What do you think? Why do Hindu opinions differ on this? Give reasons for your answer, referring to precise Hindu teaching.

- Write a brief passage to support one side of this debate: 'This house believes in animal medical research.'

Islam:
Religion and medical ethics 1

The next two pages will help you to:

- explore Muslim attitudes to abortion
- investigate Muslim ideas and teachings on euthanasia and suicide.

Muslim attitudes towards abortion

According to Islam, Allah created the world and everything which is in it (see Surah 42, Topic 1, page 21). This means that Allah makes every decision about when a person will be born or die and that no one should try to interfere with this.

As you saw in Topic 1, Islam does permit **contraception** under certain circumstances. However, it does not allow **abortion**. The foetus is seen as a human being, and abortion is considered murder. The person responsible for the abortion could be required to pay blood money to the family of the foetus.

What is meant by loneliness?

However, where a doctor believes that the continuation of a pregnancy will result in the death of the mother, an abortion is allowed. Some Muslims believe that ensoulment does not take place until 120 days after conception, so the foetus is not seen as a person. For the first four months of a pregnancy, the rights of the mother are greater than those of the foetus; after this time, their rights are equal. If an abortion is needed, it should be done early. Other Muslims believe that 'the soul is breathed in by the first 42 days of pregnancy'.

Before the time of Muhammad ﷺ, baby girls were often buried alive because they were not wanted by the family. The rules of the Qur'an about this are now also applied to abortion.

> **Surah 17:31**
> *Kill not your children for fear of want: We shall provide sustenance for them as well as for you. Verily the killing of them is a great sin.*

AO1 skills ACTIVITIES

Think/pair/share
Look at the image and think about what loneliness means. With a partner, discuss whether your views are similar or different and why. Consider whether other people might have different views.

AO1+AO2 skills ACTIVITIES

- Explain what is meant by 'ensoulment'.
- Explain how a Muslim couple might decide whether the woman should have an abortion.

Euthanasia and suicide

Neither **euthanasia** nor **suicide** are allowed by Islam because, again, it would be interfering with Allah's plan.

> ### Surah 2:155–156
> *Be sure we shall test you with something of fear and hunger, some loss in goods or lives or the fruits (of your toil), but give glad tidings to those who patiently persevere, Who say, when afflicted with calamity: 'To Allah We belong, and to Him is our return'*

> ### Surah 4:29
> *Nor kill (or destroy) yourselves: for verily Allah hath been to you most Merciful!*

When people suffer, Islam says that this is a test of their faith. However, nothing that happens to anyone is a good enough reason to end their life.

Muhammad ﷺ taught that anyone who killed themselves would go to hell.

> ### Hadith
> *Anyone who throws themselves down from a rock and commits suicide will be throwing themselves into Hell. A person who drinks poison and kills themselves will drink it for ever in Hell. A person who stabs themselves will stab themselves for ever in Hell.*

The time of someone's death is controlled entirely by Allah.

> ### Surah 16:61
> *When their Term expires, they would not be able to delay (the punishment) for a single hour, just as they would not be able to anticipate it (for a single hour).*

> ### Surah 3:145
> *Nor can a soul die except by Allah's leave, the term being fixed as by writing.*

Anyone committing suicide is taking a life that belongs to Allah, not to them, and is also seen as showing a failure of the **ummah** (the worldwide community of Muslims) to care for them.

Euthanasia is also forbidden. It is considered **zulm**, something wrong done against Allah.

Muslims do not believe that people should be kept alive by artificial means.

❝ *If, however, a number of medical experts determine that a patient is in a terminal condition, there is no hope for his/her recovery and all medication has become useless, then it could be permissible for them, through a collective decision, to stop the medication.* **❞**

(Muzammil Siddiqui of the Fiqh Council of North America)

RESEARCH NOTE

Research the law on abortion in the UK.

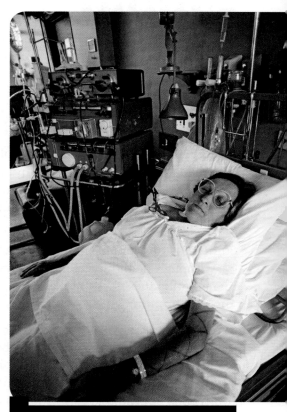

When should life-support machines be turned off and who should decide?

FOR DEBATE

- Consider whether there are any circumstances in which Muslims might say that someone was right to commit suicide.
- Consider how the response of a non-religious person might be different.

AO1+AO2 skills ACTIVITIES

- How might a Muslim doctor respond to someone who wants to die?
- 'It is up to the individual when they die.' Discuss. Remember to give your own view and to support it with argument.

Islam:
Religion and medical ethics 2

The next two pages will help you to:

- investigate Muslim responses to the issues raised by fertility treatment and cloning
- evaluate Muslim beliefs about the use of animals in medical research.

Muslim attitudes to fertility treatment

Children are seen as a natural part of a Muslim **marriage**. When a family cannot have children, they may look for comfort in the teachings of the Qur'an where, for example, Ibrahim and Sara and Zakariya and Ishbra were unable to have children until they were very old.

Some Muslim women may also look at the life of Muhammad ﷺ. Although he did have children with his first wife Khadijah, he had only one other child although he had nine more wives. His son Ibrahim, whose mother was Mariyah, died in infancy.

Some Muslims may say that infertility is Allah's will, but others believe that it is a disease and that there is a duty to find a cure for it. Science has offered one possibility with **IVF**. Although some of the eggs implanted as part of this process will die, Islam does not see this as a problem as they are not human beings. The important issue is that spare embryos could be used for stem cell research, but cannot be given to another woman because a child born in this way would be illegitimate.

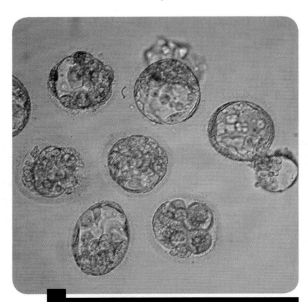

How far should humanity experiment with life?

> **Surah 25:54**
> *It is He Who has created man from water: then has He established relationships of lineage and marriage: for thy Lord has power (over all things).*

Cloning

Cloning human beings is a technology that has not yet been developed. However, already there are Muslim responses and discussion about the issue.

Reasons against human cloning

- May cause danger to the human personality.
- May cause danger to human dignity and honour.
- Allah is the Creator, not humans. We have no right to interfere with Allah's plan.
- Loss of kinship, as the clone does not really have an identifiable mother or father.
- Harmful to society/nature – may have grave consequences if this ability were to create superior beings.

ACTIVITIES

Look at the picture. Make two lists of arguments for and against using science to help someone to become pregnant. Which list do you think is most convincing and why?

RESEARCH NOTE

Read the stories of Ibrahim and Sara in Surah 51:28 ff, and of Zakariya and Ishbra in Surah 21:89 ff.

FOR DEBATE

Consider how a Muslim couple might deal with finding out that one of them is infertile.

- May cause disruption in nature, due to possibilities of overpopulation and famine.
- Unnatural – a way of reproduction that is contrary to what Allah has given humans.

Arguments in favour of human cloning

- Cloning is a form of creation that is created from materials we have, rather than from nothing, which is Allah's ability only.
- Islam encourages research and investigation.
- Cloning technology can be used for good purposes, such as new cures for diseases and medical conditions.

Generally, Muslims accept cloning in respect of plants and animals, but not for human beings.

The use of animals in medical research

Islam teaches that all life belongs to Allah.

Surah 6:38

There is not an animal (that lives) on the earth, nor a being that flies on its wings, but (forms part of) communities like you. Nothing have we omitted from the Book, and they (all) shall be gathered to their Lord in the end.

Animal experimentation for scientific purposes is allowed if it helps humans, but the importance of the animals must also be taken into account.

Surah 24:41

Seest thou not that it is Allah Whose praises all beings in the heavens and on earth do celebrate, and the birds (of the air) with wings outspread? Each one knows its own (mode of) prayer and praise. And Allah knows well all that they do.

There are also stories of Muhammad ﷺ showing care for animals, as on the occasion when he ordered a fire to be put out because there were ants walking towards it.

Later Muslim thinkers

There is a 13th-century bill of legal rights for animals, written by a Muslim lawyer called Izz ad-Din ibn Abd as-Salam.

In 1986 Dr Abdullah Omar Nasseef made a speech at the World Wide Fund for Nature International conference in which he said:

❝ *[Allah's] trustees are responsible for maintaining the integrity of the Earth, its flora and fauna, its wildlife and natural environment… we will be answerable for how we have… maintained balance and harmony in the whole of creation around us.* ❞

So, all life is important because it is part of Allah's creation, but this does not mean that, with suitable precautions, medical research cannot be conducted on animals if it is designed to help human wellbeing.

ACTIVITIES

Do you think that Muslim attitudes towards fertility treatment and cloning are justifiable or are they just old-fashioned? Give reasons for your answer.

FOR DEBATE

'Muslim attitudes towards animal research cannot stand up to the arguments of animal activists.' Discuss.

ACTIVITIES

Do you think that humans have the right to use other animals for food and in medical experiments? Give reasons for your answer.

Judaism:
Religion and medical ethics 1

The next two pages will help you to:

- explore Jewish attitudes to abortion
- explore Jewish attitudes to euthanasia and suicide.

What should people do to help someone who is suffering?

AO1+AO2 skills **ACTIVITIES**

Think/pair/share
What action would you be prepared to take to prevent someone suffering? With a partner, discuss your views. Are they similar or different? Why? What other views might people have? Be prepared to explain to the class why you think people have different views on this.

Jewish teachings on the sanctity of life

In the first chapter of Genesis, in the Torah, it explains that G-d created the world and during this creation he also created all life, including men and women. Judaism teaches that because G-d created everything, G-d is in charge of whether something or someone lives or dies.

Jewish attitudes towards abortion

Because of the teaching from Genesis and the instruction to 'Be fertile and increase, fill the earth', Judaism teaches that **abortion** would interfere with G-d's plan for the world.

However, the Torah also teaches that the life of a human being is more important than the life of a child that is not yet born.

Genesis 1:26–28
And G-d said, 'Let us make man in our image, after our likeness. They shall rule the fish of the sea, the birds of the sky, the cattle, the whole earth, and all the creeping things that creep on earth.' And God created man in His image, in the image of G-d He created him; male and female He created them. G-d blessed them and G-d said to them, 'Be fertile and increase, fill the earth and master it; and rule the fish of the sea, the birds of the sky, and all the living things that creep on earth.'

Exodus 21:22–25

When men fight, and one of them pushes a pregnant woman and a miscarriage results, but no other damage ensues, the one responsible shall be fined according as the woman's husband may exact from him, the payment to be based on reckoning. But if other damage ensues, the penalty shall be life for life, eye for eye, tooth for tooth, hand for hand, foot for foot, burn for burn, wound for wound, bruise for bruise.

You should note that this passage, together with other similar ones, does not say that people should literally take an eye for an eye, but that the financial penalty imposed should not be greater than the loss that has been caused.

As with some other religions, the argument about abortion depends, in part, on when the foetus is judged to have become a human being, or receives its soul. After much discussion, the Rabbis decided that a foetus became a person at the moment of birth and not at conception. Because of this, abortion cannot be considered to be murder.

Mishnah

If a woman is in difficult labour (to the point that her life may be in danger) her child must be cut up while it is still in her womb, since the life of the mother is more important than the life of the foetus. But if the greater part of the child has already emerged, it may not be damaged, since one life cannot be more important than another.

Following these teachings, some Jews accept that there are occasions when abortion should be allowed. It is the life and health of the mother that is placed first, but it is also the mother who must take the decision. Obviously, Jews do not approve of abortion for the sake of convenience.

Euthanasia and suicide

Judaism teaches that all human life is **sacred**, so **suicide** is seen as a sin. The Rabbis taught that 'one who intentionally takes one's life has no share in the world to come.' If a Jew commits suicide, he or she is not given the normal burial rites and is not buried near other Jews.

It is possible to argue that there are stories in the Torah of people taking their own life. One example is in Judges 16:28–30, when Samson tears down the temple, saying 'Let me die with the Philistines!' The Rabbis said that, in these sorts of circumstances, suicide is acceptable because it is done to protect others.

As Jews do not generally approve of suicide they also do not approve of **euthanasia**. An exception is found in the teachings of Rabbi Moses Isserles.

66 *If there is anything which causes a hindrance to the departure of the soul... then it is permissible to remove it.* 99

Many people see this as an argument that life-support machines should be turned off if there is no hope of the patient recovering.

As in many instances, there are differences of opinion between Orthodox and Progressive Jews.

ACTIVITIES

Explain how a Jewish mother might decide whether she should have an abortion.

ACTIVITIES

Your eyes saw my unformed limbs; they were all recorded in Your book; in due time they were formed, to the very last one of them. (Psalm 139:16)

Explain how this verse applies to Jewish teachings about the **sanctity** of life.

Judaism:
Religion and medical ethics 2

How far should we go to try to create life?

The next two pages will help you to:
- investigate Jewish responses to the issues raised by fertility treatment and cloning
- evaluate Jewish beliefs about the use of animals in medical research.

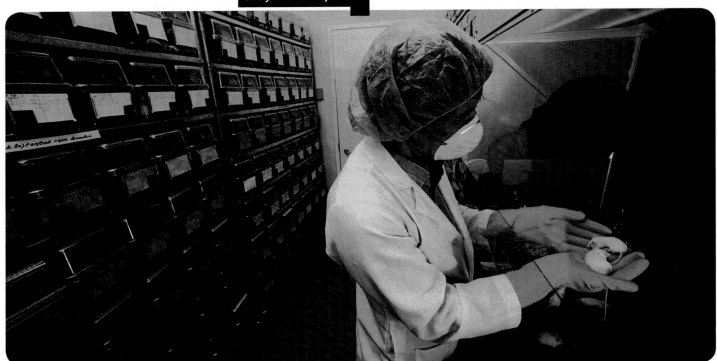

Jewish attitudes to fertility treatment

Of course, there is no specific reference to fertility treatment in the Bible because such medical advances did not exist at the time. However, there are several instances of people who wanted children but could not have them – it was usually regarded as G-d's decision that a particular woman should not have a baby.

> **1 Samuel 1:2b, 5b**
> *Hannah was childless... – for the Lord had closed her womb.*

Even so, Judaism considers that children are not only a blessing, but also a **mitzvah**, a commandment.

> **Maimonides**
> *Whoever adds even one Jewish soul is considered as having created an (entire) world.*

AO1+AO2 skills ACTIVITIES

- Find out which other women in the Bible were unable to have children. What happened to them? You could start by doing an internet search for 'barren women bible'.
- Do you think that Jewish attitudes towards fertility treatment and cloning are old-fashioned? Give reasons for your answer.

The Rabbis have been very flexible in relation to fertility treatment. There is no objection to the husband's sperm being used in **AIH** treatment. In some circumstances, **AID** is also permitted. The donor is seen as the father of the child according to Jewish law, but it is taught that no sin has taken place because of this and the child is accepted as legitimate by the Jewish community.

Cloning

The technology to clone human beings has not yet been developed, but already there are Jewish discussions about the issue.

Cloning is seen as being a long way from the ideal methods of creating human life. However, if nothing else works, Jewish law might consider cloning to be a mitzvah for infertile couples – or, at the least, an action which is neither good nor bad in itself. What is stressed is that clones are fully human and must always be treated with the respect shown to any other human being.

The use of animals in medical research

On the sixth day of Creation, according to the first account in Genesis, G-d created humans and animals. If you take a look at the sacred text from Genesis 1:26–28 on page 52, you can see that this appears to place all other forms of life in a position below that of humans.

However, there is no doubt that the Jews saw animals as valuable, as they were offered as daily sacrifices in the Jerusalem Temple. There are also passages in the Tenakh which show that animals are to be treated with respect:

> **Deuteronomy 25:4**
> *You shall not muzzle an ox while it is threshing.*

> **Proverbs 12:10a**
> *A righteous man knows the needs of his beast.*

The way animals are referred to in the Ten Commandments also shows the great respect that should be shown to them.

The use of animals in the Ten Commandments

It is clear from the Jewish scriptures that animals are to be shown respect and should be treated well. On the other hand, humans are told that they are in charge of the animal world. Medical research on animals is allowed provided that the animals do not suffer any more than is absolutely necessary. Animals may also be used for organ transplants: even the use of heart valves from pigs is permitted, despite the fact that pigs are generally seen as unclean by Jews.

> **Exodus 20:8–10**
> *Remember the sabbath day and keep it holy. Six days you shall labour and do all your work, but the seventh day is a sabbath of the Lord your G-d: you shall not do any work – you, your son or daughter, your male or female slave, or your cattle, or the stranger who is within your settlements.*

AO1 skills ACTIVITIES

Think of all the reasons people might want a baby. Now consider which of these reasons are selfish and which are not. Ignore the selfish reasons and explain the importance of those that remain.

FOR DEBATE

Having read these two sections, are Jews in favour of fertility treatment and cloning or not?

Consider the arguments for and against, and also the practical difficulties that may be involved.

AO2 skills ACTIVITIES

Write a letter from a Jewish point of view to an MP, explaining why you believe that medical research on animals should be allowed even though other people may oppose it.

AO1 skills ACTIVITIES

Look carefully at the passage from Exodus. What does it tell you about the status of animals in a Jewish home?

Sikhism:
Religion and medical ethics 1

Sikh views on abortion

Sikhs have different attitudes towards **abortion**. The Guru Granth Sahib Ji teaches that all life is **sacred**, especially human life, since it has the essence of God contained within it. Sikhs also believe in the **reincarnation** of the soul, so in this respect, life begins at fertilisation for a great many Sikhs. Abortion in line with these teachings is strictly condemned as wrong and going against the Will of God.

However, Sikh women, like other Indian women, may be pressurised into producing male heirs. Many women are forced by family members or, indeed, decide themselves, to abort female foetuses. Female infanticide is a practice that the Sikh Gurus spoke out against strongly. Destroying a foetus by abortion is in effect, according to Sikh teachings, the destruction of a sacred life that has been granted the human body according to the Grace and Will of God.

Abortion is, however, permissible if the mother has become pregnant as a result of rape or if her life is at risk if she continues with the pregnancy.

Fertility treatment and cloning: does science have the right to play God?

There are no teachings about Sikhs turning to fertility treatments such as **IVF** if they cannot conceive children naturally. However, an examination of the principles of God's Will (Hukam) and Grace (Nadar) show that a Sikh should, in adherence to religious philosophy, accept infertility as the Will of God.

> **Guru Granth Sahib Ji, page 5**
> *Pilgrimages, Austerities, Mercy, Charity,*
> *Bring but honour small and paltry.*
> *One must Hear, Believe, Love the Name.*

The next two pages will help you to:

- develop your knowledge and understanding of Sikh attitudes towards abortion and fertility treatment
- analyse the importance of Sikh religious teachings about the sanctity of human life and the Will of Waheguru
- make links between these concepts and attitudes with what you think/believe.

 **AO1+AO2** skills **ACTIVITIES**

Write down as many reasons for and against abortion as you can. With a partner, discuss if you agree or disagree with the opinions. Can everyone agree on the issue of abortion? In pairs, discuss what you think the term 'medical ethics' refers to.

AO1+AO2 skills **ACTIVITIES**

Think/pair/share
In small groups, think of three scenarios in which a pregnant woman might consider abortion, for medical or personal reasons. Firstly, in your own group, have a discussion about what the mother should do in each case and whether it is considered ethically right or wrong. After this, swap your scenarios with another group and do the same.

Contribute to a whole-class discussion on the scenarios you have considered. Remember to justify your opinions.

However, this is not always what happens in practice. Sikhism constantly stresses the importance of the life of a householder and the bearing of children. In the more narrow-minded Sikh communities, a woman who cannot have children is considered unlucky during special events and ceremonies. So some Sikhs couples will turn to treatments such as IVF in hope of having children. The ever-demanding social strain on Sikh women to produce male children has caused an increase in Sikh couples attending 'gender clinics', where they can determine the sex of their future child.

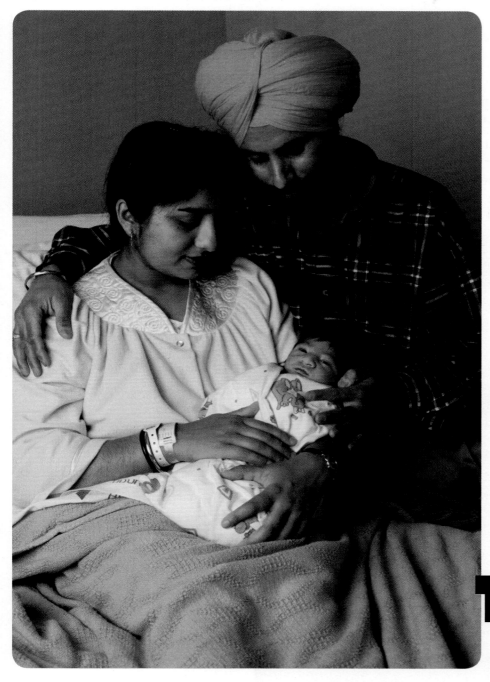

Sikhism stresses the importance of children and the family.

It should be stressed that not all Sikhs have such traditional notions, and many would treat male or female children equally. The Sikh Gurus strongly condemn the practice of gender selection, as they emphasised the **equality** of men and women.

AO2 skills ACTIVITIES

What do you think Guru Nanak Dev Ji's advice would be to a couple having difficulty conceiving?

Sikhism:
Religion and medical ethics 2

What is a Sikh's attitude towards euthanasia and suicide?

The important Sikh belief of the immanence of God would place doubt on the practice of **euthanasia** and on **suicide**.

Although taking pain relief is acceptable for Sikhs, there is no overall teaching that accepts the practice of euthanasia. Life is considered **sacred** and everyone's life will come to an end in accordance with God's will. However, Sikhs will give consent if needed, for a life-support machine to be switched off.

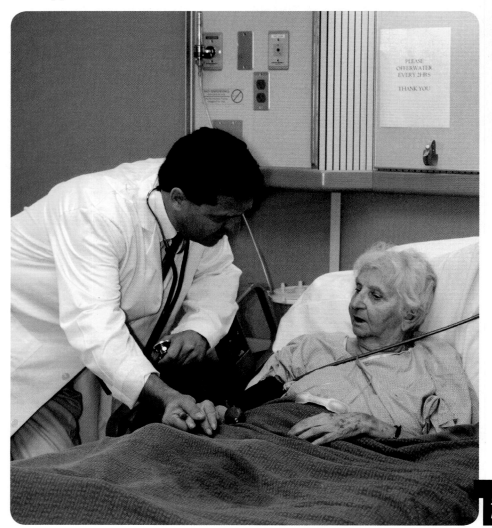

The next two pages will help you to:

- develop your knowledge and understanding of Sikh attitudes towards euthanasia and suicide
- examine Sikh views on the use of animals in medical research
- make links between these concepts and attitudes with what you think/believe.

AO2 skills ACTIVITIES

Think/pair/share
What would you do if a close family member, whom you deeply loved, was constantly in pain and asked for your help in ending their life? Think carefully about your response to this dilemma. Talk to another person in the class to see if they agree or disagree with your answer. Now discuss the issue as a class; you should have enough differences of opinion to form two broad responses.

Sikhism teaches that life will come to an end in accordance with God's will.

Committing suicide is strictly against the teachings of Sikhism. Counselling would be offered to the person concerned and the whole family would show their support. Taking your own life, or asking another person to end it for you, is regarded as interfering with the Hukam of God. Committing suicide would accumulate bad **karma/ karam** and hence be a major hindrance to the goal of liberation, referred to as **mukti** – the 'release' from the cycle of reincarnation.

Would breakthroughs in medicine be possible without research on animals?

The use of animals to conduct medical experiments is acceptable among Sikhs. This experimentation does, however, need to be for ethical and medical reasons. Many Sikhs would object to the testing of cosmetics on animals. All life is seen as sacred by Sikhs. However, Sikh teachings often allude to the idea that humans are the highest of God's creation.

Many Sikhs train as scientists and are involved in animal experimentation to find cures and breakthroughs in medicine that would benefit society as a whole.

 GradeStudio

AO1

QUESTION

Explain Sikh attitudes towards abortion. [6 marks]

You could build an answer like this:

Level 1
First, let the examiner know that you are aware what the question is about. For example,

'There are different attitudes towards abortion amongst Sikhs.'

Level 2
Next, go on to explain the teaching about the immanence of God within humans; this means that life begins at conception. Abortion is not generally acceptable unless the pregnancy is a result of rape or if the mother's life is at risk. The issue of female infanticide can also be discussed.

Level 3
Finally, mention that the destruction of a human life is equated to interfering with the Will of God.

AO1 skills **ACTIVITIES**

What can counselling offer to people who have attempted suicide?
You have been put in charge of preparing literature for the gurdwara where the President is hoping to set up a Counselling Service. This Counselling Service will also be for victims who have attempted to commit suicide. How will the service offered enable your literature to be used positively?

 FOR DEBATE

Currently, euthanasia is illegal in Britain. If found guilty of assisting someone with euthanasia, the accomplice can be tried for murder. The administering of euthanasia is legal in countries such as Germany and Switzerland. Do you think euthanasia should be made legal in Britain? Would a Sikh think the same as someone who is not a Sikh? Explain your answer with as much justification as possible.

 **AO1+AO2** skills **ACTIVITIES**

Make a poster to show Sikh attitudes towards the use of animals in experiments. Remember there are differing attitudes amongst Sikhs. You need to address the various points of view in your work. Show your poster to the rest of the class.

GradeStudio

Welcome to the Grade Studio

Grade Studio is here to help you improve your grades by working through typical questions you might find on an examination paper. For a fuller explanation of how Grade Studio works, and how the examiners approach the task of marking your paper, please see p. 30.

AO1
Question

Explain Christian attitudes to the use of animals in medical research.

[6 marks]

Student's answer

Christians believe that God placed humans in charge of the world and in charge of the animals. Some Christians believe that, because humanity was placed in charge of the animals, we can eat them and do anything else that we wish with them. If animals can help save human lives, this is a good reason to conduct medical research on them.

Examiner's comment

The candidate has given a satisfactory answer to the question. There are two relevant points, but they are not explained in any detail. In order to reach Level 3, the answer needs to give more information and examples. The candidate could also use more technical terms from the specification to show the breadth of their knowledge and understanding.

Student's improved answer

Christians believe that God placed humans in charge of the world and in charge of the animals. Some Christians believe that, because humanity was placed in charge of the animals, we can eat them and do anything else that we wish with them. If animals can help save human lives, this is a good reason to conduct medical research on them.

Some Christians might say that this is using animals as a type of lesser creation, and that there is no basis for this. Many people are also concerned as to what experiments take place on animals. While some people may be reasonably happy with experiments on animals that lead to cures for human diseases, especially if there is no other way of carrying out the research, they may be much less happy with experiments to test cosmetics or other tests which are not necessary and are simply taking place for human convenience.

Examiner's comment

This is now a good answer to the question. The candidate has shown a clear understanding of the question. There is good description and explanation of a variety of different responses that Christians might have in relation to animals. The candidate has shown good analysis in dealing with the question of experiments on animals. The information is presented clearly and there is good use of technical terms.

AO2

Question

'Every woman has the right to have a baby.' Discuss this statement. You should include different, supported points of view and a personal viewpoint. You must refer to Christianity in your answer. **[12 marks]**

Student's answer

Christians might say that women are designed to have babies and that therefore every woman has the right to have one. Some Christians might also say that, if a woman is not able to have a baby by natural means, she should be able to have fertility treatment because God has enabled scientists to discover this.

Examiner's comment

The candidate has given a limited answer to the question. There are two relevant points but neither is expanded very far. In order to reach Level 4 the answer needs to give alternative viewpoints and to include a personal response.

Student's improved answer

Christians might say that women are designed to have babies and that therefore every woman has the right to have one. Some Christians might also say that, if a woman is not able to have a baby by natural means, she should be able to have fertility treatment because God has enabled scientists to discover this.

Other Christians might say that a baby is a gift, not a right, and that if God wanted a woman to have a baby then she would have one. The fact that she cannot conceive naturally means that she was not intended to have a baby. Others may say that this sort of statement means that single mothers and lesbians would also have the right to have babies, and they would not approve of this.

My personal opinion is that there is no simple answer to this question. I do understand that many women are desperate to have a baby and may not be able to have one naturally, so they will want fertility treatment. However, it is also true that there are a lot of questions to be answered about single women choosing to have a baby without a father.

Examiner's comment

This is now a good answer to the question. The candidate has shown a clear understanding of the question and has presented a range of views supported by evidence and argument. The answer explains Christian views, amongst others, and includes a personal viewpoint, which is also supported.

These specimen answers provide an outline of how you could construct your response. Space does not allow us to give a full response. The examiner will be looking for more detail in your actual exam responses.

These examples only use Christianity but you could use the Grade Studio to apply to any of the religions you are studying and the structure of the answers would work in the same way.

Topic 3: Religion, poverty and wealth

The Big Picture

In this Topic, you will be addressing religious beliefs and teachings about:

- wealth and the causes of hunger, poverty and disease
- concern for others
- the uses of money
- moral and immoral occupations.

What?

You will:

- develop understanding of the causes of hunger, poverty and disease, including religious understanding and practice of charity, and the teachings on the use of money and on moral and immoral occupations
- explain how these key teachings are important to a believer and analyse the impact of these teachings on the life of a believer
- evaluate how these beliefs affect a religious person by creating a reasoned response.

Why?

Because:

- understanding the causes of poverty and the uses of wealth will help you to set your own priorities regarding how you use money
- you will gain a greater understanding of the issues concerning poor people
- understanding these beliefs helps you to compare and contrast what others believe and to think about your own ideas and beliefs about poverty and wealth.

How?

By:

- outlining the key beliefs and teachings about poverty and wealth, showing how a believer would respond to the needs of others
- illustrating how beliefs about poverty and wealth affect the life of an individual and how they would treat other people
- relating these teachings to your own thoughts about money, comparing your own experiences with those of the religions studied.

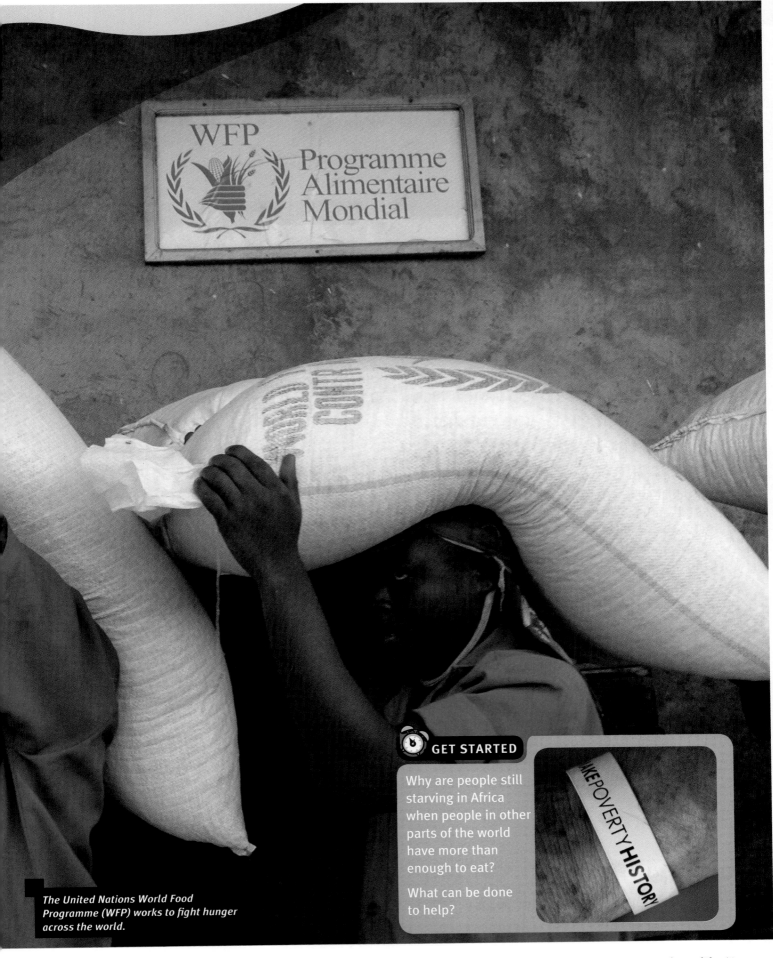

WFP
Programme
Alimentaire
Mondial

The United Nations World Food Programme (WFP) works to fight hunger across the world.

Religion, poverty and wealth

Beliefs about the causes of hunger, poverty and disease

In the world today there is a big gap between rich and poor. There are inequalities of power and wealth between the North and South. People of all religions believe that they should try to make the world a better, more equal place for everyone.

Responses of different religious groups to the needs of the starving, the poor and the sick

- Buddhists believe material goods do not lead to happiness, but everyone should help others to meet their basic material needs by giving.
- Christians believe they have a duty to help people who are suffering.
- Many Hindus believe people are poor because of wrongdoing in a previous life. They believe it is important to look after the poor by giving them money or employment.
- The Qur'an commands Muslims to share their money with the poor. One of the Five Pillars is **zakah**, which is a tax to help poor people.
- The Torah requires Jews to give a percentage of their income to the poor: this is **tzedaka**, which means 'righteousness' or an act of **charity**.
- Sikhs believe it is the responsibility of the rich to look after the poor.

REMEMBER THIS

In Buddhism and Hinduism, **ahimsa** means non-violence and respect for all living things.

'If there are poor on the moon, we shall go there too!'
(Blessed Mother Teresa)

Design an illustration for the quote from Blessed Mother Teresa and write a slogan for the picture of the two hands.

The teaching of different sacred texts about caring for others

- The Buddha taught that the greatest wealth is contentment, not material possessions.
- Christians believe the teaching of Jesus in the Parable of the Sheep and the Goats (Matthew 25) means that people will be judged according to how well they have cared for others.
- The Laws of Manus teach Hindus that wealth should be shared. Not helping the poor goes against the Hindu belief in **ahimsa**.

KEY QUESTIONS

KNOWLEDGE AND UNDERSTANDING
Explain Christian teachings about ways of earning a living and compare them with the teachings of other religions you have studied.

ANALYSIS AND EVALUATION
Are there some ways of earning a living that you would never consider because they are morally wrong? Explain your reasons.

- The Qur'an teaches Muslims to give extra charity – **sadaqah** – to the poor.
- The Torah teaches Jews to share their wealth with the poor.
- Many Sikhs follow the teaching of Guru Amar Das Ji by giving a tenth of their surplus money to the community, called **daswandh**.

Different ways in which religious people put charity into action

- Buddhists believe that giving to others is a positive action, and can generate good **kamma** if the motivation is to help.
- Christians support organisations such as Christian Aid and CAFOD.
- Hindus try to give a little to the poor every day.
- Muslims support people in less developed countries through organisations such as Muslim Aid and Islamic Relief.
- Jews support the poor through organisations like Jewish Relief.
- Sikhs give time and talents as **sewa** as well as money.

Religious teachings about the use of money

- Buddhists believe that money should be used to help others and reduce dukkha.
- Christians believe money should only be used for good purposes. Wealth should be shared and used to help others in need.
- Hindus believe wealth should be shared. Not sharing it is the same as violence.
- Islam teaches Muslims not to lend money at interest and to let people off their debts if they cannot pay. Gambling and lotteries are not allowed.
- Jews think that lending money at no interest is one of the best ways of helping others.
- Sikhs believe gambling, lending and borrowing are not good uses of money.

Teachings about moral and immoral occupations

- Buddhists follow the Noble Eightfold Path, which teaches them to follow only a 'right livelihood' – a way of earning a living that does no harm.
- Christians believe money should only be made in good ways.
- Many Hindus believe it is good to be wealthy so long as money is not earned in ways that harm others.

- Muslims follow the teaching of the Qur'an on what work they should not do.
- Jews are encouraged to work and earn money, but Jewish law says that all business transactions must be honest.
- Sikhs believe in **kirat karna** – the obligation to earn a living by honest means.

KEY WORDS

atman: the soul, or real self

charity: to give help or money to people in need

compassion: sympathy and concern for others

dalits: the lowest of the social groupings in Hindu and Sikh society (outside the four varnas), previously known as the 'outcastes' or 'untouchables'

daswandh: Sikh practice of giving 10 per cent of surplus money to the poor

dhan: the Sikh word for helping others through giving to charity or giving time to help those in need

forgiveness: to forgive (stop feeling angry towards) someone who has caused you hurt

immoral: not conforming to accepted standards of behaviour

kamma: intentional 'action' in Buddhism

kirat karna: Sikh belief in earning a living honestly

live in poverty: to be extremely poor

Sabbath or **Shabbat:** Jewish day of spiritual rest, starting at sunset on Friday and ending at nightfall on Saturday

sadaqah: extra charity that Muslims give to the poor

secular: not religious

sewa: Sikh idea of service to the community

tithe: the Christian act of giving a tenth of your income to charity (formerly taken as a tax by the church)

tzedaka: an act of charity in Judaism, for example the practice of giving 10 per cent of your income to help the poor

vand chhakna: the Sikh principle of sharing one's wealth and goods with those who are less fortunate

varnas: the four Hindu social groups

zakah: paying money to the Muslim community to help the poor

FOR INTEREST Did you know that, although Britain is thought of as a rich country, one in five people don't have enough to live on? What are the reasons and what can be done? You can find out more on the Oxfam website.

Buddhism:
Religion, poverty and wealth 1

The next two pages will help you to:

• explore Buddhist beliefs about wealth
• explore Buddhist beliefs about the causes of poverty.

Does money bring happiness?

AO1+AO2 skills **ACTIVITIES**

Think/pair/share
• Look at the pictures and decide which person is most happy. Share your conclusion with a partner. Do you agree? Why/why not?
• In your pairs, list those things that lead people to be happy. Highlight those factors related to money or material possessions in one colour and those related to emotions or attitudes in another. What conclusions can you reach about the causes of happiness by looking at your list?

Wealth and poverty

Buddhists believe in following the middle path in life. The Buddha lived a life of both extreme luxury and extreme asceticism before reaching enlightenment. The Buddha felt that neither path relieved **dukkha**, and he therefore recommended a middle way between the two. The Buddha felt that those living a life of luxury could become complacent about dukkha and fail to seek a solution to it. On the other

REMEMBER THIS

• **Dukkha** can be translated as suffering, ill, unsatisfactoriness or imperfection.
• Intentional actions that affect one's circumstances in this and future lives are called **kamma**.

hand, those living in **poverty** can be so busy trying to survive physically that they cannot find the time to seek a solution to the more spiritual problem of dukkha.

Material wealth did not bring the Buddha happiness.

In an individual sense, whether a person is wealthy or not is determined by **kamma**. Wealth in this life might be a result of generosity in past lives, and poverty might be a result of having been mean and unsupportive of those in need in the past. This does not mean that Buddhists blame those in poverty for their previous bad kamma, or will not seek to help them. Indeed, in helping the poor a Buddhist can develop positive kamma and ensure a more favourable **rebirth** in the future. A wealthy person cannot just enjoy the rewards of their previous good kamma either. If they do not make good use of their fortune in this life, and act in accordance with Buddhist teachings, they will gain bad kamma and their next rebirth will be less favourable.

Craving

Buddhists believe that dukkha is caused by craving, so the aim within Buddhism is to stop craving for things people do not have and to accept life as it is. This aim applies equally to both the wealthy and the poor. Some Buddhists believe it is harder to achieve this aim in more wealthy and materialistic societies, where a person's worth is often judged by what they have rather than what they do.

Buddhists do not approve of gambling because it causes craving and therefore dukkah (suffering). In the Buddhist sacred text the *Jatakas* lending money at interest is forbidden. By the second century CE it became generally accepted that Buddhists could lend at interest provided the interest rate was not too high.

REMEMBER THIS

The Four Noble Truths are the Buddha's diagnosis of the cause of suffering.

- First Noble Truth – there is dukkha
- Second Noble Truth – dukkha is caused by craving
- Third Noble Truth – dukkha can be stopped
- Fourth Noble Truth – following The Eightfold Path or the middle way is the way to stop dukkha.

ACTIVITIES

Do you think it is possible to stop craving for things entirely? Do you agree that this might be harder to do in more wealthy and materialistic societies? Why/why not?

FOR DEBATE

'If a person's wealth is a result of previous good kamma, they should be encouraged to enjoy the rewards for their good behaviour. If poverty is a result of previous negative kamma, people should be left to suffer the consequences of their kamma.'

What do you think?

Buddhism:
Religion, poverty and wealth 2

Concern for others

The Buddha did not reject wealthy followers. He encouraged them to use their wealth in ways that helped others. During the time of the Buddha, wealthy patrons donated land or food to the **bhikkhus** (monks). Some were encouraged to donate food to other, less fortunate Buddhists.

This Buddhist tradition of helping others has been continued until the present day. Some monasteries donate alms that they do not require to the poor, and many monasteries are engaged with helping the needy in other ways. Helping others might be seen as a positive form of the first precept, and so is encouraged.

Compassion

Buddhists are also encouraged to show **compassion** through stories of the Buddha's previous lives, such as *The Hungry Tigress*, which the Buddha told to Ananda. These stories are often told to children or repeated at festivals.

> ### The Bodhisattva and the Hungry Tigress
>
> *In the remote past, there lived a King with three sons: Mahapranada, Mahadeva and Mahasattva. The princes were enjoying the beauty of a park when they came across a thicket of bamboo. In the thicket they saw a tigress, surrounded by five cubs. Hunger and thirst had exhausted the tigress. The princes noted that the tigress was too weak to catch prey and thus would either eat her cubs or die, leaving the cubs to die as well. Mahasattva thought to himself that he should sacrifice himself. The body he was using was going to die anyway, and he could choose to leave it at a time when it could aid others. This sacrifice would help him to achieve enlightenment. So out of compassion, Mahasattva threw himself down in front of the tiger. Noticing she was too weak to move to kill him, he used a sharp bamboo stick to cut his throat, whereupon the tigress ate him, leaving only bones. The Buddha then revealed to Ananda that he had been Mahasattva.*
>
> **(adapted from E. Conze, Buddhist Scriptures)**

In Mahayana Buddhism, a Buddha is seen as one who has perfected both wisdom and compassion, and thus compassion and support for others, including the poor, is encouraged. However, it is important to note that both compassion and wisdom are to be developed: It is possible in Buddhist thought to be compassionate, but to act in a way which does not help others through lack of understanding.

The next two pages will help you to:

- evaluate Buddhist responses to poverty
- explain Buddhist attitudes to different kinds of occupation.

AO1 skills **ACTIVITIES**

'Compassion must be balanced by wisdom.' Why? What might happen if you did not balance the two and only showed compassion?

Compassion must be matched by wisdom.

Right livelihood

In The Eightfold Path, one of the areas to be perfected is right livelihood. As with all areas of The Eightfold Path, how this is applied to daily life is open to interpretation. However, most Buddhists feel that the livelihood they follow should be compatible with other Buddhist beliefs, such as the five precepts.

Many Buddhists would feel that being a butcher breaks the first precept of non-harming. Other Buddhists, however, engage in butchery or fishing, because the consumption of meat or fish is necessary for survival in the areas in which they live. Some Buddhists might feel that participation in the pornography industry would break the third precept because it might encourage people to engage in sexual misconduct or might harm the people being filmed or photographed. Some Buddhists feel they should avoid involvement in the gambling industry because it harms those with addictive personalities, and can harm families as a by-product.

Such decisions about following right livelihood are not clear cut. For example, would working in a restaurant that was not vegetarian be appropriate? On the one hand, the employee is not directly involved in killing or harming animals; on the other, they could be seen as encouraging the eating, and thus killing, of animals. Each Buddhist must decide for themselves how to interpret this teaching.

The duties of employers and employees

Whichever employment is followed, Buddhist employees and employers both have responsibilities to meet.

Employers should show appropriate compassion and support to their employees. In order to meet the first precept they also need to ensure proper health and safety procedures are followed and that the employee's psychological wellbeing is protected.

Employees have a responsibility to work hard and ensure the success of the business they are employed in. Misusing an employer's time or resources (for example, by phoning a friend for a chat in work time) could be seen as breaking the fourth precept, as you are taking time (and thus money) from the employer.

... AND DO YOU KNOW WHAT JANE DID ON SATURDAY NIGHT?

Is this the same as stealing from her employer?

ACTIVITIES

- Do you think a Buddhist should remain unemployed rather than take a job that was incompatible with their beliefs? Why/Why not?
- Do you think Buddhist expectations of employees and employers would make a business more or less productive? Explain your answer.

Grade Studio

AO1

QUESTION
Why might Buddhists give money to charity? **[6 marks]**

Level 1
You might begin by saying that Buddhists want to help other people, and giving money to charity is one way to do this.

Level 2
Continue by referring to specific Buddhist concepts. You might say that in helping other people, Buddhists could gain good kamma, which will help them gain a better rebirth.

Level 3
You could also make reference to other specific aspects of Buddhist ethics, for example Right Action in the Eightfold path. In questions like this, it is easy to give generic responses, which could apply to anyone. Try to remember to relate your answer to Buddhism more directly to access the higher levels.

Christianity:
Religion, poverty and wealth 1

The next two pages will help you to:

- explain what Christians think about wealth
- investigate what Christianity teaches about the causes of hunger, poverty and disease.

Christian attitudes to wealth and poverty

Many Christians would feel comfortable about being wealthy. You may agree that there is nothing wrong with wealth. However, it is important that a Christian does not allow their personal wealth to prevent them from understanding the needs of others, or to helping those who are less well off. Jesus did not say that it was wrong to be rich, but that riches sometimes made it hard for people to behave in a caring and sympathetic way.

 RESEARCH NOTE

Visit the Gates Foundation website then write a fact sheet about Bill Gates to explain how he made his wealth and what he is doing with it.

> **The Sermon on the Mount, Matthew 6:19–20a, 21**
>
> *Do not store up riches for yourself on earth, where moths and rust destroy, or robbers break in and steal. Instead, store up riches for yourself in heaven... For where your treasure is, there your heart will be also.*

> **Matthew 19:24**
>
> *Again I tell you, it is easier for a camel to go through the eye of a needle than for a rich man to enter the kingdom of God.*

> **1 Timothy 6:10**
>
> *For the love of money is a root of all kinds of evil.*

 **ACTIVITIES**

- Explain what Jesus and Paul taught about wealth.
- What might Christians think are the dangers of wealth?
- List some 'riches' other than money that could be used to help others.

What does Christianity say about the causes of hunger, poverty and disease in the world?

Natural disasters

These include events that humans cannot control, such as earthquakes, hurricanes and tsunamis. Severe droughts (lack of rainfall) lead to famine (not enough food) as crops cannot be grown and livestock die.

Some Christians believe that natural disasters are the work of the Devil. They think that the Devil is making people suffer through these disasters so that people might lose their faith in God because it appears that he is not helping them.

Others might think that many of these disasters are caused by changes to the environment because of the way in which it has been exploited. They would then say that this is the result of greed by individuals and businesses who are not showing respect for the environment.

Disease and education

In some countries, health care is not available to many people. Illnesses that would be cured in richer countries can kill in poorer areas. In developing countries, the problem of HIV/AIDs has had a devastating effect on communities.

Many Christians might see the **poverty** of the developing world as the result of greed and exploitation by the developed world. There are a minority of Christians who see the problem of HIV/AIDS as God's punishment on homosexuals.

Trade

Many trade practices are unfair as they benefit rich, developed countries and put less developed countries at a disadvantage. Multinational companies take advantage of poor workers and cheap labour – often the people who make certain goods will never be able to afford to buy them!

Products that poorer countries do produce to sell in the global market are controlled by high taxes, so they can only sell raw materials at a low price. The profit is then made by rich countries who turn the raw materials into manufactured goods, which they then sell back to the developing countries.

In many ways, the developed world takes advantage of developing regions, which prevents them from growing economically. This keeps many people in poverty.

Debt

In the past, poor countries were encouraged to take out large loans from rich countries. Over time the debt increased and they are now unable to pay off the interest, let alone clear the debt completely.

Many Christians would say that the trade practices of the developed world and the way in which Western banks have lent money at high interest rates have both contributed to poverty and suffering in the world. All these practices go against Christian teaching and, in particular, against what Jesus said was the second most important Commandment: 'Love your neighbour as yourself' (Mark 12:31a).

Tourists photographing poor children in South Africa.

RESEARCH NOTE

Find out more about Fairtrade at the Fairtrade website.

AO1+AO2 skills **ACTIVITIES**

Imagine you are an MP for a rich government. Write a speech to persuade your country to invest fairly and support poorer nations.

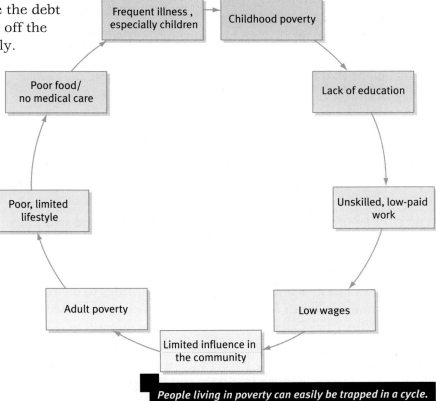

Frequent illness, especially children → Childhood poverty → Lack of education → Unskilled, low-paid work → Low wages → Limited influence in the community → Adult poverty → Poor, limited lifestyle → Poor food/ no medical care → Frequent illness, especially children

People living in poverty can easily be trapped in a cycle.

Christianity:
Religion, poverty and wealth 2

How might Christians respond to the needs of the starving, poor and sick?

Christians believe that they have a responsibility to care for the poor. The ethical commandments (also known as the Golden Rule) can be found in the gospel according to Mark, where Jesus says

> **Mark 12:29–31**
>
> *The most important [commandment] is this:... 'Love the Lord your God with all your heart and with all your soul and with all your mind and with all your strength.' The second is this: 'Love your neighbour as yourself.' There is no commandment greater than these.*

Jesus taught that the poor were as important as the rich:

> **Luke 6:20b**
>
> *Blessed are you who are poor, for yours is the kingdom of God.*

Christians should not make a big show of their support, but should do what they can, such as working as a volunteer in a **charity** shop.

Jesus taught that the size of the gift is not important:

> **Luke 21:1–4**
>
> *As he looked up, Jesus saw the rich putting their gifts into the temple treasury. He also saw a poor widow put in two very small copper coins. 'I tell you the truth,' he said. 'This poor widow has put in more than all the others. All these people gave their gifts out of their wealth; but she out of her poverty put in all she had to live on.'*

The parable of the sheep and the goats shows that God will judge people by the way they have cared for the poor (Matthew 25).

How do Christians try to support the poor?

Many Christians give a percentage of their earnings to charity. In the Old Testament, a tenth of the harvest was given to God's work. This is called a **tithe**. Christians may give the money directly to their church, or they may support a charity such as Christian Aid or CAFOD. These organisations work in many parts of the world. Other charities that may be supported include those that help children or the sick. There is no rule about which groups to support, as long as they are helping others.

The next two pages will help you to:

- examine a variety of Christian responses to the needs of the starving, poor and sick, including giving to charity
- identify Christian teachings about the use of money
- explore the notion of moral and immoral occupations and the effect this has on believers.

AO1 skills **ACTIVITIES**

Find out about the work of one of these charities, and design an advert to show their work.

- Cafod
- Christian Aid
- Make Poverty History.

Aid workers in the aftermath of Hurricane Katrina.

Christian teaching about money

Everyone needs money to enable them to have food, clothing and somewhere to live. Adults earn money in order to support themselves and their families. However, some may become greedy and crave more than they need, forgetting that there are other people who are in need of support.

Jesus taught that it was wrong for people to keep too much for themselves, because what people have on earth cannot be taken with them when they die. The parable of the rich man who stored all his goods in large barns shows this, as the man dies just as he completes building new, larger storage for his possessions. St Francis of Assisi is an example of a rich young man who gave his possessions away and devoted his life to others.

St Francis of Assisi (1181–1226).

Moral and immoral occupations

The Bible does not have a list of good and bad occupations. However, there are certain principles that can be applied using teaching from the Bible. Christians believe that all humans are made in the 'image of God' (Genesis 1) and that people should respect God's creation. Jobs that involve helping others would be seen to be **moral** and would support the teachings of the Golden Rule.

Occupations that degrade humans in some way would be seen to be **immoral**, such as anything to do with pornography, prostitution or gambling. Christians might also try to avoid working for companies that exploit the poor, or do not care for the environment.
Christian teaching does not approve of gambling because it can bring poverty and suffering to people and their families. In the past, Christians were very opposed to lending money.

Matthew 6:24

No one can serve two masters. Either he will hate the one and love the other, or he will be devoted to the one and despise the other. You cannot serve both God and Money.

REMEMBER THIS

Moral means conforming to accepted standards of behaviour.

 **ACTIVITIES**

Make two lists: one showing jobs that you think are moral (good), the other showing those that you think are immoral (bad).

Luke 6:35

'... love your enemies, do good to them, and lend to them without expecting to get anything back.'

GradeStudio

AO1

QUESTION
Explain what Christians believe about the right use of money. **[6 marks]**

Level 1
First, let the examiner know that you know what the question is about. For example, Christians believe that money can be used in different ways. Some of these ways may just be selfish while others are to help the less fortunate.

Level 2
Next, go on to explain in more detail Christian teachings about how they should use their money to help the poor, giving examples.

Level 3
Finally, explain this belief in detail. Christians believe that they cannot serve two different masters, money and God. They believe that they should give some of their money to the poor, perhaps a tenth as in the old idea of tithing. They also follow the teachings of Jesus in the Parable of the Widow's Offering and the Parable of the Rich Man.

Hinduism:
Religion, poverty and wealth 1

The next two pages will help you to:

- explain the attitudes Hindus have to poverty
- evaluate how Hindu beliefs influence their actions towards the poor.

Which image shows the greatest poverty? Why do you think this?

What does it mean to be poor?

The *Oxford English Dictionary* defines **poverty** as 'the state of being extremely poor... the state of being insufficient in amount.'

There are many causes of poverty, disease and hunger. These include flood, drought, poor education and lack of a health service to help when ill. Poverty can be measured as absolute, where it is a struggle to live – or as relative, where you have enough to live but are not as wealthy as the average person in the country you live in.

For Hindus, giving to the poor is part of their **dharma**, or religious duty. India has a great deal of poverty, and it is important that those who are richer try to help the poor. India does not have an unemployment benefit, so it is thought important that the poor should be employed by the rich as servants in order to help them. This will help the rich to build up good **karma** for doing a helpful thing, and it will protect the poor from doing jobs or actions that they might otherwise be forced into, which might add to their bad karma, the condition known as **samsara**.

Many Hindus believe that the principle of **dana** (giving) such as in charitable giving should be central to their lives as it will remove bad **karma** from their lives. You can never know if the wealth you have might be taken from you, so you need to be reflect on this. Many

Hindus try to avoid throwing away items like clothes or shoes that could continue to be used by others, as they feel that there is always someone who could benefit from them. They may offer food to help those in need.

Gandhi on poverty and wealth

Gandhi taught that there was a responsibility to care for the poor. Since all people had an **atman** – a part of the divine spark within them – then all people should be treated with respect, regardless of their wealth. He was also worried about the way in which the **caste** system reinforced the poverty in India. He wrote:

> ❝ *My greatest worry is the ignorance and poverty of the masses of India, and the way in which they have been neglected by the classes, especially the neglect of the Harijans [the untouchables, or* **dalits***, see p.77] by the Hindus.*
>   *Let there be no distinction between rich and poor, high and low.* ❞
>
> (Mahatma Gandhi)

Hindu teaching about money

Many Hindus are greatly influenced by some key ideas about how to gain wealth. One of these is dharma, which means that a person should try to fulfil their duty. Another is **artha**, in which all money must be gained by lawful and **moral** means. If you gain money dishonestly or in a way that does harm to the poor by exploiting them, this money will be a factor that will lead to bad karma.

The Hindu writer Kautilya saw artha as one of the most important of all parts of Hindu morality as he made a link between being rich and power. He taught that, if a person had great wealth, they had a responsibility to use that power for constructive, good ends and not just to reinforce their existing state.

The reality of poverty may well force tough choices for the poor and so it is important that Hindus find a way to help them escape from the temptation to use crime to help feed their families or pay their bills.

The principle of **kama**, or enjoyment of the good life, means that Hindus who are wealthy should not lead lives that are excessive. They should think about trying to be moderate in their habit and to consider the needs of others.

Money should not be wasted. Hinduism teaches that gambling encourages the waste of money and is against karma, therefore it can lead to bad consequences.

In c.500 BCE the Hindu lawmaker Vasishtha made a special law that stopped people exploiting each other by charging interest on a loan. However, by the second century CE lending at interest was allowed providing that the rate was not too high.

> **Bhagavad Gita 17:26**
> *Charity given out of duty without expectation of return, at the proper time and place and to a worthy person is considered to be the quality of goodness.*

FOR DEBATE

What could you do to help someone who is poor? What could a class of people do?

AO1+AO2 skills **ACTIVITIES**

- Explain the importance of kama, artha and dhamma when a Hindu is thinking about how they can help a poor person.
- 'Hinduism is right to talk about the deserving and the undeserving poor.' What do you think? Give reasons for your answers, making sure that you refer to Hindu teaching in your answer as well as your own opinion.

Hinduism:
Religion, poverty and wealth 2

The next two pages will help you to:

- analyse why Hindus make a distinction between moral and immoral occupations, giving clear reasons as to why each fits each category
- evaluate the Hindu ideas about occupations and be able to explain the practical consequences of their beliefs.

Modern Hindus may work in areas such as IT, where moral questions are less easy to identify.

Can Hinduism still help its followers choose their jobs?

Have you thought about the job or career you would like to pursue? Why do you want to do it? Is it for the wealth, or for the satisfaction that it could give you?

There are many reasons why we choose to do what we do, but are they all equally acceptable? Hinduism believes that not all the reasons for choosing a career are **moral**. Some jobs might be seen as **immoral** because they will encourage us to participate in doing wrong or supporting others who are doing wrong.

Hinduism divides people into groups called **varnas**. Each varna has a particular duty or set of obligations that are unique to it. These groups have been in existence since early Hinduism. People have made varnas into a form of social division. Families belong to one of the varnas, and each person in the family should try to find a job or occupation appropriate to that group. Within each varna are sub-groups called jatis. **Marriage** between varnas is not encouraged.

AO1+AO2 skills ACTIVITIES

- Working in pairs, look at the following list of jobs and occupations and put them in an ordered list from most useful to society at the top, to the least useful at the bottom. You will have to justify your choices to the class.
  Post deliverer; Doctor; Van driver; Refuse collector; Hairdresser; Soldier; TV presenter; Teacher; Prison officer; Farmer; Shopkeeper.
- What do Hindus think about moral and immoral occupations?

The structure of Hindu society reflects how it began. The Brahmins are the priests and teachers, who lead in the religious life of Hinduism as well as in the varnas. The Kshatriyas are the warriors, the political rulers and leaders of society, as they had been when India was often under attack. Then come the Vaishyas who are traders, shopkeepers and involved in business. The next group, the Sudras are involved in manual work such as farming or construction.

The Hindu book, the **Bhagavad Gita**, teaches Hindus that each varna has its own dhamma and that, as a consequence, they should do different types of jobs. It also teaches that some varnas are better suited to some roles than others. The qualities of a Brahmin should include peace, **forgiveness** and wisdom, which suit them for being priests. The Kshatriyas' qualities include heroism and the ability to be resourceful, so that suits them to be fighters or political leaders. Sudras are well suited to jobs like hospital orderlies, but it would be inappropriate for them to aspire to be doctors.

The dalits are usually seen as an underclass in Hindu society.

As well as the four varnas, there is a fifth group of people in Hindu society. They were once called 'the untouchables' but are now known as **dalits**. 'Dalit' means 'oppressed', reflecting the fact that they were often not allowed to take a full part in Hindu society. Gandhi called them Harijans, the children of God, and campaigned to remove their lowly status.

The Indian government banned the idea of untouchability in 1950, but many traditional Hindus still act differently towards those with a dalit background. Dalits in the past were the only people who were allowed to do jobs that might have led to ritual impurity, such as moving corpses or dealing with rubbish. Now the government has tried to encourage the integration of dalits into society by allocating them jobs in government departments and university study places.

As well as the varna structure, there are other jobs that Hindus might consider inappropriate. Many are vegetarians, so there are few butchers. Some Hindus believe so strongly in **ahimsa**, or non-violence, that they will avoid any career where they will in any way cause harm to others. As many Hindus believe that women should try to dress in a modest way, a career that encourages them not to do so, such as a fashion model or rock singer, might be seen as inappropriate.

As Indian society has developed and new trades have emerged, the varnas have begun to be a little more fluid. People with talent or effort can often find work in trades and occupations very different from those traditionally accepted as the ones appropriate for the group into which they were born.

AO1+AO2 skills **ACTIVITIES**

- 'Varnas are totally inappropriate for the 21st century.' Write arguments for two Hindus, one who supports the statement and one who does not.
- 'Morality should not be a big part in choosing the career you follow.' What do you think? What might Hindus say? Show that you have thought about it from more than one point of view.

Islam:
Religion, poverty and wealth 2

Wealth and poverty

The next two pages will help you to:

- explore Muslim beliefs about the causes of poverty and wealth
- evaluate Muslim responses to poverty
- explain Muslim attitudes to different kinds of occupation.

Islam is very concerned about **poverty** and suffering. Muslims do not attempt to explain why some are poor and others rich as this is something that only Allah can know. However, they are required to do what they can to help the poor and suffering.

> **Surah 3:110**
>
> *Ye are the best of peoples, evolved for mankind, enjoining what is right, forbidding what is wrong, and believing in Allah.*

Muhammad ﷺ wanted to show that Islam was concerned for the poor and to react against the greed of the merchants of Makkah. His aim was to show that the material world was part of Allah's creation and that the spiritual teachings of Islam should be combined with daily life. The practice of praying on five occasions a day at fixed times reflects this.

When the Prophet reached al-Madinah, he was able to do this because there were so many poor and suffering people there, as well as his own followers who had left everything behind in order to be with him.

Islam is opposed to the hoarding of money and possessions, and believes that wealth should circulate in the community so that everyone can benefit. Lending, investing or borrowing money at interest is also forbidden.

Muslims believe that everything comes from Allah and is intended to benefit everyone.

Zakah

One of the Five Pillars of Islam is **zakah** (purification of wealth by payment of welfare due):

> **Surah 2:110**
>
> *And be steadfast in prayer and regular in charity: and whatever good ye send forth for your souls before you, ye shall find it with Allah: for Allah sees well all that ye do.*

As well as being one of the Pillars, zakah is an act of **ibadah** – duty and worship – and plays a very important role within the **ummah**, the worldwide community of Muslims.

What reasons can there be for people to suffer like this?

AO1 skills ACTIVITIES

Think/pair/share
Look at the pictures. Discuss with a partner: What reasons can there be for people to suffer like this?

Giving zakah protects people from their wealth because it has been purified. It is not charity, but an obligation to give 2.5 per cent of surplus income. Obviously, rich people give more than the poor, and the very poor pay nothing.

Here is how zakah is calculated:

Cattle	one per 30 animals
Five camels	one sheep or goat
Goats and sheep	one per 40 animals
Mining produce	20%
Money and savings	2%
Precious metals	7%
Produce from artificially irrigated land	5%
Produce from naturally irrigated land	10%
Rent	2%

In Muslim countries, zakah acts like social security – essentials including housing, medicine and education can be provided for everyone.

Giving zakah is one of the Five Pillars of Islam.

Surah 9:60

Alms are for the poor and the needy, and those employed to administer the (funds); for those whose hearts have been (recently) reconciled (to the Truth); for those in bondage and in debt; in the cause of Allah; and for the wayfarer.

Muslims pay additional zakah at the festival at Id-ul-Fitr.

Voluntary charitable contributions are called **sadaqah** lillah (for the sake of Allah)

Surah 2:177

It is not righteousness that ye turn your faces towards East or West; but it is righteousness – to believe in Allah and the Last Day, and the Angels and the Book, and the Messengers; to spend of your substance, out of love for Him, for your kin, for orphans, for the needy, for the wayfarer, for those who ask, and for the ransom of slaves...

The Hadith teaches that charity should be given privately:

Hadith

There is a man who gives charity and he conceals it so much that his left hand does not know what his right hand spends

Poor people do not see zakah as a charity, but as their right. To withhold zakah is to steal money from the poor. By accepting zakah, the poor are also worshipping Allah and submitting to his will.

Muslim charities

There are many Muslim charity organisations, including:

- **Islamic Aid**, which works to help immediately when people are suffering from poverty, war or natural disaster
- **Islamic Relief Mission**, which works to end the long-term suffering of the poor around the world
- **Muslim Aid**, which works around the world in short- and long-term situations to help the poor deal with the causes of poverty.

MUST THINK ABOUT!

Remember – **zakah** is not charity, it is an act of duty and worship.

FOR DEBATE

'The rich have worked hard for their money, so they should not have to give it away.'

ACTIVITIES

- Explain why Muhammad ﷺ wanted to make changes in al-Madinah.
- Explain the differences between zakah and sadaqah.

RESEARCH NOTE

Choose one of these Muslim charities. Find out exactly what it does and how it raises money.

Islam:
Religion, poverty and wealth 2

The next two pages will help you to:

- examine Muslim attitudes to different types of occupation
- find out why work is important to Muslims.

Muslim banks allow people to borrow money without interest being charged on the loan.

Muslim attitudes to different kinds of occupations

The Qur'an is clear about the activities and occupations that Muslims are forbidden to do.

Money-lending

Any money-lending for interest (riba) is not allowed:

> **Surah 30:39**
> *That which ye lay out for increase through the property of (other) people, will have no increase with Allah.*

Also, Muslims should always be understanding to someone who owes them money:

> **Surah 2:280**
> *If the debtor is in a difficulty, grant him time till it is easy for him to repay. But if ye remit it by way of charity, that is best for you if ye only knew.*

Gambling and alcohol

Gambling of any form, including lotteries, is forbidden, as is making any profit from alcohol:

> **Surah 5:91**
> *Satan's plan is (but) to excite enmity and hatred between you, with intoxicants and gambling, and hinder you from the remembrance of Allah, and from prayer: will ye not then abstain?*

This means that Muslims cannot accept lottery money towards community projects.

Making money

Making money from prostitution is forbidden:

> ### Surah 24:26
> *Women impure are for men impure, and men impure for women impure, and women of purity are for men of purity, and men of purity are for women of purity. Allah, and from prayer: will ye not then abstain?*

as is lying, fraud and burglary:

> ### Surah 2:188
> *And do not eat up your property among yourselves for vanities, nor use it as bait for the judges, with intent that ye may eat up wrongfully and knowingly a little of (other) peoples' property.*

The importance of work for Muslims

The importance of working is stressed in the Qur'an:

> ### Surah 37:96
> *But Allah has created you and your handiwork!*

The way in which work is carried out in accordance with the principles of Islam is found in two of the Five Pillars: **salah** (prayer) and **sawm** (fasting).

Salah – praying five times a day – means that normal **secular** activities have to stop so that Muslims can spend time thinking about Allah.

It is important to remember that Salat-ul-Jumu'ah – weekly Friday prayers – are not part of a day of rest. Islam teaches that Allah did not rest after creation therefore there is no weekly rest day for Muslims. Attendance at Friday prayers helps strengthen the **ummah**, the community.

Sawm – the month-long fast from sunrise to sunset – also shows that Muslims focus on good and not on bodily needs.

Working to support others

Muslims do believe that they should work to support charities and send money to Muslim communities abroad.

> ### Hadith
> *The generous man is near God, near Paradise, near men and far from Hell, and the ignorant man who is generous is dearer to God than a worshipper who is miserly.*

> ### Hadith
> *Every day, each person has two angels near him who have descended from heaven. One says, 'O Allah!, compensate the person who gives to charity,' the other says, 'O Allah! Inflict a loss on the person who withholds his money.'*

Muslims praying on the last Friday of Ramadan at the Tajul Masjid mosque in Bhopal, India.

FOR DEBATE

Explain how Muslims might deal with a situation where they are offered money to build a new mosque.

AO1+AO2 skills ACTIVITIES

- In pairs, draw up a list of different jobs. Now try to sort these into those a Muslim can do and those they cannot.
- Explain Muslim teaching about zakah and how it helps the ummah.
- 'Everyone should give part of their income to charity.' Discuss. Remember to give your opinions and arguments.

Judaism:
Religion, poverty and wealth 1

The next two pages will help you to:

- explore Jewish beliefs about the causes of poverty and wealth
- evaluate Jewish responses to poverty.

 **ACTIVITIES**

Think/pair/share

- Look at the picture. Discuss with a partner: What causes some people to be rich and others to be poor?
- If all people are created equal, why do some suffer poverty while others have more money than they can spend?

How can there be such differences in the world between people?

Wealth and poverty

The Tenakh and Talmud contain Jewish teaching on **poverty** and wealth.

Jews do not attempt to explain why some are poor and others rich, as this is something which only G-d can know. However, they are required to do what they can to help the poor and to alleviate suffering.

Jews should give a tenth of their wealth as **tzedaka**, or righteousness. Judaism teaches that this money belongs to the poor, and that not to give it to them is the same as stealing it from them. Everyone from rich to poor should try to give tzedaka.

There are different ways in which tzedaka can be given.

- Handing someone money is the worst way.
- Lending someone money indefinitely with no intention of charging them interest is the best way, because you are not embarrassing the person with a gift.

The hope is that, by helping someone, they will be able to support themselves.

> **The best way of giving is to help a person help themselves so that they may become self-supporting.**

(Maimonides)

Many Jewish homes have pushkes or collection boxes for tzedaka where children are encouraged to give part of their pocket money to help those who are less fortunate.

Here are some of the teachings on wealth and poverty that are found in the Torah:

Deuteronomy 15:7–8

If, however, there is a needy person among you, one of your kinsmen in any of your settlements in the land that the Lord your G-d is giving you, do not harden your heart and shut your hand against your needy kinsman. Rather, you must open your hand and lend him sufficient for whatever he needs.

Excess wealth should also be used to help the poor. In agricultural terms, this is found in Leviticus 19. Farmers are instructed that they should not harvest to the edges of the fields. They should leave these so that the poor can gather food from there for themselves. Vineyard owners are also told not to pick all the grapes or pick of the fallen fruit so that poor people can harvest them.

Jews continue to try and put these beliefs into practice today by caring for the poor both in the Jewish community and outside.

Although Judaism is completely against materialism, it also says that people should not waste their money or give it all away, and so end up poor and a burden on others.

Talmud

It is better to make your Sabbath like a weekday than to need other people's support.

The Torah also teaches that loving money can lead people away from the worship of G-d.

Deuteronomy 8:12–14a

When you have eaten your fill, and have built fine houses to live in, and your herds and flocks have multiplied, and your silver and gold have increased, and everything you own has prospered, beware lest your heart grow haughty and you forget the Lord your G-d...

Another way in which Jews may try to help the less fortunate is Gemilut Hasadim – 'kind actions'. This includes any sort of charity work, including work for international organisations such as Tzedaka, which works to help people all over the world.

RESEARCH NOTE

Look up the Book of Ruth and find out what it says about gleaning.

Proverbs 23:4–5

Do not toil to gain wealth;
Have the sense to desist.
You see it, then it is gone;
It grows wings and flies away,
Like an eagle, heavenward.

AO1 skills ACTIVITIES

Research the work of Tzedaka and explain what it does in no more than 50 words.

FOR DEBATE

'If people are poor, it is their own fault.' Discuss this statement with a partner, then join in a whole-class debate on the subject.

Judaism:
Religion, poverty and wealth 2

The next two pages will help you to:

- explain Jewish attitudes to work
- explore Jewish ideas about different kinds of occupation.

Jewish attitudes to work

Work

From the time that Adam and Eve were forced to leave the Garden of Eden, work has been an essential part of Jewish life.

This is echoed by Maimonides:

> **❝** *Great is work. God's presence only rested upon the Jewish people when they began occupying themselves with useful work.* **❞**

As well as stressing the need for work, Judaism also insists that time is allowed for studying the Torah.

In Deuteronomy 31 Jews are told that men, women, children and even visitors should all be encouraged to spend time listening to the Torah so that they can follow its teachings. This was repeated at the time of Ezra:

Genesis 3:19
By the sweat of your brow
Shall you get bread to eat,
Until you return to the ground –
For from it you were taken.
For dust you are,
And to dust you shall return.

II Chronicles 17:7–9
In the third year of his reign he sent his officers Ben-hail, Obadiah, Zechariah, Nethanel, and Micaiah throughout the cities of Judah to offer instruction. With them were the Levites, Shemaiah, Nethaniah, Zebadiah, Asahel, Shemiramoth, Jehonathan, Adonijah, Tobijah and Tob-adonijah the Levites; with them were Elishama and Jehoram the priests. They offered instruction throughout Judah, having with them the Book of the Teaching of the Lord. They made the rounds of all the cities of the Lord and instructed the people.

Permitted occupations and Shabbat

When it comes to permitted occupations, Judaism requires that all business transactions must be honest. The vendor is also responsible for the quality of the goods that they are selling.

Leviticus 19:35–36a
You shall not falsify measures of length, weight, or capacity. You shall have an honest balance, honest weights, an honest ephah, *and an honest* hin.

Judaism forbids the same general types of occupation as most religions: prostitution, murder, selling drugs and gambling.

However, Judaism also places restrictions on what can be done during **Shabbat** – this is one of the most important aspects of Jewish life relating to work.

Judaism insists that all business transactions are honest.

In the Talmud, there are 39 different types of work that cannot be done on the **Shabbat**. These are divided into six main categories:

- growing and preparing food
- making clothing
- leatherwork and writing
- providing shelter
- creating fire
- work completion.

There are also three further restrictions:

- Muktzeh – objects that cannot be used or handled on the Shabbat
- Sh'vut – a Jew cannot ask someone else to do something on the Shabbat which they cannot do, unless this is arranged in advance
- Uvdin d'chol – weekday things.

All of these rules can be broken in the case of pikuakh nefesh. This **mitzvah**, commandment, means that almost any Jewish law can be broken in order to save life.

Mishnah

Whoever destroys a single life is considered as if he had destroyed the whole world, and whoever saves a single life as if he had saved the whole world.

RESEARCH NOTE

What is an ephah? What is a hin? Do some research at the library or on the Internet to find out.

AO1+AO2 skills **ACTIVITIES**

- In pairs, draw up a list of different jobs. Now try to sort these into those a Jew can do, and those they cannot.
- Look carefully at the list of Shabbat restrictions. How do you think these might affect a Jew in their working life? Try to find positive and well as negative responses.

Sikhism:
Religion, poverty and wealth 1

The next two pages will help you to:

- develop your knowledge and understanding of Sikh views about wealth and the causes of poverty
- explain the meaning and importance behind giving to charity (**daswandh**).

ACTIVITIES

Do you think it is our duty, as humans, to help those who may be less fortunate than ourselves? Give reasons for your answer.

Nelson Mandela, former President of South Africa. The Make Poverty History campaign, led by a number of celebrities, aimed to raise awareness of extreme poverty in the developing world.

ACTIVITIES

In pairs, make a list of causes or factors that you think contribute to world hunger and poverty.

ACTIVITIES

Think/pair/share
In pairs, think about how you would begin your own campaign to relieve world poverty. How are you going to get the public interested in what you have to say? Importantly, how are you going to convince people in the West to part with their money, and hopefully their time, to either help promote the campaign or to offer the poor countries aid?

Remember: for your campaign to make an impact on the lives of the poor and hungry, administration costs must be kept to a minimum.

Poverty

There are many causes of hunger around the world and many causes of **poverty**. These include being caught in war, poor harvests and world debt. Millions of people lack the basic amenities that we take for granted in the West, such as clean water and free education. Also, the greed of developed countries such as the USA and UK mean that resources are distributed inadequately. Many charity and pressure group campaigns, often led by celebrities, aim to make people in more developed countries aware of the problems with hunger and poverty in developing countries, and to bring about practical changes to help redress the balance.

How should Sikhs be concerned for the poor and hungry?

Sikh teachings have many references in them as to how we should help those who are less fortunate than ourselves. The Sikh principle of **vand chhakna** is very important. This means to share one's wealth and goods with those who are less fortunate. Sharing one's food and wealth is a noteworthy action according to Sikh teachings. Sikhs are, however, encouraged not to give to beggars and not to beg themselves. This is due to the principle of **kirat karna**, which means earning one's money or meal from an honest day's work.

Helping others, without wanting glory for oneself, generates good **karma** and so enables the individual to step closer to achieving **mukti** – release from the cycle of reincarnation.

Are there inappropriate uses of money?

Sikhs are encouraged to use their wealth appropriately, since it has been earned by hard work and honesty. On the other hand, gambling or wasting money on irrelevant objects or activities is strongly discouraged.

The Sikh principle of **daswandh** is very important here. This was started by the third Sikh Guru, Guru Amar Das Ji, who instructed Sikhs to give one tenth of their income to charitable causes to help the needy. Also, the practice of **sewa** in Sikhism is strongly linked to the principle of giving to charity. It means offering one's service voluntarily for the benefit of the society in which one lives. Sewa means that it is a privilege to help clean and cook in the gurdwara, the Sikh meeting hall. Many Sikhs are involved in voluntary work through which they can help others.

RESEARCH NOTE

There have been many campaigns and concerts to raise awareness of the poverty and hunger in Third World Countries. Research the activities of Live Aid and Band Aid and write down what their aims were and how they set about achieving them.

AO1 skills **ACTIVITIES**

Make a poster to show why a Sikh would take part in charity events to raise money for the poor. Make sure you include the practical nature of teachings about giving to charity such as sewa, daswandh and vand chhakna (also referred to as vand ke chakko).

AO1+AO2 skills **ACTIVITIES**

Think/pair/share
Give some examples of where you think a person has spent their money well. Now think of some examples where you believe an individual has wasted their money on inappropriate objects or activities.

In pairs, what similarities or differences have you come up with? Share your answers with the rest of the class, and from the feedback, make a list of:

- appropriate uses of money
- inappropriate uses of money.

The practice of Sewa is central to Sikh life and belief.

Sikhism:
Religion, poverty and wealth 2

What makes someone a good person?

As you read in the previous section, **sewa** and the giving of **daswandh** are key concepts for Sikhs striving to be good people. As long as they are done unconditionally, they enable the individual to be a **gurmukh** – a god-orientated rather than self-orientated individual. **Dhan**, the practice of giving charity to others is also a very important part of Sikh teachings.

There is a good story among Sikhs of how Guru Nanak Dev Ji dealt with **immoral** people who earned their living by robbing others.

The story of the thief, Sajjan Thug

Sajjan Thug owned a resthouse, where weary travellers stopped the night during their travels. During the day, Sajjan Thug welcomed his guest with a smile, pretending to have their welfare at heart. However, during the night, he would steal the travellers' goods and money while they slept. One day, Guru Nanak Dev Ji and his musician friend Mardana stopped off at Sajjan Thug's resthouse. During his stay, Guru Nanak Dev Ji taught listeners about the importance of being a good person at heart: he taught that an outward show of pretentious goodwill

The next two pages will help you to:

- explore Sikh teachings and ideas about moral and immoral occupations
- make links between Sikhs attitudes towards poverty and wealth with what you think/ believe.

AO1 skills ACTIVITIES

Sikhs are discouraged from robbing and begging. Why do you think this is so? Discuss with a partner, then with the whole class.

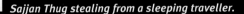
Sajjan Thug stealing from a sleeping traveller.

FOR DEBATE

Do you think Guru Nanak Dev Ji's message would have been just as strong as if he had openly confronted Sajjan Thug? Would Sajjan Thug have openly admitted he was an evil man if approached in this manner? Give reasons for your answers and compare them to those of others in the class.

was not enough if the person had evil thoughts and ways. Guru Nanak Dev Ji taught about the damaging effects to one's soul of robbing and cheating others. These teachings made a huge impact on Sajjan Thug, who realised what an evil man he was because of his cheating and robbing people who trusted him. Sajjan Thug soon changed his ways and became an ardent follower of Guru Nanak Dev Ji.

What is a moral occupation?

According to Sikh teachings, any occupation or job which allows an individual to earn their money by hard and honest means is **moral**. Begging, robbing, prostitution and selling intoxicants are all immoral occupations and should not be considered.

The principle of **kirat karna** – earning one's living by honest means – is pivotal to the role of the breadwinner. Since Sikhism promotes the stage of the householder, grihasta, the householder is expected to work hard and honestly to provide for the family. This is an example set by the Sikh Gurus themselves. Any occupation that causes harm to others, either physically or mentally, must be avoided. Sikhs should not give in to the lure of 'easy money', as this would contradict the principle of hard work.

Guru Granth Sahib Ji, page 75

With virtue he has not traded, and good actions he has not made his friends.

Guru Granth Sahib Ji, page 952

He, who with his body gives in charity and alms all he can; That house-holder is pure like the Ganges-water.

Guru Granth Sahib Ji, page 1245

He who eats what he earns through his earnest labour and from his hand gives something in charity; he alone, O Nanak, knows the true way of life.

AO1+AO2 skills **ACTIVITIES**

Suppose you are the producer of a West End show. The performance is all about how being a moral person does not necessarily have to be a result of religion, but rather a consequence of the free will and conscience that we as human beings have. In groups, write a script for a performance in which sometimes our circumstances and situations in life can dictate whether we are moral or immoral people. You also need to address the concept of forgiveness and helping others. Act your performance out in front of the rest of the class.

AO1+AO2 skills **ACTIVITIES**

Read the quotations from the Guru Granth Sahib Ji. In pairs, discuss the impact of each of these sayings on the moral behaviour and caring for others that Sikhs should display.

GradeStudio

AO1

QUESTION

Explain why a Sikh might regularly give money to charity.
[6 marks]

You could build an answer like this:

Level 1

First, let the examiner know that you are aware what the question is about. For example,

'Sharing one's wealth with those who are less fortunate, known as vand chhakna, is one of the main principles of Sikhism.'

Level 2

Next, go on to explain how giving to others with an unselfish attitude generates good karma and hence brings the individual a step closer to mukti, which is escape from the cycle of reincarnation. The practice of daswandh also needs to be explained as giving a tenth of one's income to help the poor and needy.

Level 3

Finally, go on to discuss the concept of service to others, sewa, as indicating one's duty to give to charitable causes. You could also mention that giving money to charity is an act of compassion for all individuals.

Welcome to the Grade Studio

Grade Studio is here to help you improve your grades by working through typical questions you might find on an examination paper. For a fuller explanation of how Grade Studio works, and how the examiners approach the task of marking your paper, please see p. 30.

AO1

Question

Why might Christians give money to charity?.

[6 marks]

Student's answer

Christians are nice people who want others to like them, so they will always give money to charity. Christians also believe that the Bible says they must give to charity. Some Christians give money in church every Sunday when there is a collection so that the church can work to help others.

Examiner's comment

The candidate has given a satisfactory answer to the question. The opening sentence is very weak. There are two relevant points but neither is explained in any detail. In order to reach Level 3 the candidate needs to give more information and examples. The candidate could also use more technical terms from the specification to show the breadth of their knowledge and understanding.

Student's improved answer

Christians are nice people who want others to like them, so they will always give money to charity. Christians also believe that the Bible says they must give to charity. Some Christians give money in church every Sunday when there is a collection so that the church can work to help others.

Some people, as well as giving to a weekly collection, may also give a tenth of their income to the church to help the less fortunate – this is called tithing. Charity has always been part of Christian life and teaching since the time of the deacons in Jerusalem who looked after the widows. Also, Jesus told the Parable of the Widow's Mite as an example of how and why people should give to charity.

Examiner's comment

This is now a good answer to the question. The candidate has shown a clear understanding of the question. There is good description and explanation of a variety of different reasons why Christians might give to charity. The candidate has shown some analysis. The information is presented clearly and there is good use of technical terms.

AO2

Question

'People must look after their family before they worry about the poor.' Discuss this statement. You should include different, supported points of view and a personal viewpoint. You must refer to Christianity in your answer.

[12 marks]

Student's answer

The proverb says 'charity begins at home', so of course people should look after their own family first. Some Christians might also say that their family is their first responsibility and so they must look after the needs of their family before they can worry about people outside of it.

Examiner's comment

The candidate has given a limited answer to the question. There are two points but they both address the same point of view and neither is expanded. In order to reach Level 4 the candidate needs to give alternative viewpoints and also include a personal response.

Student's improved answer

The proverb says 'charity begins at home' so of course people should look after their own family first. Some Christians might also say that their family is their first responsibility and so they must look after the needs of their family before they can worry about people outside of it.

Some people, on the other hand, might think that because of the amount of suffering, disease and poverty in the world, as Christians they have an obligation to look after the poor. Jesus told his followers to look after the poor and not to concern themselves with their own wellbeing.

My personal opinion is that Christians have to strike a balance between the two positions. Of course, they have to look after their family but, when it comes to things that are simply luxuries, they need to be concerned with taking care of the poor first.

Examiner's comment

This is now a good answer to the question. The candidate has shown a clear understanding of the question and has presented a range of views supported by evidence and argument. The answer explains Christian views, amongst others, and includes a personal viewpoint, which is also supported.

These specimen answers provide an outline of how you could construct your response. Space does not allow us to give a full response. The examiner will be looking for more detail in your actual exam responses.

These examples only use Christianity but you could use the Grade Studio to apply to any of the religions you are studying and the structure of the answers would work in the same way.

Topic 4: Religion, peace and justice

The Big Picture

In this Topic, you will be addressing religious beliefs and teachings about:

- attitudes to war
- violence and pacifism
- crime and punishment
- social injustice.

What?

You will:

- develop your knowledge of religious beliefs about war and the use of violence, including attitudes towards punishment, criminals and responses to social injustice

- explain how these key teachings are important to an individual and analyse religious responses to peace and justice in the world

- evaluate, using a variety of sources and viewpoints, how these beliefs affect a religious person.

How?

By:

- exploring the key attitudes to peace and justice by using a variety of key teachings

- discussing how beliefs and teachings about peace and justice affect the life of an individual

- relating these teachings to your own thoughts about peace and justice by comparing and evaluating your own experiences with those of the religions studied.

Why?

Because:

- you will understand the issues relating to peace and war, and justice and injustice, and the differing approaches to them

- understanding religious beliefs about peace and justice will help you to empathise with how and why people react to the unfair treatment of others

- understanding the beliefs of others will help you to reflect on your own reasons and values towards issues of peace and justice.

DON'T ATTACK IRAQ

MAB

DAILY Mirror

MAKE TEA NOT WAR

Stop the War Co...

NOT IN MY NAME
DON'T ATTACK IRAQ

NO

PEACE WITH JUSTICE

Anti-war protests are often held outside the Houses of Parliament.

GET STARTED

The International Prayer for Peace
Lead me from death to life, from falsehood to truth;
Lead me from despair to hope, from fear to trust;
Lead me from hate to love, from war to peace;
Let peace fill our heart, our world, our universe.

Look carefully at the words of the 'International Prayer for Peace' by Satish Kumar. Is it a good example of a prayer for world peace that can be said by members of all religions? Give your reasons.

Form an Opinion Line across your classroom in response to the statement: 'War is necessary to keep world peace.'

Religion, peace and justice

Attitudes to war, violence and pacifism and the reasons for these attitudes

- Buddhists are essentially peaceful and do not support violence as a way to solve conflict.
- Although the Christian ideal is that everyone should live together in peace, most Christians believe that war is sometimes necessary to prevent worse things happening, known as a 'Just War'. Some Christians, such as Quakers, are **pacifists**, who believe war is always wrong.
- Hindus believe in **ahimsa** and try not to do harm to anyone.
- Islam means 'the peace attained by following the will of Allah' and Muslims will try to oppose evil by performing greater jihad 'to struggle in the way of Allah'. Muslims believe it may sometimes be necessary to fight a Holy War – **Harb al-Muqadis** – to protect Islam.
- Judaism emphasises peace and **justice**. Jews believe that most wars are wrong and that people should always try to find peaceful solutions first.
- Sikhs believe that war can be justified in the defence of righteousness – called **dharam yudh**.

Crime and punishment and the concept of justice

- Buddhists emphasise non-violence and compassion for all life. They believe that inhumane treatment of offenders does not solve the problem and that offenders should be helped to make amends and reform. The taking of life

REMEMBER THIS

- **Ahimsa** is the Buddhist and Hindu principle of non-harming, showing respect for all life.
- **Kamma** (or **karma**) means intentional actions that affect one's circumstances in this and future lives.

ACTIVITIES

'Hatred does not cease by hatred; hatred ceases only by love. This is the eternal law.'
(The *Dhammapada*, Buddhist sacred text)

How would the world be different if everybody lived by this Buddhist teaching?

is not acceptable, so Buddhists do not condone capital punishment, although it is still practised in some Buddhist countries.

- Christians believe that people who break the law should be punished but should also be helped to become a better person. Most believe that life is sacred, but some support the death penalty. They believe prisoners should be treated properly and helped to reform their lives when they are released.

KEY QUESTIONS

KNOWLEDGE AND UNDERSTANDING
Explain the 'Just War' argument, with reference to Christianity and any other religion you have studied.

ANALYSIS AND EVALUATION
Is it always right to solve conflicts by using violence?

- Hindus believe that people who break the law should be punished but that they should also be helped to become better people.

- In Muslim countries, Shari'ah (Islamic Law) is used to punish criminals. Victims of crime are allowed compensation. Capital punishment is allowed for some crimes in all Muslim countries, although there is variation in the extent to which it is practised.

- Jews believe criminals must always have a fair trial. Jews believe in the **sanctity** of human life. In 1954, Israel abolished the death penalty, except for Nazi war criminals. Some Jews look to the **lex talionis** for the idea of the punishment being in proportion to the crime committed.

- Sikhs believe that life is given by God and is therefore **sacred**. There is no clear teaching on Sikh views about capital punishment.

Attitudes and responses to social justice and social injustice

 **REMEMBER THIS**

Sanctity means **sacred** or holy.

- The Buddha taught that following the principles of the Eightfold Path would help develop **compassion**, loving kindness, generosity and **forgiveness** towards others. Buddhists try to put these principles into practice in their everyday lives.

- Christians believe that they have a responsibility to work to make the world a fairer place for everyone and are often involved in projects to help vulnerable groups in society, such as homeless people.

- Hindus are born into one of four **varnas** (social groups) as a result of their past lives. Each has a different place in society, which they cannot change except in a future life. The lowest group are known as **dalits** – the oppressed. Many Hindus now feel that this is an unfair way of treating people.

- Muslims ensure that orphans, elderly people, people who are poor, disadvantaged or disabled, and travellers who are beggars are given special care and attention.

- Jewish teaching gives very clear guidance on how other people should be treated. Jews fight hard against injustice and give help and support to anyone in need.

- Sikhs are required to live their lives in the selfless service of others, called **sewa**. This includes **dhan** – helping others through giving to charity or giving time to help those in need.

REMEMBER THIS

In Hindu society there are four **varnas,** or social groups, which are subdivided into **castes**.

Sewa is the Sikh principle of voluntary service to others.

FOR INTEREST   The great Hindu leader Mahatma Gandhi taught that violence is always wrong, regardless of the circumstances. He practised satyagraha (peaceful, non-violent protest). Find out more about his life by watching the 1982 film of his life, *Gandhi*.

Buddhism:
Religion, peace and justice 1

The next two pages will help you to:

- explore Buddhist attitudes to violence and pacifism
- evaluate Buddhist attitudes to war.

So what exactly do Buddhists believe about violence and pacifism?

Violence and pacifism

For some people Buddhist attitudes to violence and pacifism might seem contradictory. On the one hand, the first precept, **ahimsa** or non-harming might indicate that violence should be avoided at any cost. On the other hand Buddhist practitioners in Japan and other Asian countries often practise martial arts, which could be seen as a form of violence.

This use of martial arts can be explained in two main ways.

Martial arts as a meditative technique

For many Buddhists martial arts are not practised in order to engage in violent activity itself. They are used as a meditative technique. Through the practice of martial arts a person can become intensely aware of their own bodies, and of their surroundings. This develops many of the skills required within Buddhism. This focus can be seen in the highly ritual nature of many of the martial arts, and the great respect that participants are required to show to each other.

AO1+AO2 skills **ACTIVITIES**

Draw up a questionnaire and carry out a class survey to find out what people believe about Buddhist attitudes to violence and pacifism. Are the views similar or do people have different ideas about Buddhist attitudes.

When you have finished this topic, repeat the survey and see if people's attitudes have changed. If they have, explain why this might have happened.

Skilful means (upaya)

Mahayana Buddhism advocates the use of 'skilful means' or upaya. Essentially, a Buddha or **bodhisattva** can use any technique, even those that would not normally accord with Buddhist teachings, in order to achieve the aim of bringing everyone to enlightenment or **nibbana**. When Buddhism spread to Japan, the Japanese culture would not have accepted a completely **pacifist** faith. Thus Buddhism adopted martial practices in order to achieve the ultimate aim of bringing the Japanese culture to accept Buddhism. They then provided new meaning for these practices in order to bring them into more accord with Buddhist attitudes.

However, the majority of Buddhist teachings advocate peace.

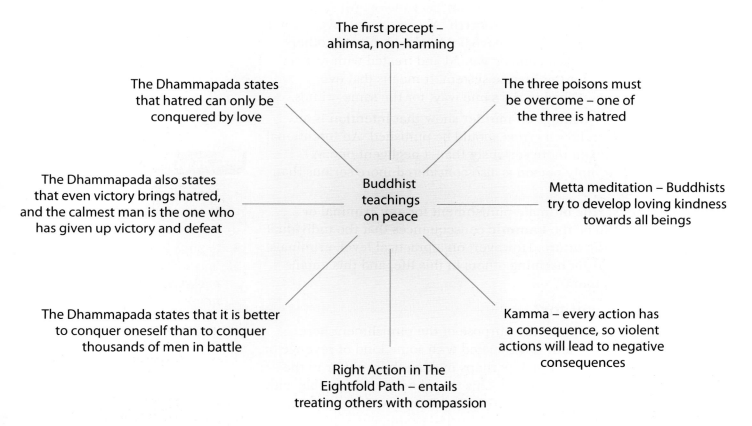

The first precept – ahimsa, non-harming

The three poisons must be overcome – one of the three is hatred

The Dhammapada states that hatred can only be conquered by love

Metta meditation – Buddhists try to develop loving kindness towards all beings

The Dhammapada also states that even victory brings hatred, and the calmest man is the one who has given up victory and defeat

Buddhist teachings on peace

Kamma – every action has a consequence, so violent actions will lead to negative consequences

The Dhammapada states that it is better to conquer oneself than to conquer thousands of men in battle

Right Action in The Eightfold Path – entails treating others with compassion

Attitudes to war

The Buddhist teaching on **ahimsa** would generally lead Buddhists to disapprove of war. In early Buddhism, it was the slaughter of war which led Asoka, an Indian king, to turn to Buddhism, and one of his first acts was to refrain from further wars.

However, most Buddhist countries have standing armies, and are prepared to go to war if they feel it to be necessary. When China invaded Tibet in 1950, there were mixed views within Tibet about whether the Buddhist population should fight back or not. In the end many Buddhists fled to India over the Himalayas rather than fight back.

 **ACTIVITIES**

Think/pair/share
Think of as many reasons for and against being a pacifist as you can. In pairs, rank these reasons in order, putting the best reason for either point of view at the top and the worst at the bottom. As a pair, decide whether pacifism is a realistic option. Share your views with the class.

Buddhism:
Religion, peace and justice 2

The next two pages will help you to:

- investigate Buddhist beliefs about crime and punishment
- explore ideas of social justice within Buddhism.

Crime and punishment

Justice

Buddhists believe that every sentient being has equal worth. This derives from the Buddhist belief in **rebirth**. At some point, every being will be a King and an ant, and will have been related to every other. This means that all beings should be valued and treated with respect. This has implications for the **justice** system. It means that every criminal should be punished in the same way, for the same crimes.

However, Buddhist teachings on murder show that intention is an important element in how a crime should be punished. An intentional murder should be taken more seriously than a negligent one. A murder of a good or holy person is also considered more serious than other murders.

In a spiritual sense, the ultimate punishment for any criminal or **immoral** action will be the **kammic** consequences that the individual will experience in the future. However, on a practical level, criminals must be prevented from harming others in this life, and this entails some sort of punishment.

What is punishment for?

It is important to distinguish the purpose of the punishment here. Often the term punishment is associated with some kind of revenge or retaliation towards the criminal, perhaps making them suffer in the same way they made others suffer. This would not be compatible with the first precept of non-harming within Buddhism. Additionally such motivation on the part of those punishing the criminal would be negative, and result in negative kamma for them.

In Buddhism, the purpose of punishment should be threefold:

- to protect society from further harm from the criminal
- to protect the criminal from developing further negative kamma
- to rehabilitate the criminal and help them develop a more positive attitude.

Ideally for Buddhists, criminals should be given the opportunity to study Buddhism. Only by understanding the kammic system will people be able to understand the consequences of their actions, and the importance of acting positively. Buddhists believe that, once the purpose of acting positively can be understood, then people will be more able to develop the self-control required to do so. Buddhist

> **REMEMBER THIS**
>
> - **Immoral** means 'not conforming to accepted standards of behaviour'.
> - In Buddhism **kamma** means 'intentional actions that affect one's circumstances in this and future lives'.

Buddhists believe prisoners should have the opportunity to learn and rehabilitate.

techniques of self-control can then be used to help the criminal to change their behaviour. These changes can be quite small initially, but Buddhists believe they can make a big difference to someone's life.

The treatment of prisoners in different Buddhist countries will vary, but **bhikkhus** (monks) will often visit prisoners. Buddhist practitioners are involved in prison visits in the UK.

Capital punishment

Buddhists do not support the use of **capital punishment** for several reasons:

- it breaks the first precept – do not harm
- it does not allow for people to change
- it does not stop the problem for the individual punished – they carry their negative attitude on to the next life with them.

However, in some Buddhist countries the death penalty does exist, such as Thailand and Burma.

Social injustice

Buddhists believe that everyone has equal value, and all have an equal chance to achieve nibbana. The Buddha clearly rejected as unfair the **caste system** present in India when he was living. This can be related to many modern issues of **equality**: for example, racism, mistreatment of the poor, and disability issues. Since the Buddha also accepted women into the monastic sangha, many Buddhists argue that he was opposed to sexism. In essence, Buddhists will oppose any unfair treatment of others since it causes **dukkha** for both the victim and, in the long term, for the perpetrator. You can read more about this in Topic 5.

Although Buddhists do not generally approve of violence, this does not mean they are complacent when it comes to issues of social injustice. Buddhists can, and do, protest against matters they feel are unfair. They generally do so with non-violent actions, such as marches and sit-ins. Occasionally, bhikkhus have sacrificed themselves, setting themselves on fire, to highlight issues they felt to be important.

In the recent past, there have been protests against China's treatment of Tibet, and Buddhists have also joined recent protests about matters of environmental concern.

 GradeStudio

AO1

QUESTION

Give two examples of what Buddhists may consider to be social injustice.

[2 marks]

In this question, you are simply required to give two examples that Buddhists might consider to be social injustice.

You might briefly explain why Buddhists consider these to be unjust or unfair. It is important, however, not to waste precious exam time by going into too much detail. There are only two marks available for this question, so it would be better to use your time on questions that can gain more marks with increased detail.

 FOR DEBATE

Does it matter who the victim is in determining the punishment given to a murderer? Why/why not?

 **REMEMBER THIS**

- Hindu society is based on the **caste system**, class divisions which are based on heredity.
- **Equality** means treating people as equals regardless of gender, race or religious beliefs.
- **Dukkha** means suffering or unsatisfactoriness.

Many Buddhists are actively engaged in promoting social justice.

 ACTIVITIES

- Write a 50-word summary explaining why the intention of the murderer is important in determining the punishment in Buddhism.
- Do you think every criminal can be rehabilitated? Would Buddhists agree with you? Why/ why not?
- Are Buddhists right to punish criminals, or is this interfering in the system of kamma?

Christianity:
Religion, peace and justice 1

Christian attitudes to war

Christians believe that violence is never an acceptable way of dealing with conflict. A key teaching for Christians is that God would like everyone to live together in peace. Jesus spoke to his followers in The Sermon on the Mount:

> ### Matthew 5:43–44
> *You have heard that it was said, 'Love your neighbour and hate your enemy.' But I tell you: Love your enemies and pray for those who persecute you.*

However, this is an ideal, and most Christians accept that it is sometimes necessary to use force to prevent worse things happening.

The 'Just War' Theory

In the 13th century, a Christian philosopher Thomas Aquinas put forward some 'rules' to help leaders consider whether fighting was the right action in a given situation.

- War should only be started by government or those in authority, not by any group or individual.
- Any war should be started for a good reason – for example, self defence, rather than to gain land or power or for revenge.
- When the war is over, things should be better than before it started – the victors should not leave the losers in a worse state.

Other rules have been added.

- War should be the last resort – all other options (discussion, negotiation) should have been tried first.
- The minimum amount of force necessary should be used.
- Civilians, especially women and children, should not be targets of the fighting.
- There should be a reasonable chance of success.

The next two pages will help you to:

- examine Christian attitudes to war, including the 'Just War' Theory
- analyse Christian attitudes towards violence and pacifism.

AO1 skills **ACTIVITIES**

Conflict can take place on a number of different levels. Write the following headings and identify two different forms of conflict for each one.

- personal (e.g. battling with addiction)
- between two people
- between groups
- national
- international
- global (e.g. World War).

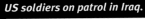

RESEARCH NOTE

Investigate one conflict that has taken place in the last five years and explain whether it was a 'Just War' in your view.

US soldiers on patrol in Iraq.

Christian attitudes towards violence and pacifism

Violence

Some Christians, such as members of the Church of England and the Roman Catholic Church, feel that there are times when violence is necessary as a last resort in order to achieve peace, or in self-defence.

Christian teachings on violence

Joshua 8:1

Then the LORD said to Joshua, 'Do not be afraid; do not be discouraged. Take the whole army with you, and go up and attack Ai. For I have delivered into your hands the king of Ai, his people, his city and his land.'

Joel 3:9–10a

Proclaim this among the nations:
   Prepare for war!
   Rouse the warriors!
   Let all the fighting men draw near and attack.
   Beat your ploughshares into swords
   and your pruning hooks into spears.

One of the Ten Commandments says 'do not murder', but many Christians would argue that killing during a war is not the same as murder.

However, the Old Testament also suggests that ideally there will be a time when fighting is no longer necessary and that people will live in peace.

In the New Testament, there is an account of Jesus using violence when he feels that traders are abusing God's temple (Mark 11:15–17).

Micah 4:1a, 3b–4a

In the last days... They will beat their swords into ploughshares and their spears into pruning hooks. Nation will not take up sword against nation, nor will they train for war anymore. Every man will sit under his own vine and under his own fig tree, and no one will make them afraid

Pacifism

Some Christian denominations believe that there is never any justification for war. For example, the Quakers maintain that Jesus' example shows that believers should love all people, including their enemies. They should also pray for those who **persecute** them.

Matthew 5:44–45a

But I tell you: Love your enemies and pray for those who persecute you, that you may be sons of your Father in heaven.

Matthew 5:9

Blessed are the peacemakers, for they will be called sons of God.

Christians who believe that violence is always wrong are called **pacifists**. They may take part in non-violent protests, or try to resolve problems through other peaceful methods – using boycotts, sanctions or protests to make their point. Pacifists will not carry weapons in a war, although they may support troops with medical aid or supplies.

 AO2 skills **ACTIVITIES**

Use the quotations and your opinions based on research to write a speech in support of or against a war.

Christianity:
Religion, peace and justice 2

The next two pages will help you to:

- explore the Christian attitudes towards crime and punishment, including capital punishment
- analyse Christian responses to social injustice.

Crime and punishment

Christians believe that everyone makes mistakes and should be forgiven. In the New Testament, when a woman was to be stoned to death, Jesus said: 'If any one of you is without sin, let him be the first to throw a stone at her' (John 8:7a). No one could, as everyone had done something wrong in their lives. However, Christians do not believe that criminals should go unpunished. Society should be protected against wrongdoing.

Punishment

Theory	Aim	Example
Protection	To protect society from anti social or harmful behaviour	Secure imprisonment for a serial killer
Retribution	To give a punishment that fits the crime (an eye for an eye)	Shorter sentence for a lesser crime
Reform	To give the offender an opportunity to change and not offend again	Community punishment and to reintegrate offender in to society
Deterrence	To act as a warning to the criminal and others	Fine – payment might put people off similar crimes

Some Christians believe in the process of **restorative justice**, where the criminal and their victim meet so that both sides can gain insight into the other's feelings or behaviour, perhaps leading the victim to feel better and the criminal to reform.

Capital punishment

Some Christians also believe in **capital punishment** because it was mentioned in the Bible: 'whoever kills a man must be put to death' (Leviticus 24:21b).

However, other Christians do not agree that capital punishment is ever acceptable, as they believe that life is **sacred** (holy) and no one has the right to take another's life. Criminals should have the opportunity to reform.

Overall, Christians believe that they have a duty to try to protect society and to help to reform criminals. They would condemn the crime, but seek to forgive the criminal.

ACTIVITIES

Put the crimes below into rank order, with the most serious at the top of your list.

Compare with others in the group, justifying your decisions.

Robbing a bank

Murder

Rape

Drink driving

Accidentally causing death

Stealing office equipment to use at home (pens, sellotape, printer paper)

Stealing medicines to save someone's life

Assisting a terminally ill person to die

Telling a lie resulting in another person being falsely imprisoned

ACTIVITIES

Look at Luke 15:11–32, the Parable of the Lost Son. Describe what happens in your own words. Explain how this shows forgiveness as well as justice.

Social injustice

Christians believe that all human beings should be treated equally, with dignity and respect. Some people are given fewer rights in society, and Christians believe that they should challenge this. Many famous people have stood up for the rights of those who are oppressed.

Christians believe that God notices what is being done and that people who act unjustly will be punished.

Leviticus 25:17a

Do not take advantage of each other, but fear your God.

They are encouraged to protect the weak and to help them.

Leviticus 19:33–34

When an alien lives with you in your land, do not mistreat him. The alien living with you must be treated as one of your native-born. Love him as yourself, for you were aliens in Egypt. I am the LORD your God.

Liberation theology

In some countries Christians have made a stand against corrupt governments who are oppressing their people. Liberation theology is the name given to the idea that God wants believers to take a stand against injustice by protesting or by helping the oppressed to challenge abuses of power. Some supporters, such as Óscar Romero, have been killed for their beliefs.

GradeStudio

AO2

QUESTION

'War is always wrong.' **[12 marks]**

Discuss this statement. You should include different, supported points of view and a personal viewpoint. You must refer to Christianity in your answer.

Level 1

First, show that you understand the question, and state an opinion. For example, many Christians believe that war is always wrong because people are killed.

Level 2

Justify this point of view by referring to a religious teaching, such as the commandment 'Do not commit murder'. Many Christians believe that killing people in war is murder. Many Christians also believe that Jesus was a pacifist because he said 'for all who draw the sword will die by the sword.'

Level 3

Offer a deeper explanation. For example, sometimes Christians say that a war is a 'Just War', meeting a number of conditions, therefore it is justified and people should be allowed to fight in it. Remember to give your own opinion.

Level 4

Now offer a deeper explanation of the second viewpoint. When the 'Just War' theory is used, every care has to be taken to ensure that the conditions are all fulfilled. In my own opinion, war is almost always wrong and particularly when it is fought so that one country can take over another one. However, there are occasions when the 'Just War' theory can be applied. You need to give your own opinion and support it with argument and evidence.

Hinduism:
Religion, peace and justice 1

The next two pages will help you to:

- explain the attitudes Hindus have to crime and punishment
- evaluate how Hindus' beliefs influence their actions about crime and punishment.

Hindu women in prison. Many Hindus believe that punishment may not just come in prison but through the bad karma caused by a person's actions.

Do Hindus believe in punishment?

Hindus believe that crime is the result of a person being caught up in ignorance about reality, coming to the belief that a selfish action will lead to their benefit. Crime has an effect on the **karma** of an individual or a group who commit it, as well as on those who are the victims and those who may have the responsibility for punishment.

The Laws of Manu, an important Hindu text, give advice as to what punishment is appropriate for each offence. When a person is punished, treating the offender in an inhumane or cruel way will not solve their misdeeds or help humanity. It will certainly not encourage them to seek the way of the **dharma** – the way of peace and wisdom.

Any punishment should be appropriate – not excessive to the offence. Shoplifting is a crime, but it should not have the same level of punishment as a bank robbery or a murder. There may be times when offenders need to be deprived of their freedom by being held in prison, but prisons should be places where they can be reformed not just punished. Many Hindus have become prison visitors.

ACTIVITIES

Working with a partner, look at the following list of crimes:

- shoplifting by a woman in her seventies
- vandalism by a 13-year-old
- murder of a violent husband by an abused wife in her forties
- bank robbery, using firearms to threaten, by a 30-year-old man.

What punishment would you give to them and why? Does the age and the context of the offender matter with regards to the sentence you give them?

REMEMBER THIS

- In Hinduism **karma** means 'actions that affect one's circumstances in this and future lives'.
- Ahimsa is the principle of non-violence and respect for all loving things.
- A person's **atman** is their soul, or real self.

A life for a life?

For many people, murder is a crime that should be punished not by a prison sentence, but by execution. This is known as **capital punishment**. Although banned in the European Union, it is still practised in many countries, such as the USA.

Many Hindus believe that the taking of a life is against the principle of **ahimsa**, which sees all life as valuable and containing the image of the divine, or the atman, in each person.

Some Hindus teach that capital punishment cannot be used because it does not give an offender sufficient opportunity to reform; it is just about punishing, getting revenge on a deed seen to be evil rather than trying to overcome the karmic consequences of the deed. The system also lacks **compassion** (concern for others), which many Hindus believe is absolutely central to any ethical issue.

The use of capital punishment means that the society has to employ an executioner. For many Hindus that would be an unacceptable job as it would inevitably involved the taking of life. This would bring negative karma to the person who carries out the execution.

Hindus believe that there is a collective karma as well as an individual one. If a group or a whole country decided to have a punishment that includes execution, the karmic effects would not just be felt by the offender or the executioner, but would have consequences for all of society.

Then why do some Hindu countries execute people?

Capital punishment was used in India following Mathatma Gandhi's murder. His assassin, Nathuram Godse, had killed him as he thought Gandhi had given too much away to the Muslims. When Godse was found guilty, Gandhi's family protested to Nehru (the Prime Minister), as they said this went against Gandhi's message. Godse was executed. Nehru argued that his attack had been not just on one man, but on the whole of India.

Many Hindus believe that the rule of law and a country's traditions are of importance to maintaining order, which they see as dhamma. Perhaps they have seen their countries suffering from political and economic unrest and feel that strong leadership is needed in order to give people an opportunity to develop their spiritual choices. They may believe that, as karma means that all actions have consequences, execution is an appropriate consequence for murder.

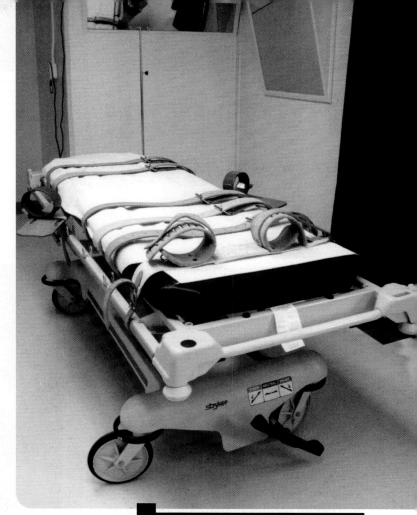

Can it ever be right to take a life for a life?

 RESEARCH NOTE

Using the Internet, try to find out how many countries where Hinduism is the majority faith practise capital punishment.

AO1+AO2 skills **ACTIVITIES**

- Using Hindu teachings, write a letter to Nehru, as a member of Gandhi's family, asking that Godse be spared.
- 'Capital punishment creates only bad karma.' What do you think? What might a Hindu say? Give reasons for your answer, showing that you have thought about it from more than one point of view.

Hinduism:
Religion, peace and justice 2

The next two pages will help you to:

- explain the differing attitudes Hindus have to war and peace
- evaluate how these beliefs, especially ahimsa, affect their actions in this area.

Can a Hindu fight?

One of the most important Hindu ideas is that of ahimsa. This is the belief that there should be no harm done to any other living thing. Many Hindus have therefore become pacifists, feeling that violence can never be justified. Gandhi particularly encouraged his followers to use non-violent methods such as marches and boycotts to make their protests, rather than violence.

Hindus are divided over whether to use violence and whether it can be acceptable to join the armed forces.

In 1919, following a massacre of unarmed civilians by the British Army at Amritsar, many in the independence movement began to use violence. Gandhi was appalled and called on the movement to stop its campaign until they could return to peaceful ways of objecting to the injustice. They did this and then Gandhi allowed the protests to resume. He believed that violence was not following the way of truth, which he believed was to be released by people following the soul-force of truth or satyagraha as it is called in Hindu thought.

Many Hindus also believe that the person who uses violence will bring bad **karma** on themselves, and will most likely end destroyed by becoming a victim of this aggression themselves.

However, this is only one Hindu approach to the issue of war and peace. Many Hindus believe that there can be good, **moral** reasons for either fighting in a war or using force or violence in some situations. A war might be acceptable:

- to remove a tyrant from power
- when a country is attacked
- if people feel oppressed by an occupying power.

> **Bhagavad Gita 2:31**
> *Think also of your duty and do not waver. There is no greater good for a warrior than to fight in a righteous war.*

Teachings on war and violence in Hindu scriptures

In the Hindu scriptures the Vedas, the gods talk about their battles and are asked in prayer to deal with soldiers. They determine whether a person killed in a battle can enter **moksha** or whether they will be reborn.

The Laws of Manu are a set of Hindu writings that are believed to date back to the first human. They set out the rules for war. They say that the Kshatriyas should fight as their religious duty but that they should make sure that they do so with mercy, respect and care. They say that they only fight other soldiers, not civilians. They should try to fight fairly: for example, making sure that they do not attack when people are asleep or have surrendered.

Some Hindus believe that these rules still apply: others say that they come from so long ago that they cannot be applied to the ways wars are fought today: in an age when we have nuclear, chemical and biological weapons, the instruction not to hurt innocent civilians can not be followed.

The Bhagavad Gita is a Hindu holy book that is a debate between good and evil. It describes the story of a soldier called Arjuna who on the eve of a battle is tempted to leave and become a wandering holy man. The god Krishna appears to Arjuna in the form of his earthly servant, encouraging him to fight. The god says that fighting in a war does not affect the eternal destiny of a person, as the soul after death will travel onto a new place.

Arjuna should feel that his sacred duty – his dharma – is to be a good soldier. Although he may kill people who are relatives, this is not an excuse to avoid this necessary war. The war about to be fought is a lawful, sacred duty, to make sure that society is upheld. Although the story can be read as symbolic of the struggle within each human to live a good life, it has been used to encourage Hindus to see that war can be justified.

REMEMBER THIS

Moksha is the release from the cycle of reincarnation.

AO1+AO2 skills ACTIVITIES

- 'The teaching about ahimsa is the most important in Hinduism and therefore fighting can never be right.' What do you think? What might Hindus say? Give reasons for what you think. Make sure you reflect on a diversity of Hindu views.
- Research the Bhagavad Gita in detail. Write a two-hundred-word summary of its main teachings.

GradeStudio

AO1

QUESTION

Explain what Hindus believe about war. **[6 marks]**

Level 1

First let the examiner know that you know what the question is about: for example, 'Hindus believe that war has too many reasons for being fought, all of which are not equally moral.'

Level 2

Next, go on to explain in more detail about how Hindus have differing opinions that influence their attitude to war and explain a couple of ideas that influence shape their thinking: for example,

'The idea of ahimsa is seen as important to many Hindus in determining their attitude to war and fighting.'

Level 3

Finally explain how this is a difficult issue to resolve. Hindus believe that there are many different factors that will influence a person whether or not to fight in a war. Their religious teachings encourage them to think about the value of human life (ahimsa), but they also have to balance this against a sense of duty (dharma). They should also think about the consequences for their individual karma and the collective karma of their nation.

Islam:
Religion, peace and justice 1

The next two pages will help you to:

- explore Muslim attitudes to violence and pacifism
- look into the meaning of greater jihad and lesser jihad.

Soldiers are sometimes needed to keep the peace as well as to fight in wars.

Violence and pacifism

The word 'Islam' means 'peace' as well as 'submission'. In Muslim teaching, peace does not mean that people should accept any situation regardless of whether it is just or not. Rather, it means that enemies should be fought with **justice** and without hatred or revenge as motives; once the fighting is over, peace must be restored.

> **Hadith**
> *Hate your enemy mildly; he may become your friend one day.*

The Qur'an teaches that everyone is created equal, and stresses that everyone should be treated equally.

> **Surah 30:22**
> *Of His Signs is the creation of the heavens and the earth, and the diversity of your tongues and colours.*

> **Surah 49:14**
> *O mankind, We have created you from male and female; and We have divided you into tribes and sub-tribes for greater facility of intercourse. Verily, the most honoured among you in the sight of Allah is he who is the most righteous among you. Surely, Allah is All-Knowing, All-Aware.*

AO1 skills **ACTIVITIES**

Take a straight 'yes' or 'no' vote in your class: 'Does the media represent Islam fairly?'

Draw up a questionnaire and carry out a class survey to find out what people believe about Muslim attitudes to violence and pacifism.

When you have finished this Topic, repeat the vote and see if people's attitudes have changed. If they have, explain why this might have happened.

The aim of Islam is world peace without any prejudice or discrimination on any grounds. Islam says that this is the right way forward for humanity and it teaches a message of peace. Greater Jihad is the daily struggle of every Muslim to submit to the will of Allah and to work towards this goal.

Attitudes to war

Jihad is an Arabic word that is often wrongly translated as 'Holy War'. In fact, jihad means 'a personal individual struggle against evil in the way of Allah'.

Greater jihad

The struggle against evil is a daily task for all Muslims, which is often called Greater jihad; someone who struggles in this way is called Mujahid.

> ### Hadith
> *The most excellent jihad is the uttering of truth in the presence of an unjust ruler.*

Lesser jihad

Jihad can be seen as a struggle against evil in a wider sense and may including fighting to protect Islam. Such a fight would be Harb al-Muqadis, a Holy War.

> ### Hadith
> *The Prophet was asked about people fighting because they are brave, or in honour of a certain loyalty, or to show off: which of them fights for the cause of Allah? He replied, 'The person who struggles so that Allah's word is supreme is the one serving Allah's cause.'*

Muhammad ﷺ fought at the Battle of Badr (624 CE) to protect Muslims in al-Madinah. Although Islam permits self-defence as a reason for fighting, they are forbidden from making the first attack.

There are many conditions that prevent a war from being described as jihad, such as when:

- an individual person declares war without the backing of the Muslim community
- innocent women and children are put at risk
- peaceful ways of solving the problem have not been tried
- the purpose of the war is to force people to convert to Islam
- the purpose of the war is to gain land or power
- the war involves the destruction of homes or places of worship
- the war is aggressive, not defensive
- the war is started by a political leader rather than a religious leader
- trees, crops and animals have not been protected.

Muslims are not allowed to start a war, and if there is an offer of peace they must lay down their weapons.

ACTIVITIES

- 'Greater jihad affects every aspect of a Muslim's life.' Discuss.

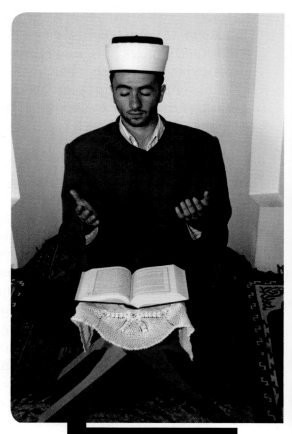

Prayer is something which Muslims must do five times a day to fulfil the will of Allah.

AO1+AO2 skills ACTIVITIES

- Make a table showing the differences and similarities between the conditions for Lesser jihad and those for a 'Just War'.
- Look at newspaper reports about jihad. Which ones, if any, are really examples of Greater jihad?

Islam:
Religion, peace and justice 2

The next two pages will help you to:

- investigate Muslim beliefs about crime and punishment
- evaluate Muslim attitudes to social injustice.

Muslim beliefs about crime and punishment

Shari'ah is Islamic law based on the teachings of the Qur'an. In Muslim countries, it is used to determine the trial, judgement and treatment of criminals. Shari'ah means the 'way to water' or the 'source of life'. Living according to Shari'ah is part of the way in which Muslims can follow the wishes of Allah.

Shari'ah recognises three types of sin:

- **shirk** – associating something or someone with Allah (this is why pictures or statues are not allowed in mosques)
- zulm – crimes such as theft, murder, suicide and illegal sexual intercourse
- a third category covering crimes such as lying, swearing and envy.

The purpose of punishment in Islam is not to remove sin; only Allah can do this when a person truly repents and asks for **forgiveness**. The main aim of punishment is to protect and strengthen society.

Certain crimes carry certain punishments, and the circumstances of the crime cannot be taken into account because, again, only Allah can know what the person was thinking and what actually happened.

For this reason, the penalties given out as punishments are called hudood – boundaries. They re-establish boundaries between what is right and what is wrong.

Hudood is used for crimes that are mentioned in the Qur'an:

- Murder – The only defence that can be given for murder is that the victim is a murderer or has tried to lead other people away from Allah's teachings. Even then, the killing must take place by legal means.
- Stealing.
- Adultery (when a married person has sex with a person other than their spouse).
- Destroying someone's reputation.

Under Islamic law, a person who has suffered because of a crime is entitled to compensation.

Pattern is used in mosques, as using pictures or statues would be shirk.

 **ACTIVITIES**

Write down as many things as you can which might mean destroying a person's reputation.

 **FOR DEBATE**

How does the system of justice of Shari'ah law compare with that in the United Kingdom? Do you think that one is fairer than the other? Why/why not?

Surah 2:178

O ye who believe! The law of equality is prescribed to you in cases of murder: the free for the free, the slave for the slave, the woman for the woman. But if any remission is made by the brother of the slain, then grant any reasonable demand, and compensate him with handsome gratitude. This is a concession and a Mercy from your Lord. After this, whoever exceeds the limits shall be in grave penalty.

These punishments can be seen as harsh, particularly to non-Muslims. However, it is important to remember some of the other conditions of Shari'ah: once a person has been punished and has asked Allah for forgiveness, their guilt is cleared and they must be treated normally.

Often, the punishments are not imposed and what happens may depend on the country in which the crime takes place. Shari'ah law is designed to protect society, not primarily for punishment. In different countries, hudu may be interpreted in different ways – Muslims remember that Allah is forgiving and therefore people should do the same.

Fātiha, or The Opening Chapter.

1. In the name of Allah, Most Gracious, Most Merciful.

2. Praise be to Allah, The Cherisher and Sustainer of the Worlds;

3. Most Gracious, Most Merciful;

4. Master of the Day of Judgment.

5. Thee do we worship, And thine aid we seek.

6. Show us the straight way;

7. The way of those on whom Thou hast bestowed Thy Grace, Those whose (portion) Is not wrath, And who go not astray.

Surah 1 of the Qur'an.

Social injustice

The Qur'an stresses the importance of **equality**. However, there are three particular groups of people who are seen as being most in need of care: the needy, orphans and travellers. This reflects the bad ways in which Muhammad ﷺ saw these groups being treated in Makkah and the ways in which he tried to change society in al-Madinah.

In the same way that Muslims believe that elderly relatives should be cared for by their families and not placed in homes, they hope that orphans should, whenever possible, be brought up by relatives and know about their family. They should also receive any inheritance that is due to them from their parents.

The group called the needy are all those who are in **poverty**, or who are handicapped or disadvantaged in some way:

Caring for the elderly is a very important aspect of Muslim teaching.

Surah 24:61

It is not fault in the blind, nor in one born lame, nor in one afflicted with illness.

Travellers, in this context, are not people on a particular journey, but beggars and people without hope who wander from place to place.

The final group to consider is the elderly. Older people are seen as part of the wealth of a Muslim community because of the contribution they have made through their lives:

Surah 17:23–24

Thy Lord hath decreed that ye worship none but Him, and that ye be kind to parents. Whether one or both of them attain old age in thy life, say not to them a word of contempt, nor repel them, but address them in terms of honour. And, out of kindness, lower to them the wing of humility, and say: 'My Lord! Bestow on them thy Mercy even as they cherished me in childhood.'

FOR DEBATE

Consider the ways in which Muslims treat orphans and elderly people. Do you think this is a good way of helping families or is it better for these people to be in homes or orphanages?

AO1+AO2 skills ACTIVITIES

- Write a 50-word summary explaining how Shari'ah law compares with punishment theory.
- How should Muslims react when they see social injustice?

Judaism:
Religion, peace and justice 1
Violence and pacifism

The next two pages will help you to:

- explore Jewish attitudes to violence and pacifism
- investigate Jewish attitudes to war.

Jewish teachings are very ancient being based on the word of G-d found in the Torah and the teachings of the Talmud. There is no country today where state law is based purely on Jewish teachings but the essential teachings about peace and justice remain as a major influence in Jewish life.

Judaism is committed to peace and **justice**. This is found in the Tenakh as well as the Talmud and remains an essential part of Jewish life and belief today.

Soldiers at a checkpoint in Israel. These soldiers are needed to keep the peace in an area that has seen much conflict in recent years.

> **Psalm 29:11**
>
> *May the Lord grant strength to His people;*
> *may the Lord bestow on His people wellbeing*

> **Talmud**
>
> *But he stands highest who establishes peace among the nations*

> **Ethics of the Fathers 1:18**
>
> *The world endures on three things – justice, truth and peace.*

Love of justice is very important to Jews. Often the following passage is interpreted incorrectly as showing that Judaism is a religion based on revenge:

> **Exodus 21:23–24**
>
> *But if other damage ensues, the penalty shall be life for life, eye for eye, tooth for tooth, hand for hand, foot for foot, burn for burn, wound for wound, bruise for bruise.*

This passage is known as **lex talionis** (the law of retaliation). However, it does not say that people should literally take an eye for an eye, but that the financial penalty imposed should not be greater than the loss that has occurred.

Judaism teaches **forgiveness**, but believes one person cannot forgive on behalf of another person. Therefore, Jews alive today cannot forgive the deaths of the six million who died in the 20th-century Holocaust; only G-d can forgive this.

AO1+AO2 *skills* **ACTIVITIES**

Draw up a questionnaire and carry out a class survey to find out what people believe about Jewish attitudes to violence and pacifism.

When you have finished this Topic, repeat the survey and see if people's attitudes have changed. If they have, explain why this might have happened.

Attitudes towards war

Judaism teaches that wars are essentially wrong and that after fighting peace must be the aim.

Judaism is not a pacifist religion, but teaches that peace must always be the aim.

Teachings on war from Isaiah

> **Psalm 34:15**
>
> *Shun evil and do good,*
> *seek amity and pursue it.*

> **Isaiah 2:2–4**
>
> *In the days to come,*
> *The Mount of the Lord's House*
> *Shall stand firm above the mountains*
> *And tower above the hills;*
> *And all the nations*
> *Shall gaze on it with joy.*
> *And the many peoples shall go and say:*
> *'Come,*
> *Let us go up to the Mount of the Lord,*
> *To the House of the G-d of Jacob;*
> *That He may instruct us in His ways,*
> *And that we may walk in His paths.'*
> *For instruction shall come forth from Zion,*
> *The word of the Lord from Jerusalem.*
> *Thus He will judge among the nations*
> *And arbitrate for the many peoples,*
> *And they shall beat their swords into ploughshares*
> *And their spears into pruning hooks:*
> *Nation shall not take up*
> *Sword against nation;*
> *They shall never again know war.*

Types of war

There are cases of war in the Jewish scriptures. There are Holy Wars, in which the Jews were trying to maintain their religion when other people opposed them. The scriptures talk of some wars that appear to be 'Just Wars' (see below), but also of others that now may appear to be unjustified.

Jewish thinking allows for three different types of war, as follows:

1   Milchemet mitzvah: This is a war commanded by G-d – therefore similar to a Holy War. This includes the war against Amalek and Joshua fighting to return to the Promised Land. The conditions for this type of war are that the enemy has attacked first or that there is a need to pre-empt an attack.

2   Milchemet reshut: This is an 'optional war' – or it could also be described as a 'Just War'. For a war to be just in this sense:
   - the war should be a last resort
   - non-violent approaches should have been tried first
   - civilians should not be targeted
   - damage should be limited.

   There has been no example of this since the fall of the Temple in 70 CE.

3   Pre-emptive war: This may only be fought when there is risk of an imminent attack upon Israel. This happened in 1967, when Israel attacked the airfields of Egypt and Syria in the Six Day War.

Jews are required to protect themselves and other Jews. They must also fight to help other countries in order to prevent the war from spreading. Self-defence is also permitted: 'If a person intends to kill you, be first to kill him' (Talmud). Judaism also teaches that wars must be fought properly and humanely.

 RESEARCH NOTE

Find out more about the rules of war in Deuteronomy 20:10–13, 19–20.

 **ACTIVITIES**

Think/pair/share
Think of as many reasons for and against being a pacifist as you can. In pairs, rank these reasons in order, putting the best reason for either point of view at the top, and the worst at the bottom. In your pair, decide whether you think pacifism is a realistic option. Share your views with the class.

> **Proverbs 25:21**
>
> *If your enemy is hungry, give him bread to eat;*
> *If he is thirsty, give him water to drink.*

Judaism:
Religion, peace and justice 2

The next two pages will help you to:

- investigate Jewish beliefs about crime and punishment
- evaluate Jewish attitudes to social injustice.

Jewish beliefs about the punishment and treatment of criminals

Judaism teaches that criminals must always be treated fairly and must have a fair trial before any sentence is passed.

Traditional Jewish law lists 36 serious crimes, including adultery, sodomy, idolatry, witchcraft and murder. Each of these should incur one of four types of death penalty: stoning, burning, beheading or strangling.

In practice, the Rabbis did everything they could to avoid the death penalty. As well as conducting a thorough examination of all the witnesses, the judges had to be sure that the defendant was aware of the punishment before they had committed the crime. In addition, if the judges were unanimous in a guilty verdict, the rules stated that they must be prejudiced, and therefore the verdict must be wrong.

On the occasions when a death penalty was issued, every effort was to be made to overturn it. Finally, if the sentence was to be carried out, the prisoner was drugged, and executed in the most humane way possible. The death penalty was abolished in 30 CE. The State of Israel only permits the death penalty for war crimes, in particular for those involved in the Holocaust.

Traditional law proscribed a further 207 crimes, including perjury, incest and eating of forbidden foods, for which criminals were whipped for a maximum of 39 strokes. However, the same rules about knowing the penalty in advance and holding a strict trial were still applied. A doctor was also brought in to inspect the prisoner to ensure that they were fit enough to receive the punishment.

Finally, minor crimes received a much milder punishment of makkat mardut, or disciplinary lashes.

Jewish law tries to limit punishment and to safeguard the criminal, so that violence and suffering is kept to a minimum. Although traditional Jewish law does not apply in any particular state, Jews today still look to apply these ancient principles of justice in their everyday lives.

How should someone be punished for this sort of crime?

AO1 skills ACTIVITIES

Should there be the same punishment whoever has committed the crime? Have a class discussion.

FOR DEBATE

How does the system of justice under Jewish law compare with that in the United Kingdom? Do you think that one is fairer than the other? Why/why not?

Social injustice

Judaism has very clear teaching about justice and injustice, showing how other people should be treated.

> ### Leviticus 19:33–34
>
> *When a stranger resides with you in your land, you shall not wrong him. The stranger who resides with you shall be to you as one of your citizens; you shall love him as yourself, for you were strangers in the land of Egypt: I the Lord am your G-d.*

There are many instances in the Jewish scriptures where the prophets condemn social injustice among the people.

Teachings from the prophet Amos

> ### Amos 6:3–6
>
> *Yet you ward off [the thought of] a day of woe*
> *And convene a session of lawlessness.*
> *They lie on ivory beds,*
> *Lolling on their couches,*
> *Feasting on lambs from the flock*
> *And on calves from the stalls.*
> *They hum snatches of song*
> *To the tune of the lute –*
> *They account themselves musicians like David.*
> *They drink [straight] from the wine bowls*
> *And anoint themselves with the choicest oils –*
> *But they are not concerned about the ruin of Joseph.*

AO1+AO2 skills ACTIVITIES

Take some of the key phrases from the passages on social justice and find out what they mean: for example, 'the ruin of Joseph'.

> ### Amos 5:23–24
>
> *Spare Me the sound of your hymns,*
> *And let Me not hear the music of your lutes.*
> *But let justice well up like water,*
> *Righteousness like an unfailing stream.*

Judaism teaches that Jews have a responsibility to help other people and other countries, both with money and with practical support for development. So, as well as trying to combat social injustice, they must also make a practical difference to people's lives. One way in which this is done is by giving a tenth of their wealth as **tzedaka** (see page 82).

AO1+AO2 skills ACTIVITIES

- Write a 50-word summary explaining how the death penalty might finally be reached in a Jewish court.
- How should Jews react when they see social injustice?
- How might a Jew ensure that they protect and look after people who are weaker than themselves?

Sikhism:
Religion, peace and justice 1

The next two pages will help you to:

- develop your knowledge and understanding of key Sikh attitudes towards war, pacifism and justice
- find out about Sikh justification for **dharam yudh** and the reasons why Sikh militancy developed.

DAILY NEWS

7 June 1984

GOLDEN TEMPLE MASSACRE

On Sunday evening (5 June) the Indian army stormed the most holy place in Sikhism, the Golden Temple (or Harmandir Sahib) in Amritsar, the Punjab.

The Temple had become a haven for Sant Jarnail Singh Bhindranwale, a politically ambitious Sikh preacher, and his followers, and had been surrounded by huge numbers of army units since Friday. The Indian government had been using Bhindranwale to oppose renewed Sikh calls for an independent homeland in the Punjab. His activities had led to widespread disruption and the Indian President, Indira Gandhi, apparently decided that he must be captured.

Demands for a peaceful surrender were met with volleys of gunfire from within the confines of the temple. The resistance was so strong that the army had to bring in tanks and heavy artillery to suppress gun fire. After 24 hours the army successfully took control of the temple.

The Indian government stated that 83 army personnel were killed and 249 injured. Sikh casualties were 493 killed and 86 injured. However, the Associated Press reports that Indian observers assert the number of Sikh casualties to be at least 800.

It remains for the next few days to show the eventual outcome of such an act of violence perpetrated by a country religiously committed to pacifism.

AO1+AO2 skills ACTIVITIES

- Read the newspaper article. What do the terms 'violence' and 'pacifism' mean?
- Do you think violence should be confronted with violence? Try to explain your answer in detail.

AO1+AO2 skills ACTIVITIES

Think/pair/share
Imagine you have the opportunity to carry out an interview with the leader of the Ministry of Defence. In pairs, think of four questions you would like to ask him/her about the country's policy on war. As a class, one person can sit in the 'hot seat' and attempt to answer the questions. Make sure you include some questions that elicit the leader's personal opinion on matters of war.

AO1+AO2 skills ACTIVITIES

Carry out a survey among your class, asking who believes that violence is justified, and who is totally pacifist, and why. Compile the reasons they give for their views in a table, like this:

Reasons FOR violence	Reasons AGAINST violence
Defending the weak and oppressed	Causes death and grief

Do Sikhs support war?

Sikhs are encouraged to protect the weak and oppressed – and if this means going to war, then violence is justified.

The concept of the **dharam yudh** or 'war of righteousness' is very important in Sikhism. Sikhs are encouraged to defend themselves and others from tyrants. The symbolism behind the **kirpan** – one of the five khandas of Sikhism – encourages a Sikh to be brave and fight against tyranny and oppression.

However, going to war without strong enough reasons is not condoned. The tenth Sikh Guru, Guru Gobind Singh Ji, laid down strict rules and regulations about when a war is justified. Selfish gain or hidden agendas did not constitute a dharam yudh.

The Zafar-nama is a letter of instruction, apparently written by Guru Gobind Singh Ji, which clearly states that, if peaceful means have failed, then the use violence is justified in terms of a dharam yudh. The letter, composed in Persian, was undertaken in the aftermath of the Guru having lost all four of his sons (the Sahibzadi) as a result of persecution from the Mughals.

How Sikh militancy developed

The martyrdom of the fifth Sikh Guru, Guru Arjan Dev Ji marks an important stage in the development of Sikhism. The fifth Guru's son, Guru Hargobind Ji, introduced the concept of militancy into the Sikh faith when he became the sixth Guru. Guri Hargobind Ji instructed his son Guru Har Rai Ji that he should always have 2200 soldiers and horses with him. Many Sikhs are of the opinion that the first five Sikh Gurus were pacifists, but that militancy had to be institutionalised so that the Sikh people and their faith could continue to develop. Guru Gobind Singh Ji and his followers were often under attack. Many battles were fought against the Mughal emperor. The Guru died of stab wounds in 1708.

Also, the history and development of Sikhism has a strong martial tradition, starting when Sikhs were under threat of conversion to Islam from the Mughal invaders of India.

Guru Hargobind Ji.

RESEARCH NOTE

Find out more about the five conditions, laid down by Guru Gobind Singh Ji, that justify carrying out dharam yudh, the war of righteousness.

ACTIVITIES

Visit a Sikhism website and look at the composition of the Zafar-nama. What are your initial thoughts about the emotions and feelings that a distraught father is showing?

What courage and attitudes do you think Guru Gobind Singh Ji is encouraging the Sikh community to develop?

ACTIVITIES

Think and share

- How would you feel if you were a Sikh living in the Punjab in the early 18th century and the Zafar-nama had just been read out to you?

- If previously pacifist, would you now turn to militancy to protect your community from the Mughal invaders? Explain why.

- Share your answers with other people in the class.

Sikhism:
Religion, peace and justice 2

Sikhs, violence and pacifism

While many Sikhs agree that violence is justified in terms of defending oneself and the oppressed or weak, others, especially Namdhari Sikhs, are staunch pacifists, and are totally opposed to violence. They can never justify the use of violence and have carried out protests, especially against the rulers of the British Raj. Guru Ram Singh, heralded by the Namdharis as the twelfth Sikh Guru, led the freedom struggle through non-violent means. Due to their pacifist outlook, Namdharis do not wear the kirpan.

There are no specific pacifist teachings in Sikhism but, even though it is not supported by evidence, many Sikhs believe that Guru Nanak Dev Ji was a pacifist.

The Mughal invader – Babur

Babur was a cruel Mughal who invaded India at the time of Guru Nanak Dev Ji. Babur appears a number of times in the writings of Guru Nanak Dev Ji as the unjust ruler who eventually gave in to his evil ways. Lalo was a devout Sikh who accompanied Guru Nanak Dev Ji on many of his travels.

The Mughal Emperor, Babur (1483–1531).

The next two pages will help you to:

- analyse the pacifist outlook of many Sikhs and explore this alongside attitudes towards crime and punishment
- make links between these beliefs and attitudes with what you think/believe.

 MUST THINK ABOUT!

There is a sharp distinction in Sikh teachings regarding mere violence and dharam yudh – the former is unjustified and is regarded as wrong.

 FOR DEBATE

There has been much debate amongst Sikhs as to whether Guru Nanak Dev Ji was a pacifist. The Mughal rulers were already in India at the time of Guru Nanak Dev Ji. Having read the quotations, do you think Guru Nanak Dev Ji was a pacifist? Give reasons for your answer.

Guru Granth Sahib Ji, page 722

Guru Nanak Dev Ji on Babur

As the word of the Lord comes to me, so do I utter, O Lalo.
Bringing the marriage party of sin, Babur has hastened from Kabul and
demands perforce the gift of our Land, etc, O Lalo.
Modesty and righteousness both have vanished, and falsehood moves about as
the leader, O Lalo...
Nanak sings the glories of the Lord in the city of corpses and mentions this affair,
He, who has made the mortals and attached them to pleasures, sits apart and
alone, and beholds them.

 **ACTIVITIES**

Imagine you are working in a court and have a case presented to you in which a young man is accused of robbing from an old people's home. Using the Guru Granth Sahib Ji as your basis, how would you deal with the accused and what verdict, on religious terms, would you deliver?

How should Sikhs treat criminals?

While there are no teachings about capital punishment in Sikhism as such, on a religious basis, everyone is given the opportunity to ask for **forgiveness**. Sikhs believe that, in accordance with the law of karma, every person will face the consequences of their bad actions in the next life. Sikhs follow the law of the country they are in with regard to the treatment of criminals.

Sikhism and social injustice

Sikhs believe that God is a Just Creator, and this belief should be carried out in our lives too. Sikh history contains many references to the injustice committed against the Sikhs, especially during the Mughal and British rules in India. Sikhs are encouraged to fight against social injustice; if peaceful means fail, then violence is justified. The actions of the Sikh Gurus stand as fine examples of how a Sikh should work for **justice** in society.

ACTIVITIES

Imagine you are working for Amnesty International. In groups, decide on a project that you would like to undertake and write down the aims and objectives. How will you implement this project from a Sikh point of view? What teachings and examples from Sikh history will you use to achieve your aims?

Each group will report back. Allow time for the class to ask you questions about your work.

GradeStudio

AO1

QUESTION

Explain how Sikhs might justify reasons for a war.

[6 marks]

You could build an answer like this:

Level 1

First, let the examiner know that you are aware what the question is about. For example:

'Sikhs are encouraged to fight and speak out against oppression and tyranny, especially in defence of the weak and oppressed.'

Level 2

Next, examine the institution of martial arts into the development of Sikhism as a result of the martyrdom of Guru Arjan Dev Ji by the Mughal invaders. You could go on to describe the importance of the dharam yudh in Sikhism. This is the concept of a just and righteous war in the face of tyranny and oppression.

Level 3

Finally, go on to look at the efforts of the Sikh freedom fighters who sought independence for India from the British rulers during the Raj. It is also important to analyse here the symbolism behind the kirpan, one of the five Ks of Sikhism, especially the Khalsa.

GradeStudio

Welcome to the Grade Studio

Grade Studio is here to help you improve your grades by working through typical questions you might find on an examination paper. For a fuller explanation of how Grade Studio works, and how the examiners approach the task of marking your paper, please see p. 30.

please see p. 30.

AO1
Question

What are Christian attitudes towards war?   **[6 marks]**

Student's answer

Christians are pacifists and believe that all war is wrong because Jesus was a pacifist. Some Christians believe that there are occasions such as a 'Just War' which meet certain conditions and when it is right to fight in order to protect people.

Examiner's comment

The candidate has given a satisfactory answer to the question. There are two main points but only one of them, about 'Just War', has any valid explanation. In order to reach Level 3 the candidate needs to give more information and examples. The candidate could also use more technical terms from the specification to show the breadth of their knowledge and understanding.

Student's improved answer

Christians are pacifists and believe that all war is wrong because Jesus was a pacifist. Some Christians believe that there are occasions such as a 'Just War' which meet certain conditions and when it is right to fight in order to protect people.

Some Christians say that there are examples in the Bible of wars that were fought with God's approval and help. Some of these are described as Holy Wars, fought to protect religion. There are some Christians such as Quakers (The Religious Society of Friends) who are total pacifists and will not fight under any circumstances.

Examiner's comment

This is now a good answer to the question. The candidate has shown a clear understanding of the question. There is good description and explanation of a variety of different attitudes towards war. The candidate has shown some analysis in dealing with the Quakers. The information is presented clearly and there is good use of technical terms.

AO2

Question

'All people must be pacifists.' Discuss this statement. You should include different, supported points of view and a personal viewpoint. You must refer to Christianity in your answer. **[12 marks]**

Student's answer

Some Christians say that all people must be pacifists because they believe that Jesus was a pacifist. Other Christians believe that the commandment says 'do not kill' and that therefore any fighting must be wrong because people risk being killed.

Examiner's comment

The candidate has given a limited answer to the question. There are two relevant points but one is a matter of opinion and the other is a common misinterpretation resulting in a misunderstanding. In order to reach Level 4 the candidate needs to give alternative viewpoints and also include a personal response.

Student's improved answer

Some Christians say that all people must be pacifists because they believe that Jesus was a pacifist. Other Christians believe that the commandment says 'do not kill' and that therefore any fighting must be wrong because people risk being killed.

Some people, on the other hand, might think that there are circumstances, such as during a 'Just War', when it is necessary for Christians and others to fight. The circumstances include such things as avoiding unnecessary harm, not attacking civilians, the war must be declared by a recognised authority.

My personal opinion is that it is not easy to decide whether to be a total pacifist or whether there are circumstances, such as during the Second World War, where people have a duty to fight in order to protect their country from being overrun by evil.

Examiner's comment

This is now a good answer to the question. The candidate has shown a clear understanding of the question and has presented a range of views supported by evidence and argument. The answer explains Christian views, among others, and includes a personal viewpoint, which is also supported.

These specimen answers provide an outline of how you could construct your response. Space does not allow us to give a full response. The examiner will be looking for more detail in your actual exam responses.

These examples only use Christianity but you could use the Grade Studio to apply to any of the religions you are studying and the structure of the answers would work in the same way.

Topic 5: Religion and equality

The Big Picture

In this Topic, you will be addressing religious beliefs and teachings about:

- the principle of equality
- attitudes towards racism
- attitudes towards gender
- attitudes towards religion
- forgiveness and reconciliation.

What?

You will:

- describe teaching about equality, by demonstrating your knowledge of religious views and attitudes and by showing their importance to a member of a religion
- explain how these teachings are important to an individual and analyse the impact of these beliefs on a believer
- evaluate how these teachings affect a religious person by using evidence and creating a personal response.

Why?

Because:

- you will understand how religious people view their community and the people in it
- understanding different viewpoints will enable you to contribute to discussions of significant current equality issues, such as the role of women
- you will be able to observe how forgiveness and reconciliation have helped and healed religious communities.

How?

By:

- demonstrating your knowledge of key teachings and beliefs, showing their impact on the daily lives of a believer
- illustrating and assessing how teachings on equality affect the life of an individual
- relating these concepts to your own ideas about equality and recognising similarities and differences between your own ideas and those of the religions studied.

Changes in the world of work mean that women and men may well do the same jobs.

GET STARTED

'Women still not paid as much as men!' The BBC website.

Are you surprised that this is still the case in modern society? What do you think are the reasons for this? Is this unfair?

Religion and equality

KEY INFORMATION

The National Association of Women Civil Servants protesting for equal pay in the 1950s.

AO2 skills ACTIVITIES

'*Equality may perhaps be a right, but no power on earth can ever turn it into a fact.*'   Honoré de Balzac

Do you think that this is true?

Religious teachings about equality

- Buddhists believe everyone possesses the 'Buddha-nature', therefore all are worthy of respect.
- The Bible teaches Christians that everyone is equal in the sight of God.
- Hindus are born into one of four **varnas** (social groups) depending on the actions of their past lives. Living a good life leads to being reborn into a higher varna.
- Muslims believe Allah created all people equal.
- Jews believe that everyone is descended from Adam and all are equal, whatever their beliefs.
- Sikhs regard everyone as equal regardless of **caste**, creed, race or gender.

Attitudes to discrimination on grounds of race and gender

- For Buddhists, discrimination of any kind is not compatible with living in accordance with **dhamma**.
- Christians believe that racial or gender **discrimination** is always wrong.
- Many Hindus believe prejudice against someone because of their race or gender is wrong.
- Muhammad ﷺ taught that there should be no discrimination on grounds of race or colour.

REMEMBER THIS

In Buddhism **dhamma** means universal law or ultimate truth.

- Jews remember their experiences of **racism** and persecution and believe they should always welcome people from other races.
- Sikhs follow the example and teaching of the Gurus who stressed the **equality** of all humans.

Beliefs about the role of women

- Buddhists regard men and women as spiritually equal and both may be monks or nuns.
- Some Christians believe that God created men and women to have different roles; others think that they should have the right to choose.

KEY QUESTIONS

KNOWLEDGE AND UNDERSTANDING
What is interfaith dialogue? Give examples of how it works in practice in Christianity and any other religion you have studied.

ANALYSIS AND EVALUATION
'Religious Education in schools is a good way of promoting understanding of the differences between religions.' Do you agree? Give reasons for your view. What other ways are there to promote understanding between religions in our local and national communities?

- In Hinduism, men and women have different roles. Women are expected to be good wives and mothers, bringing up their children to follow Hinduism.
- Islam teaches that men and women are equal but have different rights and duties.
- Progressive Jews treat men and women equally: they pray together and women can become rabbis. In Orthodox Judaism, women sit separately in the synagogue.
- Sikhs follow the teachings of Guru Nanak Dev Ji, who emphasised the equality of men and women.

Attitudes to other religions

- Buddhists promote understanding between faiths, and there are examples of people being both Buddhist and Christian.
- Some Christians think Christianity is the only true religion and that all other religions are false. Many Christians are committed to **evangelism**, while others work to develop **interfaith** understanding.
- Hindus believe that different religions should respect each other.
- Muslims believe Islam is the only true religion and that all people are born to be Muslims – this is called **fitrah**. In Britain, Muslims are often involved in interfaith dialogue in their local communities.
- Jews believe everyone should follow their own religion, according to the **Noachide code**. They do not encourage people to convert to Judaism.
- Sikhs believe people should have freedom to practise their religion.

Beliefs about forgiveness and reconciliation

- In Buddhism, to become enlightened is to be an example of deep knowledge and compassion. Buddhists try to practise **forgiveness** and to work for peace and **reconciliation**.
- Christians follow the teaching of Jesus in the Lord's Prayer that they should forgive others.
- Hindus believe that their behaviour will be rewarded or punished in their next life. They believe that bearing a grudge against someone hurts the person who has these feelings.
- Muslims believe that Allah forgives people who admit wrongdoing and Muslims must follow this example.

- Jews are taught to pray for forgiveness daily. Judaism teaches Jews to forgive others, but that only G-d can forgive on behalf of others.
- Sikhs respect others, teach tolerance and seek **justice**.

KEY WORDS

discrimination: unjust or prejudicial treatment because of race, age or gender

ecumenical movement: people who work to improve understanding between Christian groups

equality: treating people as equals regardless of gender, race or religious beliefs

Eucharist: the Christian ceremony commemorating the Last Supper, in which bread and wine are consecreted and consumed

evangelism: persuading others to share your faith

fitrah: the teaching that Islam is the only true religion and that all people are born to be Muslims

interfaith dialogue: discussions and work to help understanding between different faiths

mitzvot (pl.): the 613 commandments by which Jews should try to live their lives (singular is mitzvah)

Noachide code: seven commandments given to Noah by G-d after the flood

ordination: the process by which individuals are consecrated, or set apart, as clergy to perform various religious rites and ceremonies

prejudice: making judgements not based on reason or actual experience

proselytising: trying to convert people to one's own religion

racism: prejudice, discrimination or ill treatment against someone because of their race

reconciliation: restoring friendly relations

repentance: sincere regret or remorse from one's actions

sexism: prejudice, stereotyping or discrimination, typically against women, on the basis of sex

varnas: Hindu social classes believed to have existed since the beginning of the world

FOR INTEREST

Do you know what interfaith activities take place in your area? Do some research to find out. You can visit the Interfaith Network for the UK for listings of regional and local activities.

Buddhism:
Religion and equality 1

The next two pages will help you to:

- explore Buddhist teachings about equality
- investigate Buddhist views of women.

Would you like to be treated differently because of your beliefs?

ACTIVITIES

Think/pair/share
Think of as many different types of prejudice as you can. In pairs, decide why people show prejudice in these ways. Can you think of any ways in which these prejudices can be overcome? Share with the class.

Are all beings equal?

Buddhism developed from the Hindu tradition. In Hinduism, there is a **caste** or **class system**. This is based on the **varna** or class of your parents, and determines religious and social obligations; at the time of the Buddha, it also determined your occupation. The Buddha rejected the caste system as unfair. He felt that a human's worth should be determined by his actions in this life, rather than the caste or class he was born into.

Some Buddhists go further than this, and declare that every sentient being is of equal value. Since every being has been, or will be human, animal, etc., they all have equal value. This is not a view shared throughout Buddhism. Some Buddhist writers have claimed that killing small animals results in less negative **kamma** because the effort required to kill them is less than that required to kill large animals. Buddhist commentaries on the murder of humans also indicate that killing a good or holy person should attract a more serious punishment than that of anyone else.

Prejudice

The Buddhist attitude to all forms of prejudice, including racism, is that it derives from ignorance or delusion. This is one of the three poisons, along with greed and hatred. In the Buddhist worldview, being deluded or ignorant of the way the world really is allows people to feel greed and hate. If they truly understood the world, they would know that greed and hatred are pointless, and would seek to overcome them.

RESEARCH NOTE

Research the structure and organisation of the Hindu caste system, to help you understand what the Buddha was rejecting.

REMEMBER THIS

In Buddhism **kamma** means 'intentional actions that affect one's circumstances in this and future lives'.

REMEMBER THIS

The three poisons are shown at the centre of the wheel of **samsara** as a pig, cockerel and snake. The three poisons are the factors that keep beings tied to the wheel of samsara. If delusion, greed and hatred were overcome, enlightenment could be achieved.

Essentially Buddhists feel that prejudice derives from a false understanding of self. By thinking they have an eternal self, people become selfish. Buddhists believe that if we recognised the truth of **anatta**, or no-self, they would see how pointless it is to be selfish. If we have no eternal self, then there is no 'I' to be selfish about. Buddhists believe that when people recognise the truths of the three marks of existence, they can see all people as having equal value and status.

A popular Buddhist **meditation** practice is metta meditation. Metta means **compassion**, or loving kindness. In metta meditation, practitioners try to extend feelings of loving kindness towards all beings.

Do women have equal status in Buddhism?

This is a difficult question to answer. Based on the information provided above it would seem that all humans should be regarded equally, including men and women. The Buddha accepted women into the monastic community and most Buddhists see women as having equal spiritual status and rights. However, there are issues of gender inequality within Buddhism. These are often more pronounced in poorer Buddhist countries, and some may be a result of cultural rather than religious influence.

Can women achieve enlightenment?

Some Buddhist writers have claimed that a female rebirth is less favourable than a male rebirth. This may reflect the society in which they were living, where women may have had less freedom to determine their own lives, or found it harder to follow a spiritual path within the monastic sangha.

Some people have claimed that within Buddhism women cannot gain enlightenment, and that a male rebirth is necessary. While this view may have been popular in some patriarchal societies, modern Buddhist scholars believe that the Buddha said that both men and women could gain enlightenment.

The status of the bhikkhunis

According to Buddhist scriptures, when the Buddha was initially asked to institute an order of **bhikkhunis**, he refused. He relented on the condition that bhikkhunis followed extra rules.

It is difficult to accord this view with the Buddha's other teachings. One explanation might be that, within the patriarchal Indian society of the time, such additional rules were necessary for the bhikkhunis to be accepted at all. Another might be that women may be more susceptible to physical dangers, and that placing the bhikkhunis under the protection of the bhikkhus would offer them additional protection.

In many Buddhist countries, the lines of bhikkhunis died out. Cultural influences may have made it hard for women to leave their family lives in order to pursue a spiritual life. It is currently a matter of debate within Buddhism whether these **ordination** lines can be re-established by the bhikkhunis of other traditions, or by the bhikkhus. Until the matter is decided, women who wish to follow a spiritual life in these traditions cannot seek full ordination as a bhikkhuni.

REMEMBER THIS

The three marks of existence in Buddhism are **dukkha**, **anatta** and **anicca**.

REMEMBER THIS

A **bhikkhuni** is a Buddhist nun and a **bhikkhu** is a Buddhist monk.

Should bhikkhunis have the same status as bhikkhus?

FOR DEBATE

Should the rules for the bhikkhunis be changed to reflect changes in society?

AO1+AO2 skills ACTIVITIES

- Design a poster for a Buddhist temple showing Buddhist attitudes towards equality.
- Write a letter from a modern Buddhist woman explaining how they feel about the status of women within Buddhism, and whether they would like to see changes in Buddhist beliefs and practices.

Buddhism:
Religion and equality 2

How do Buddhists interact with other religions?

The next two pages will help you to:

- evaluate Buddhist attitudes to other religions
- investigate Buddhist teachings about forgiveness and reconciliation.

Buddhists have generally been tolerant of other faiths. Buddhism began in India and has spread to many other countries around the world, often co-existing with the indigenous religions in these countries. In the past, when Buddhism has spread to a new country, it has not generally tried to prevent the practice of the indigenous religions. Instead, it has tended to find points of common interest between Buddhism and the indigenous religion on which to build. In some cases, Buddhism has adopted the local practices of the country it spread to, and has given them a new meaning that coincides with Buddhist interests.

In India, King Asoka, a Buddhist supporter, was tolerant of other faiths. He encouraged his subjects to offer food to Hindu Brahmins, as well as Buddhist bhikkhus. He himself supported Hindus, Jains and other religious philosophers, as well as Buddhists. This demonstrates that, even in early Buddhist history, tolerance of other faiths was well established.

In the modern world, Buddhism has been active in the **ecumenical movements** designed to bring faiths together. Buddhist leaders have often engaged directly with the leaders of other faiths, and are tolerant of the interests of others.

The Dalai Lama, the leader of Tibetan Buddhism, is recorded as saying that it is better to have a range of faiths, to suit the range of different people within the world. He also said that learning about other faiths can enrich a person's own faith.

It could be argued that most religions teach people to behave morally, and that in so doing people are making progress along the path to **nibbana**. This might then be fulfilled in a future life, when they are reborn as a Buddhist.

AO1+AO2 skills — ACTIVITIES

- Think of arguments for and against working with other faiths on issues that concern all humanity. Do you think religions should work together or not? Explain your answer as fully as possible.
- Do you think that having a tolerant attitude to other religions means you value your own faith less? Why/why not?

REMEMBER THIS

Nibbana is the blowing out of the fires of greed, hatred and ignorance, and the state free of suffering.

Police arrest a protesting monk near the Chinese Embassy in Kathmandu.

Forgiveness and reconciliation

Buddhists believe that **forgiveness** is an important element of a person's spiritual development. Along with greed and delusion, hatred is one of the three poisons that prevent a person from achieving nibbana.

Buddhists believe that, by refusing to forgive someone, a person becomes bitter and hateful. This affects their attitudes to others, and leads them to behave in ways that lead to negative kammic consequences. A failure to forgive is as harmful to the person who is asked to forgive as it is to the person who needs forgiveness.

While Buddhists may find it as hard to forgive people as anyone else, their religion encourages them to do so. Metta meditation is one method by which a Buddhist might try to develop feelings of compassion towards those they dislike, and thus work towards forgiveness and **reconciliation** with them. The meditation can be adapted to focus on one person, or a small group, if a Buddhist is having difficulties feeling loving kindness towards them.

 **ACTIVITIES**

- Do you agree with the Buddhist view that failure to forgive hurts the person who is filled with hatred as much as the person who wants forgiveness?

- Do you think it is always possible to forgive others, or are some 'evils' too awful to forgive? Explain your answer fully.

GradeStudio

AO2

QUESTION

'Men and women are not equal.' Discuss this statement. You should include different, supported points of view and a personal viewpoint. You must refer to Buddhism in your answer. **[12 marks]**

Level 1

First, show you understand the question, and state an opinion. For example, you might say that Buddhists believe that everyone is equal, and so men and women must be as well.

Level 2

Next, justify this view by referring to a religious

teaching, you might say that in Buddhism the concept of equality is very important and found in the teaching of Siddattha Gotama, the Buddha.

Level 3

Next, offer a deeper explanation. You might show awareness of the differences between the rules for bhikkhus and bhikkhunis, and explore whether these show that men and women are not equal, or have different purposes. Remember to give your own opinion.

Level 4

Finally, offer a deeper explanation and give your own opinion and support it with evidence and argument.

Christianity:
Religion and equality 1

What does the Bible teach about equality?

Christians are told that all humans are made 'in the image of God' (Genesis 1:27). They believe that all humans matter to God, regardless of race, gender, ability, wealth or skills, and that all who pray to God will be listened to and treated without favouritism. As a result of God's attitude to humans, they should treat others with the same respect.

Christians also believe that they should treat others in the way they would wish to be treated: 'Love your neighbour as yourself' (Luke 10:27b).

On equality

> **Galatians 3:28**
> *There is neither Jew nor Greek, slave nor free, male nor female, for you are all one in Christ Jesus.*

> **James 2:1**
> *My brothers, as believers in our glorious Lord Jesus Christ, don't show favouritism.*

> **Acts 10:34–35**
> *Then Peter began to speak: 'I now realise how true it is that God does not show favouritism but accepts men from every nation who fear him and do what is right.*

Christian views on prejudice and discrimination

Christians believe that they should follow the example of Jesus, therefore all people should be treated in the same way. Jesus healed the son of a Roman centurion, even though the Romans were hated; he showed respect for women, who were seen as less important than men; and he made a Samaritan the hero of his parable, even though the people of Samaria were not respected by the Jews.

The next two pages will help you to:

- examine Biblical teachings about equality
- look at a variety of views about prejudice and discrimination in relation to race and gender, including Christian views
- evaluate Christian attitudes to the role of women.

 **ACTIVITIES**

Pair work
'All animals are born equal, but some are more equal than others.'

Discuss what this quotation from George Orwell's book *Animal Farm* means. Decide whether you agree with it and explain your opinions.

Christians believe that God loves all people equally regardless of race, colour, gender or age.

> **Luke 10:30–35a**
>
> **The Parable of the Good Samaritan**
>
> *Jesus said: 'A man was going down from Jerusalem to Jericho, when he fell into the hands of robbers. They stripped him of his clothes, beat him and went away, leaving him half dead. A priest happened to be going down the same road, and when he saw the man, he passed by on the other side. So too, a Levite, when he came to the place and saw him, passed by on the other side. But a Samaritan, as he travelled, came where the man was; and when he saw him, he took pity on him. He went to him and bandaged his wounds, pouring on oil and wine. Then he put the man on his own donkey, took him to an inn and took care of him. The next day he took out two silver coins and gave them to the innkeeper. "Look after him," he said.'*

Racism

In the past, Christians have not always set a good example: for example, there were many Christian slave owners. However, there are also a number of dedicated believers who have fought against discrimination.

Gender

Sexism is a form of prejudice based on gender, typically against women. In the past, many people felt that men and women possessed different skills, and this has resulted in their being treated differently. Some Christians believe that God made men and women differently, and this has led to a traditional view that men should go out to work to provide for the family while women bring up children and run the home.

However, many Christians now feel that men and women should be given equal opportunities and responsibilities in the workplace and at home.

Women in the Church

Christians believe in **equality**, although this may not mean that all people are able to do the same job. There is a strong feeling in some denominations that women should have no part in the Ministry of the Word of God.

In the Roman Catholic Church, women are not accepted as priests as it is felt that only men should say the words spoken by Jesus that are repeated during the Mass. It is also thought that because God came to earth in the form of a man – Jesus – his representatives on earth should only be men. St Paul also taught that women 'should be silent in church'.

However, many other denominations have long accepted women in their ministry. Methodists, Baptists and others allow both men and women to be ministers, to preach and to have equal responsibility. The Church of England accepted women as vicars in 1994. Some Anglicans disagree with this and have not been comfortable with women taking over their parish (church area).

ACTIVITIES

Make a poster based on the theme 'all humans are equal', using quotations from the Bible to support the theme.

RESEARCH NOTE

Find out about Martin Luther King Jr or Archbishop Desmond Tutu. Prepare a short presentation to describe how they fought for equality, using the BBC and Nobel prize websites to help you.

There are female Anglican vicars, but no female Anglican bishops as yet.

FOR DEBATE

If Christians believe in equality, why do some oppose women priests?

Christianity:
Religion and equality 2

The next two pages will help you to:

- examine Christian attitudes towards other religions
- identify Christian beliefs about forgiveness and reconciliation and evaluate their impact.

Christian attitudes towards other religions

Christianity is an **evangelical** religion. This means that Christians believe that they should try to encourage everyone to become members of their faith. This is because of the commission Jesus gave to the disciples:

> **Matthew 28:16–20a**
>
> *Then the eleven disciples went to Galilee, to the mountain where Jesus had told them to go. When they saw him, they worshipped him; but some doubted. Then Jesus came to them and said, 'All authority in heaven and on earth has been given to me. Therefore go and make disciples of all nations, baptising them in the name of the Father and of the Son and of the Holy Spirit, and teaching them to obey everything I have commanded you.'*

This commission is taken seriously by many Christians, who feel that they should become involved in missionary work – bringing the Christian message to people in their own country and all over the world. Christians involved in missionary work feel that it is essential to give everyone the opportunity to follow the Christian faith in order to know God. John's Gospel explains this:

> **John 14:6**
>
> *Jesus answered: 'I am the way and the truth and the life. No one comes to the Father except by me.'*

AO1 skills **ACTIVITIES**

Visit the Church Mission Society and the BMS World Mission websites to research the work undertaken by a missionary society. Produce a leaflet to highlight the variety and scope of the activities of your chosen society.

Ecumenism

This is the name given to the movement that tries to unite different Christians. There are hundreds of different Christian groups and often they have different ways of practising their faith. Many denominations – mostly Protestant and orthodox – meet as members of the World Council of Churches in order to celebrate the fact that all confess the Lord Jesus Christ, according to the Holy Scriptures, as God and Saviour. The spirit of ecumenism has been encouraged by many of the Asian and African Churches, which have demonstrated great courage in the face of persecution.

Christian beliefs about forgiveness and reconciliation

It can be hard to forgive someone, but Christians are encouraged to do so. In the Lord's Prayer Christians pray:

Luke 11:4a

Forgive us our sins, for we also forgive everyone who sins against us.

This suggests that if Christians wish to be forgiven by God, they should be prepared to forgive other people. This does not mean that a person who commits a wrong action should get away with it, but that if they **repent** (are truly sorry) they should be forgiven.

In the Roman Catholic Church, a person can ask for **forgiveness** through the Sacrament of Reconciliation (Confession), where they tell a priest what they have done and the priest helps them to make amends for their actions through prayer and **repentance**.

Christians believe that God sent Jesus to be sacrificed on the cross in order to reconcile God with humanity. Humans are forgiven through the death and resurrection of Jesus, and this is remembered in the service of the **Eucharist**, also known as Holy Communion.

ACTIVITIES

Pairs/groups
Write down three actions that you think are unforgivable. Share them with a partner and then with another pair. What do you agree on? Why?

GradeStudio

AO1

QUESTION
Explain Christian attitudes towards racism. **[6 marks]**

Level 1
First, let the examiner know that you are aware of what the question is about. For example, Christians believe that God created all of humanity, so Christians should not be racist.

Level 2
Next, explain in more detail what Christians believe about racism and how they may put these beliefs into practice in their lives.

Level 3
Finally, explain more about this belief. Christians believe that God made everyone equal and that all human beings are equal regardless of their skin colour or language. Some people say that Adam was made from different coloured soils from the four corners of the earth; some say that the sons of Noah were the fathers of different races; some say that different languages came about because of the Tower of Babel. However, Christians believe that Jesus' message was for everyone, so they should oppose racism wherever they find it.

Hinduism:
Religion and equality 1

We are all one? Hindu attitudes to race and caste

Some people believe that all human beings have common ancestors and therefore we ought to show this belief in action by the way in which we treat others.

> **The Purusha Sukta**
>
> *When the primal man was divided*
> *The Brahmin priest arose from his mouth*
> *The kshtatiyra soldier from his arms*
> *The vasishya merchant from his thighs and*
> *The shudra working man from his feet.*

Take a look at the Purusha Sukta. Does it encourage people to believe not just that all have come from an original man but that, in some way, at the point of separation some people became better than others? Within each **varna** are groups called **castes** or jatis, which are linked to occupation-based groups in society.

Although many people think that we should treat each other as if we are all equal, this is not always the case, as there many forms of prejudice to be overcome. In some cases, people have a negative view of others. These views are based on a pre-judgement, without really knowing the person or people involved. This includes racism, sexism, homophobia, ageism and a lack of respect for the disabled.

Hindu society has been structured around the idea of **varna**, which means class or social group. Many **marriage** advertisements in newspapers mention the varna of the person seeking marriage. As names can often reveal a person's varna, sometimes people may use alternative names. Although the Indian government has tried to outlaw the notion of untouchability or **dalit** people, who were seen as below the varna system, some observant Hindus still continue to follow this belief.

There is some tension in Indian society between Hindus and Muslims. And when Europeans such as the British were ruling parts of India, many Indians of the Brahmin varna refused to enter their houses, for fear of compromising their religious purity.

The next two pages will help you to:

- explain the beliefs that Hindus have on equality and justice
- evaluate how Hindu beliefs affect their attitudes to gender, race and caste
- develop your own views about creating a more just society.

 **ACTIVITIES**

What do you think causes people to be prejudiced? With a partner list as many reasons as you can.

REMEMBER THIS

- **Dalits** are the lowest of the social groupings in Hindu and Sikh society (outside of the four varnas), previously known as the 'outcastes' or 'untouchables'.
- **Dharma** means religious duty in Hinduism.

What do Hindus think about the role of women?

Traditionally, Hindu society stressed the different roles and duties of men and women. Women were expected to be supportive wives and good cooks, and to spend their time raising children. Some Hindus look to the example of Sita, who was the wife of Rama. Women were seen as less necessary than men. Many Hindus believe that an unmarried woman has not fulfilled her destiny or her **dharma**.

The Indian government wrote into their constitution that there should be equal rights for all citizens. The law clearly gives equal access to jobs. Women now have the right to own property, have access to education and are allowed into the top ranks of Indian society.

Many Hindu women have been influenced by feminism. Some believe that the elements of Hinduism that seem to be sexist can be removed without seriously damaging the faith. They also stress the importance of the idea of goddesses in Hinduism, which they claim has often been overlooked because of the men's sexist attitudes.

Campaigns to make sure that widows are not abandoned by their families have also been very successful. In the past, some widows were encouraged to commit ritual suicide – called suttee – following the death of their husbands, or to become unpaid servants in the house of one of their husband's family members. Now a widow is supported by a benefit and is free to marry again if she wishes.

Despite the fact that India has had a female Prime Minister, the Indian government has had to bring in legislation to stop parents deciding to abort female foetuses because sons are regarded as being of more value.

Indira Gandhi (1917–1984) was Prime Minister of India for a total of 15 years.

RESEARCH NOTE

Find out more about Indira Gandhi, a former Indian Prime Minister, and produce a PowerPoint presentation about her life.

AO2 skills **ACTIVITIES**

- 'It is obvious that men and women are equal.' What do you think? Give reasons for your answer, referring to Hindu teaching in depth.
- Can we ever produce a just and equal society? What do you think? Show that you have thought about it from more than one point of view.

Hinduism: Religion and equality 2

The next two pages will help you to:

- explain the attitudes that Hindus have to other religions
- evaluate how Hindu beliefs influence their actions to other religious believers
- explain Hindu teaching on forgiveness and reconciliation.

The Ten Avatars or Incarnations of Vishnu.

Hindus include the Buddha as an avatar, a human form of the God Vishnu, even though the Buddha himself denied he was a god. Are they right to make him a god against his wishes?

Only one way to truth?

Many people think that of all the world's religions, Hinduism is the most open and least threatened by the existence of other belief systems. In the past, it has often absorbed or been integrated into other religions – for example, the Buddha is regarded by some Hindus not as the leader of another religion but as one of the avatars, or forms, of the god Vishnu. They have an inclusive approach, seeing many of the other religious leaders or founders, such as Jesus, as manifestations of the divine.

The Hindu leader Gandhi tried to bring religions together. One of his ways to do this was to set up a community that he called an ashram. The word ashram means village or community. Here, Hindus, Muslims, Jews and Christians were to live together in harmony, running a small farm together as a way to show that people from different backgrounds could co-exist peacefully. For over 20 years, Gandhi lived in South Africa and so the ashram he founded was a way of showing a racist society that the divisions of race and colour did not matter.

AO1+AO2 skills **ACTIVITIES**

Write down three things you believe to be true. Explain to a partner how you came to believe the statements were true and what 'true' means in each case.

RESEARCH NOTE

Find out in detail about how Gandhi used the ashram to break down barriers.

Hindus and Muslims

There has been much religious tension between Hindus and Muslims in India. Hindus are often mistakenly thought of by Muslims as idol worshippers. Muslims stress the idea of there being only one God, and therefore find it difficult to accept the Hindu emphasis on there being one supreme God but many other divine beings.

Hinduism is not a religion that tries to persuade other people to join it, as it sees all religions as an equal attempt to find the truth about the divine. They find it offensive to claim that only one route can draw you to God.

One way in which Hindus tried to counter the idea that people needed to convert from one religion to another was through the setting up of the Ramakrishna Mission. Ramakrishna lived in India in the 19th century, when many Christian missionaries were being sent there to convert people. He taught that there were many paths to God, so there was no need to abandon the Hindu faith. He believed that Hinduism also provided an important way of expressing the importance of Indian culture. The movement became so successful that some Christians began to wonder whether they should send missionaries at all.

What do Hindus teach about forgiveness and reconciliation?

Hindus believe that every person has an **atman**, an eternal soul that, while it lives in a physical body, will go on to another life. It is important that a person should try to promote good **karma** in themselves and others by seeking **forgiveness** for any acts they may have done towards others. They should also seek to be open to being reconciled to others who may have hurt them, as this will show that they are trying to improve their lives and those of others.

Trying to do good in these ways will please the Gods. Some Hindus believe that some of the gods are especially interested in the **moral** choices that humans make.

One of the most important ideas in Hindu moral thinking is **dharma** – doing one's sacred duty. Each person in each **varna** will have particular duties to perform and they need to do these in order to build the karma that is needed to help improve life, not destroy it.

One aim of life is to develop a good life or dama. Resentment or guilt cannot help this to develop. The ultimate goal for all Hindus is **moksha** – union with Brahman and an end to **samsara** (the cycle of rebirth).

Hindus believe that the way of love should underlie all our relationships. Love can be experienced through relationships, through the senses, and through the bonds of family and friendship. Above all, the Hindu should seek to find bhakti – the spiritual love of God. Love should be about becoming a person who is a giver, a receiver and a forgiver.

REMEMBER THIS

- A person's **atman** is their soul, or real self.
- **Moksha** is the end to cycle of reincarnation (**samsara**).

ACTIVITIES

- 'All religions are the same.' Do you agree? What would Hindus say? What do you think? Make sure that you refer in detail to Hindu teachings.
- 'There are some acts that cannot be forgiven.' What do you think? What would Hindus say? Give reasons for your answer and show more than one point of view.

Islam:
Religion and equality 1

The next two pages will help you to:

- explore Muslim teachings about equality, racism and sexism.

Would you like to be treated differently because of your religion?

Muslim teaching about equality

According to the Qur'an, Allah created all people and therefore all people are equal, regardless of their tribe, nation, language or skin colour:

> **Surah 49:13**
> *O mankind! We created you from a single (pair) of a male and a female; and made you into nations and tribes, that ye may know each other (not that ye may despise each other).*

Muslim teachings about racism

Muslims are often represented in the media as a racial group. In fact, although Islam had its origins in what is now Saudi Arabia, followers of Islam are found all over the world, speaking thousands of different languages and with many different skin colours. Because of this, and because of the teachings of the Qur'an, there is no excuse for any form of racism or prejudice within Islam.

Muhammad ﷺ stressed this in his final sermon:

66 *All mankind is descended from Adam and Eve, an Arab is not better than a non-Arab and a non-Arab is not better than an Arab; a white person is not better than a black person, nor is a black person better than a white person except by piety and good actions. Learn that every Muslim is the brother of every other Muslim and that Muslims form one brotherhood.* **99**

The Prophet demonstrated these beliefs in **equality** in his own life. In al-Madinah he worked to bring peace to the warring parties who were often separated by religion. Also, his choice for the first mu'adhin (the caller to prayer) was based on who had the best voice, and the former Ethiopian slave, Bilal, was chosen.

AO1 skills **ACTIVITIES**

Think/pair/share
What do you think 'equality' really means? Is it possible to treat everyone equally? In pairs discuss these questions. Share your answers with the class and compare the responses.

AO1+AO2 skills **ACTIVITIES**

Look on the Internet, or at other forms of media, and see how many examples you can find of people being discriminated against because of their colour or religion.

Although Muslims may feel that they should fight racism wherever they see it because it goes against Allah's will, they must obey the authorities, unless they are asked to do something which goes against Allah's will.

Muslim attitudes towards women

As Islam teaches that all people are equal in the creation of Allah, so men and women are seen as being equal. In many Muslim societies women are required to dress in a certain way so that they are not stared at by men. Often their clothing may leave only their hands and eyes exposed.

Surah 33:59

O Prophet! Tell thy wives and daughters, and the believing women, that they should cast their outer garments over their persons (when abroad): that is most convenient, that they should be known (as such) and not molested. And Allah is Oft-Forgiving, Most Merciful.

Although many non-Muslims may believe that this is discriminating against women, some Muslim women say that the covering they wear gives them a sense of freedom in public, because they do not feel that men are staring at them sexually.

There are also rules that men must dress modestly and they must always be covered from the navel to the knees, even for sporting activities.

Men and women are not seen as identical, rather that they should complement each other.

Surah 4:34

Men are the protectors and maintainers of women, because Allah has given the one more (strength) than the other, and because they support them from their means. Therefore the righteous women are devoutly obedient, and guard in (the husband's) absence what Allah would have them guard. As to those women on whose part ye fear disloyalty and ill-conduct, admonish them (first), (next), refuse to share their beds, (and last) beat them (lightly); but if they return to obedience seek not against them means (of annoyance): for Allah is Most High, Great (above you all).

In terms of family responsibilities, men must work to support their families while women take care of the home and bring up the children.

Nevertheless, women have many rights in Islam: they can study, refuse a **marriage**, **divorce**, inherit, keep their own names after marriage, own property, take part in politics and run a business. These conditions are the same whether the woman is married or not.

The media often highlights cases where it appears that Muslim women are seen as subordinate to men. Some of these may be true, but they often reflect harsh and repressive governments rather than Islamic teaching.

The importance of showing respect to women was shown by the Prophet:

❝ *Paradise lies at the feet of your mother.* **❞**

(Sunan An-Nasa'i)

Muslim women's clothing often depends on the part of the world in which they live.

 MUST THINK ABOUT!

Remember the difference between complement and compliment.

 **ACTIVITIES**

- There have been many debates in recent years about the clothing some Muslim women wear. Discuss what you feel about this type of religious dress.
- Design a leaflet for a mosque explaining Muslim attitudes towards equality.

Islam:
Religion and equality 2
Muslim attitudes towards other religions

The next two pages will help you to:

- evaluate Muslim attitudes to other religions
- investigate Muslim teachings about forgiveness and reconciliation.

Although Muslims believe that all people should be shown respect, they do not accept that other religions are true. To do this would go against the teachings of Muhammad ﷺ and of the Qur'an.

However, the situation is slightly different when it comes to Jews and Christians:

Surah 2:62

Those who believe (in the Qur'an), and those who follow the Jewish (scriptures), and the Christians and the Sabians – any who believe in Allah and the Last Day, and work righteousness, shall have their reward with their Lord; on them shall be no fear, nor shall they grieve.

Jews and Christians are seen as different because, with Muslims, they are all People of the Book – this is the Divine Word of Allah, which was revealed to each group in turn until the final revelation was made to Muhammad ﷺ.

Surah 5:82

Strongest among men in enmity to the Believers wilt thou find the Jews and the Pagans; and nearest among them in love to the Believers wilt thou find those who say, 'We are Christians': because amongst these are men devoted to learning and men who have renounced the world, and they are not arrogant.

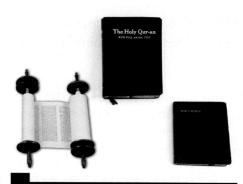

left to right: the Torah, the Qur'an and the Bible.

Islam, like Christianity, is a **proselytising** religion. They believe that they have an obligation to teach other people about their faith and to persuade them to adopt it.

Surah 3:85

If anyone desires a religion other than Islam (submission to Allah), never will it be accepted of him; and in the Hereafter he will be in the ranks of those who have lost (all spiritual good).

RESEARCH NOTE

Who were the Sabians?

In fact, Islam teaches that all people are born with the natural instinct to be Muslim – this is called **fitrah**. Fitrah is the inherent disposition towards virtue in humanity, and what endows people with the ability to differentiate between right and wrong. According to the Qur'an, it is the original state in which humans are created by Allah.

The doctrine of fitrah means that although people may belong to other religions this is because of the way in which they were brought up. So

ACTIVITIES

This definition of fitrah is complicated. Work in pairs to look up any unusual words in this passage and then write a definition in your own words.

when someone chooses to become a Muslim they are not 'converting' to Islam, but 'reverting' to their original faith.

When someone does become a Muslim, it is when they believe in their heart that the following is true: 'there is no God but Allah and Muhammad ﷺ is His Messenger.' Someone who is reverting makes this statement in front of two adult Muslims and takes a Muslim name. After this they are encouraged to associate with other Muslims to benefit from the strength and support of the **ummah** (Muslim community).

Unlike for converts to Judaism, it is not necessary for male reverts to be circumcised.

Forgiveness and reconciliation

Muslim prisoners at the US prison camp in Guantanamo Bay, Cuba.

> **Surah 1:1**
> *In the name of Allah, Most Gracious, Most Merciful.*

Islam teaches that Allah will always forgive people who acknowledge their guilt and ask for **forgiveness**.

> **Surah 41:34**
> *Nor can Goodness and Evil be equal. Repel (Evil) with what is better: then will be between whom and thee was hatred become as it were thy friend and intimate!*

Muslims believe that they must follow the example of Allah and his forgiveness.

> **Surah 7:199**
> *Hold to forgiveness; command what is right; but turn away from the ignorant.*

> **Abu Dawud, Tirmidhi**
> *Those who are kind and considerate to Allah's creatures, Allah bestows His kindness and affection on them.*

Muslim law, **Shari'ah**, is based on the Qur'an and governs how people should be tried and punished for crimes they have committed. There are strict conditions on the use of Shari'ah to protect the person on trial and, if they are found guilty, to ensure that the punishment imposed is no more than that specified for the crime they have committed.

- Bodily harm of a robbery victim is punished by cutting off a hand and a foot.
- Less serious crimes are punished by prison sentences.
- Murder of a robbery victim is punished by death.

People must be tried by a legal court.

AO1+AO2 skills ACTIVITIES

- Explain Muslim attitudes towards forgiveness and reconciliation. You should refer to Surah 7 in your answer.
- Find out in which countries Shari'ah law is the law of the land.

Judaism:
Religion and equality 1

Are all beings equal?

The next two pages will help you to:

- explore Jewish teachings about equality with respect to race and gender.

Judaism teaches that the aim of life is to live at peace with other people. Jewish teaching about how other people should be treated is very clear:

> **Leviticus 19:33–34**
>
> *When a stranger resides with you in your land, you shall not wrong him. The stranger who resides with you shall be to you as one of your citizens; you shall love him as yourself, for you were strangers in the land of Egypt: I the Lord am your G-d.*

AO1+AO2 skills **ACTIVITIES**

Think/pair/share
Think of as many different types of prejudice as you can. In pairs, decide why people show prejudice in these ways. Can you think of any ways in which these prejudices can be overcome? Share with the class the reasons why people are prejudiced, and any solutions you have devised.

The Jewish scriptures look towards a time of peace and **equality** for the whole world:

> **Isaiah 2:2, 3b–4**
>
> *In the days to come,*
> *The Mount of the Lord's House*
> *Shall stand firm above the mountains*
> *And tower above the hills;*
> *And all the nations*
> *Shall gaze on it with joy.*
>
> *...*
>
> *For instruction shall come forth from Zion,*
> *The word of the Lord from Jerusalem.*
> *Thus He will judge among the nations*
> *And arbitrate for the many peoples,*
> *And they shall beat their swords into ploughshares*
> *And their spears into pruning hooks:*
> *Nation shall not take up*
> *Sword against nation;*
> *They shall never again know war.*

The Nazi party discriminated against Jews in Germany. Do you think Western Europe is safe from ever repeating this level of discrimination?

According to the Talmud, G-d took different coloured soils from the four corners of the world in order to make Adam:

> **Genesis 2:7**
>
> *the Lord G-d formed man from the dust of the earth. He blew into his nostrils the breath of life, and man became a living being.*

Therefore, everyone of every race is descended from this first human. The scriptures say that the existence of different languages is explained by the story of the Tower of Babel.

One of the problems which has often been the cause of anti-semitism (hatred of the Jews) is the idea that the Jews are a 'chosen people'. This idea is found in the book of Exodus:

> **Exodus 19:5–6**
>
> *'Now then, if you will obey Me faithfully and keep My covenant, you shall be My treasured possession among all the peoples. Indeed, all the earth is Mine, but you shall be to Me a kingdom of priests and a holy nation.' These are the words that you shall speak to the children of Israel.*

This does not mean that the Jews have any special benefit or superiority, but that they are chosen to work harder to fulfil G-d's will and to set an example to other people of how G-d wants all humanity to live.

The Talmud makes it clear that 'the righteous of all nations will inherit the World to Come.' Therefore, it is the responsibility of everyone to ensure that people of every colour, race and religion, whether they are living with disability, wealth or poverty, should be equal.

Jewish attitudes towards women

Many people see what they consider to be traditional Jewish attitudes towards women as sexist. Some claim that this starts with the punishment of Eve in the Garden of Eden when she picked the fruit of the Tree of Knowledge and gave it to Adam.

In Orthodox synagogues, women sit separately from men in services and are not allowed to take part. Only men are bound by the 613 **mitzvot** (laws).

Although it is the woman's responsibility to prepare the house for **Shabbat** and light the candles, during the service, a husband tells his wife how valuable she is to him.

> **Proverbs 31:10–12**
>
> *What a rare find is a capable wife!*
> *Her worth is far beyond that of rubies.*
> *Her husband puts his confidence in her,*
> *And lacks no good thing.*
> *She is good to him, never bad,*
> *All the days of her life.*

However, there are some Jewish women who feel that such passages only serve to emphasise their inequality.

Many Progressive Jews believe that the scriptures should be reinterpreted for the 21st century, and consider that there should be no distinction between the way in which men and women are treated. They pray and worship together, and women can become rabbis.

RESEARCH NOTE

Read the story of the Tower of Babel (Genesis 11:6–9). Consider what the purpose of the story is.

Should women have the same status as men within Judaism?

> **Genesis 3:16**
>
> *And to the woman He said,*
> *'I will make most severe*
> *Your pangs in childbearing;*
> *In pain shall you bear children.*
> *Yet your urge shall be for your husband,*
> *And he shall rule over you.'*

 REMEMBER THIS

- **Sabbath** (or **Shabbat**) is the Jewish day of spiritual rest, starting at sunset on Friday and ending at nightfall on Saturday
- The **mitzvot** are the 613 commandments by which Jews should try to live their lives.

 FOR DEBATE

- Do you agree that all religions are equally true (or false) or do you think that one religion is better than all the others?
- Design a poster for a synagogue showing Jewish attitudes towards equality.

Judaism:
Religion and equality 2
Jewish attitudes towards other religions

The next two pages will help you to:

- evaluate Jewish attitudes to other religions
- investigate Jewish teachings about forgiveness and reconciliation.

Judaism teaches that everyone should follow their own religion, which is what G-d wanted for them. They believe that anyone who lives according to the **Noachide Code** is living according to G-d's will.

The Noachide Code

The Code consists of seven commandments, which were given to Noah by G-d after the flood:

> *Worship only G-d*
> *Do not blaspheme*
> *Do not murder*
> *Do not steal*
> *Do not commit adultery*
> *Do not be cruel to animals*
> *Establish a system of law and order so that everyone can live together in harmony.*

Jews actively discourage converts to their faith because, if people are following the Noachide Code, they are living according to G-d's will. The only people who have to live according to the 613 **mitzvot** of Judaism are those who were born of a Jewish mother.

However, if people insist on converting, they have to study Jewish laws and customs and learn Hebrew. They have to visit the **mikveh** and, if they are a man, be circumcised. When the preparations are over, they have to go to a **Beth Din** (Jewish Court), where they are tested in their commitment to the faith by three rabbis. Once they have converted, their previous, non-Jewish life, is never referred to again.

Judaism teaches that all humans are descended from Adam and Eve:

> **Genesis 3:20**
> *The man named his wife Eve, because she was the mother of all the living.*

Because the Jews were driven to live outside the Promised Land, they do not reject other people:

> **Deuteronomy 23:8**
> *You shall not abhor an Edomite, for he is your kinsman. You shall not abhor an Egyptian, for you were a stranger in his land.*

ACTIVITIES

Should people of different faiths always be tolerant towards one another? Discuss with a partner, then the whole class.

REMEMBER THIS

- The **mikveh** is a ritual bath, which is usually part of the synagogue complex.
- The **mitzvot** are the 613 commandments by which Jews should try to live their lives.

They also believe that they should work in every way possible to help other people, especially as they seek to serve G-d.

> **Isaiah 42:6–7**
>
> *I the Lord, in My grace, have summoned you,*
> *And I have grasped you by the hand.*
> *I created you, and appointed you*
> *A covenant people, a light of nations –*
> *Opening eyes deprived of light,*
> *Rescuing prisoners from confinement,*
> *From the dungeon those who sit in darkness.*

Forgiveness and reconciliation

When the Rabbis were asked if people should ask **forgiveness** for their sins before they died, they replied 'Yes'. When asked how someone could do this if they did not know when they were going to die, they said 'Repent every day'.

Teachings about forgiveness and **reconciliation** are found throughout the Jewish scriptures:

> **Leviticus 19:17–18**
>
> *You shall not hate your kinsfolk in your heart.*
> *Reprove your kinsman but incur no guilt because*
> *of him. You shall not take vengeance or bear a*
> *grudge against your countrymen. Love your fellow*
> *as yourself: I am the Lord.*

Although Judaism teaches that wrongdoers must be brought to justice, there are very strict rules about the way in which the trial must be carried out in order to protect the prisoner.

> **Amos 5:24**
>
> *But let justice well up like water,*
> *Righteousness like an unfailing stream.*

Perhaps it is the Jewish experience of persecutions over many centuries, culminating in the Holocaust of the 20th century, that has made them particularly aware of issues concerning prejudice, discrimination and persecution.

Jews believe that they should always forgive other people, but that they cannot forgive on behalf of others: that is up to G-d.

AO1+AO2 skills **ACTIVITIES**

Explain Jewish attitudes towards other religions.

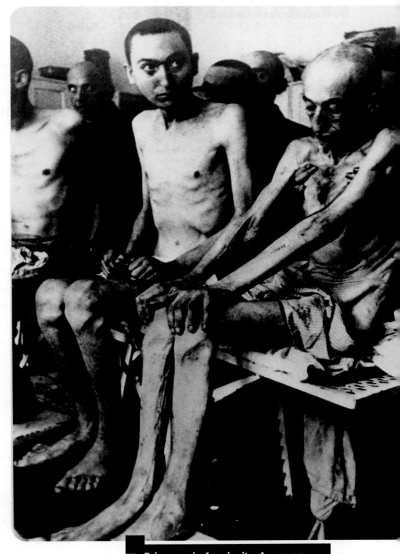

Prisoners in Auschwitz. Are some things too awful to forgive?

FOR DEBATE

Consider whether there are circumstances in which even religious people might not feel that they were able to forgive a criminal.

AO1+AO2 skills **ACTIVITIES**

Find an example of a Jew who has worked to combat racism or sexism and describe their work.

Sikhism:
Religion and equality 1
Equality and the caste system

Sikh teachings are full of references about the **equality** of all people, regardless of gender, **caste**, race or religion – a principle known as egalitarianism.

At the time of Guru Nanak Dev Ji, prejudice associated with an individual's caste was rife. The caste system was originally a Hindu social structure and, due to the Hindu background of the Gurus and their followers, it became a feature of Sikh society too, as it remains to the present day.

There are many theories about the origins of the caste system. One of these is the Hymn of the Primeval Man, Purusha Sukta. It is here that the four great classes of society are mentioned for the first time in Vedic literature, said to have arisen from the different parts of the Purusha's body:

Rig Veda, X.90

The Brahmin was his mouth, of his arms was made the warrior, his thighs became the vaishya, of his feet the shudra was born.

The next two pages will help you to:

- develop your knowledge and understanding of key Sikh teachings about equality
- explore and evaluate the apparently egalitarian nature of Sikhism in relation to the caste system and racism
- make links between these beliefs and attitudes with what you think/believe.

AO1+AO2 skills ACTIVITIES

- Do you think everyone in society should be treated the same as each other?
- Have you ever been treated differently from those around you? Try to give some examples.
- There are a group of people in India who used to be referred to as 'untouchables'. Why do you think this might have happened?

AO1 skills ACTIVITIES

- How do you think the hierarchy scale of castes was established?
- The 'untouchables' are not mentioned here: indeed, they are regarded as 'outcastes' – so polluted that they do not fit into the four level scale. Where do you think they originated from?

The Purusha Sukta teaches that people are born into a particular caste: some may be workers while others may be priests.

However, the Gurus taught that it did not matter what caste an individual belongs to.

Sikhs believe that because all people have been created by God and have the essence of God within us, there cannot be any notion of ritual purity or pollution associated with castes lower or higher than one's own. Guru Nanak Dev Ji taught that every human being has an equal chance of working towards their liberation from reincarnation:

Guru Granth Sahib Ji, page 349

Recognise the Lord's light within all and inquire not the caste, as there is no caste in the next world.

Sikh responses to racism

Because of the teaching about the immanence of God in all human beings, Sikhs would be opposed to any form of racism. The concept of egalitarianism in Sikhism means there should be no discrimination on the grounds of one's racial or cultural background.

Guru Gobind Singh Ji's creation of the **Khalsa** was aimed at promoting equality on a practical basis, by giving all Khalsa members common surnames (instead of caste-specific names). Males were to drop their family name and adopt the surname 'Singh', meaning 'lion'. Females were to adopt the name 'Kaur' meaning 'princess'.

The Sikh place of worship, the gurdwara, is open to everybody. Everyone who attends eats the langar meal, and the karah parshad is shared to symbolise that people of different faiths and backgrounds are sitting together and are, therefore, equal in all respects. This is always vegetarian, so that it does not cause offence to any person's religious beliefs.

Guru Gobind Singh Ji and the formation of the Khalsa.

RESEARCH NOTE

Find out the different theories about the origins of the caste system in Hinduism. Then look at the concepts of ritual purity and pollutions associated with different castes in India. Finally look at attitudes towards the caste system in modern-day India.

AO1+AO2 skills ACTIVITIES

In pairs, think of instances where people are treated differently because of who they are. Make up your own slogan that would promote egalitarianism to encompass every human being around the world.

AO1+AO2 skills ACTIVITIES

Think/pair/share
Think about the concept of equality in two religions other than Sikhism. In pairs, find two quotations or references about egalitarianism in these two religions and compare them with teachings about equality in Sikhism.

Share your answers with the rest of the class and make a grid of all the different religions the class has chosen to analyse, listing any similarities or differences with Sikh teachings.

REMEMBER THIS

Khalsa literally means the 'Pure Ones' and refers to those Sikhs that have taken initiation and agree to live by the rules and regulations of the Rehat Maryada.

Sikhism:
Religion and equality 2

What is the role of women in Sikhism?

The next two pages will help you to:

- explore and evaluate the apparently egalitarian nature of Sikhism in relation to men and women
- look at Sikh tolerance of other religions
- make links between these beliefs and attitudes with what you think/believe.

 **ACTIVITIES**

Think/pair/share
Can you think of any jobs that a woman would not normally do? Or a man?

Share and compare your ideas first with a partner, then with others in the class and summarise the responses.

Are men and women equal in Sikh society?

The teachings of the Sikh Gurus emphasise the **equality** of men and women. Guru Nanak Dev Ji was born into a period where women were very often regarded as second-class citizens. He promoted the ideal that, if all human beings were created by God with the immanence of God in all humans, then both men and women are equal.

Imagine the opposition that the Sikh Gurus would have faced when they began teaching that men and women are equal. Here is a quotation about gender equality from Sikh teachings:

> **Guru Granth Sahib Ji, page 473**
>
> *Within the woman, the man is conceived and from a woman he is born.*
> *With a woman he is betrothed and married...*
> *Why call her bad, from whom are born the Kings?*
> *From a woman a woman is born. Without a woman, there can be none.*
> *Nanak, only the one True Lord, is without a woman.*

FOR INTEREST

In Sikhism, sugar crystals are used in religious ceremonies.

FOR DEBATE

Do you think there is contradiction in religion generally between teachings and actual practice? Can you think of instances where teachings about gender equality are not always adhered to in practice? You can use Sikhism or another religion for your debate on gender equality.

All the Sikh Gurus encouraged the education of women and denounced child marriages, as well as the practice of suttee, in which a widow would throw herself onto her husband's funeral pyre. There is no priesthood in Sikhism, and both men and women can lead the religious service by reading from the Guru Granth Sahib Ji. In present-day society, Sikh females are encouraged to continue with their education, and many Sikh women are university graduates. The practice of **purdah** – veiling oneself – is strictly against the teachings of the Gurus. When Guru Gobind Singh Ji created the Khalsa in 1699 CE, it was his wife who mixed the sugar crystals into the water, and women were invited to become members of the Khalsa alongside men.

Religious tolerance in Sikhism

The composition of the Guru Granth Sahib Ji is a good example of religious tolerance. It is perhaps the only religious scripture to encompass the works of individuals belonging to more than one religion. Alongside the compositions of the Sikh Gurus, the Guru Granth Sahib Ji also contains hymns from both Hindu and Muslim saints. In fact, Guru Nanak Dev Ji's two closest companions were a Muslim and a Hindu. The foundation stone for the Golden Temple, originally known as Harmandir Sahib, in Amritsar was laid by a Muslim, Mian Mir. Also, as you have read, the langar in a gurdwara promotes interfaith relationships by inviting people of all faiths to sit and eat together.

Forgiveness and reconciliation

Sikh teachings emphasise the loving and just nature of the Absolute God, Waheguru. If one asks for **forgiveness** with a pure heart, it is in accordance with the Will (Hukam) of God as to whether Grace (Nadar) will be bestowed. The Khalsa, however, is not so yielding. Khalsa Sikhs who fail to keep the rules and regulations become known as patits.

 **ACTIVITIES**

In pairs, make up four sayings that could be applied to people of all faiths and none. The sayings need to promote harmony and tolerance between individuals. Design your sayings on A3 paper in the form of an open double-page spread in a book. Share your ideas with the rest of the class.

 **ACTIVITIES**

In groups, discuss why you think the Khalsa rules are so rigid. If you can, access the Sikh Rehat Maryada to find out more about Khalsa rules and patits.

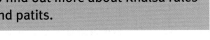

GradeStudio

AO1

QUESTION

Explain how a Sikh might respond to someone who has racist opinions. [6 marks]

You could build an answer like this:

Level 1

First, let the examiner know that you are aware of what the question is about. For example, 'Sikh teachings emphasise the concept of egalitarianism, which means that everybody should be treated the same regardless of gender or race'.

Level 2

Next, explain that the langar is a good way to combat racism as all are welcome and everybody is equal in the eyes of God. You could mention the tolerant nature of the Guru Granth Sahib Ji when he included the teachings of Muslim and Hindu saints alongside those of the Sikh Gurus.

Level 3

Finally, explain the importance of the karah parshad in promoting egalitarianism. You could also explain the importance of the teaching about the immanence of God in the hearts of all and the implications this would have for racist attitudes.

GradeStudio

Welcome to the Grade Studio

Grade Studio is here to help you improve your grades by working through typical questions you might find on an examination paper. For a fuller explanation of how Grade Studio works, and how the examiners approach the task of marking your paper, please see p. 30.

AO1
Question

Explain Christian teaching about the role of women in society. **[6 marks]**

Student's answer

Christians believe that God created men and women equal. It says in the Bible, 'male and female created he them'. Therefore they must be equal. Some Christians might also believe the story in the second creation account in Genesis, which says that Eve was made from Adam's rib. This may mean that women are inferior to men.

Examiner's comment

The candidate has given a satisfactory answer to the question. There are two relevant points but neither is explained in any detail. In order to reach Level 3 the candidate needs to give more information and examples. The candidate could also use more technical terms from the specification to show the breadth of their knowledge and understanding.

Student's improved answer

Christians believe that God created men and women equal. It says in the Bible, 'male and female created he them'. Therefore they must be equal. Some Christians might also believe the story in the second creation account in Genesis, which says that Eve was made from Adam's rib. This may mean that women are inferior to men.

Although in the past many people might have shared this view of women as being secondary to men, Christian views have changed over the last hundred years. Today most Christians would say that God made all people equal and that this includes men and women. Women have the same rights as men and, in recent years, women have been able to become priests or ministers in many denominations of the Christian church. Therefore, women should be seen and treated as equal to men in society and everywhere else.

Examiner's comment

This is now a good answer to the question. The candidate has shown a clear understanding of the question. There is good description and explanation of a variety of different attitudes towards the equality of women, with good analysis. The information is presented clearly and there is good use of technical terms.

Question

'Men and women are not equal.' Discuss this statement. You should include different, supported points of view and a personal viewpoint. You must refer to Christianity in your answer.

[12 marks]

Student's answer

Christians might say that, if God intended men and women to be equal, then he would have made them the same. Some Christians might also say that God created women to be helpmates to men, and that they are made weaker because they have to give birth to babies, while men have to work.

Examiner's comment

The candidate has given a limited answer to the question. There are two points but they both address the same issue and neither is expanded very far. In order to reach Level 4 the candidate needs to give alternative viewpoints and also include a personal response.

Student's improved answer

Christians might say that, if God intended men and women to be equal, then he would have made them the same. Some Christians might also say that God created women to be helpmates to men, and that they are made weaker because they have to give birth to babies, while men have to work.

The majority of Christians and other people would disagree with this statement. Though it might appear from the Bible that women are inferior to men, many people would say that this simply reflects the time in which it was written. Some would show how Jesus treated women as equals, while others might say that if he thought they were equal he would have had both men and women disciples.

My personal opinion is that it is obvious that men and women are equal just by looking at how they work and what they do. If any religion teaches that they are not equal, then I believe that the religion is wrong.

Examiner's comment

This is now a good answer to the question. The candidate has shown a clear understanding of the question and has presented a range of views supported by evidence and argument. The answer explains Christian views, among others, and includes a personal viewpoint, which is also supported.

These specimen answers provide an outline of how you could construct your response. Space does not allow us to give a full response. The examiner will be looking for more detail in your actual exam responses.

These examples only use Christianity but you could use the Grade Studio to apply to any of the religions you are studying and the structure of the answers would work in the same way.

Topic 6: Religion and the media

The Big Picture

In this Topic, you will be addressing religious responses to:

- the relationship between religious groups and the media
- use of the media
- censorship and freedom of speech.

What?

You will:

- develop your knowledge of the different forms of media and the influence of the media, including the portrayal of a specific belief and its religious figures, focusing on films, books and comics
- explain and analyse how media are used to convert non-believers and to educate both believers and non-believers
- evaluate, using different viewpoints, issues such as censorship, freedom of speech and the portrayal of violence and sex.

Why?

Because:

- it will help you to understand how religions choose to represent themselves in the world today
- you will develop your own ideas about issues such as censorship and freedom of speech
- you will be able to assess the effectiveness and quality of religious media.

How?

By:

- exploring the key responses of religions towards the use of the media, interpreting different attitudes and viewpoints
- illustrating how religions use the media in the modern world
- relating these beliefs and responses to your own ideas about the media by comparing your own views with those of the religions studied.

DAILY NEWS

MEDIA BLAMED FOR PETROL SCARE

What does this headline mean? What does this suggest the media caused people to do?

As a class, or in smaller groups, see how many different forms of mass media you can think of and record them on a large sheet of paper or whiteboard. Identify and discuss advantages and disadvantages of modern media.

Buddhist monks march through Yangon city centre, Union of Myanmar (Burma), in an anti-government demonstration in September 2007.

Religion and the media

 **FOR DEBATE**

'TV is chewing gum for the eyes.'
(Frank Lloyd Wright, architect)

What do you think Frank Lloyd Wright meant?

Different forms of media

The term 'media' refers to all the methods of mass communication. These include print, radio, television, art, music and all forms of communication technology.

The influence of the media

The mass media has a huge influence on how people understand the world and can be used for bad as well as good purposes. People of all faiths are concerned about possible misuses and bad influences of all forms of media.

The portrayal of different religions in the media

- Buddhism rarely appears in the Western news media, but the Buddha and Buddhist practices such as **meditation** are often caricatured in films and adverts.

- Like Buddhism, Hinduism and Sikhism attract comparatively less media attention and are often subject to **stereotyping** when they do.

- As the main religion practised in Britain, the media look to leading figures in Christianity to comment on social and ethical issues.

- Media coverage of Islam tends to focus on terrorism and other extremist behaviour, leading to **Islamaphobia**.

- Judaism has suffered frequently from media stereotyping, and many Jews feel that Judaism is often portrayed in a negative light in news stories.

The portrayal of important religious figures

- The Dalai Lama, exiled leader of Tibetan Buddhism, is frequently in the news. He is portrayed as a charismatic figure and, because so much attention is given to him, many people assume, wrongly, that he is the leader of all branches of Buddhism.

- Prominent religious leaders such as the Archbishop of Canterbury, the Pope and the Chief Rabbi attract media attention and often act as spokespeople for their faiths.

KEY WORDS

censorship: preventing publication or broadcasting of something, usually because it might be offensive to others

condones: overlooks or accepts

degradation: humiliation

Islamaphobia: negative attitudes to Islam based on fear

media (pl.): the means of mass communication (singular is **medium**)

stereotype: a fixed, over-simplified image or view of a person or group

watershed: the time after which programmes that are unsuitable for children are broadcast (9 p.m.)

KEY QUESTIONS

KNOWLEDGE AND UNDERSTANDING
Describe how Christians and the members of another religion you have studied respond to the portrayal of sex and violence in the media, explaining the reasons for their responses.

ANALYSIS AND EVALUATION
What censorship rules do you think the government should impose on the media? Explain your reasons.

Responses to films that focus on religious or philosophical messages

- Buddhists generally feel positive about the way films bring Buddhism to a wider audience.
- Films about Christianity are seen as a good way to promote understanding.
- Films of the great religious epic, the Ramayana, which tells stories of the deities, are extremely popular with Hindus.
- For some Jews, nothing relating to their religion should be represented in films, books and comics.
- Sikh culture is explored in the films *Bend it Like Beckham* and *Bride & Prejudice*.

How religions use the media to represent their faith, convert and educate

- Many Buddhists use the Internet to spread Buddhist teachings. The Pali Canon is available online.
- Radio and television programmes like *Thought for the Day* and *Songs of Praise* promote Christianity, while comedies like *Father Ted* and *The Vicar of Dibley* take a lighter view.
- Hindus contribute to Radio 4's *Thought for the Day*. The BBC has an Asian television and radio network.
- The Qur'an is available online, including sites to help teach the Qur'an to Muslim children.
- Jews do not feel they need to promote their religion through the media.
- Sikhs make positive use of Sikh television channels and publications to promote understanding of their faith and values.

Attitudes and responses to issues raised by censorship and freedom of speech

Religions have different views on the degree to which the media should be censored.

- Buddhist teachings help people to control their own behaviour rather than rely on censorship of the media.

- Some Christians would like to see greater control over the media.
- Many Jewish people are suspicious of censorship because of their experiences of Nazi propaganda.

Beliefs and attitudes towards the portrayal of violence and sex

- Most Buddhists would like to see sex and violence in the media moderated because it may influence people's actions.
- Christians believe humans are made in the image of God, so anything that promotes the **degradation** of people is unacceptable.
- Hinduism teaches non-violence and purity, so anything that leads them to be **immoral** is unacceptable.
- Muslims do not accept images that may corrupt and degrade people.
- Many Jews are concerned about the effects of violence and sex on television.
- The portrayal of sex and violence in films and other media is not compatible with Sikh values.

FOR INTEREST

The medium of the creative arts is important for representing and interpreting stories, events and people in Christianity. Artist Paul Gauguin expressed his feelings in this picture by using bright yellows and oranges. Notice that the people in the picture are dressed in the costume of the painter's own time and it is set in the French countryside where he lived. What do you think Gauguin is saying about the death of Jesus in this painting?

The 'Yellow Christ' by Gauguin (1848–1903).

Buddhism:
Religion and the media 1

The next two pages will help you to:

- explore the portrayal of Buddhism in the media
- consider the portrayal of important religious figures in the media.

In the Autumn of 1939, Heinrich Harrer, the famous Austrian mountaineer, and his countryman Peter Aufschnaiter, set out to climb Nanga Parbat, one of the highest peaks in the Himalayas.

The self-centred Harrer, whose sole preoccupation was the achievement of fame and glory, would experience an emotional awakening on his fantastic journey that would take him from the heights of conquest to the depths of internment in a British prisoner of war camp, then from escape and a harrowing two year trek through the Himalayas to the mysterious Tibetan city of Lhasa.

As a stranger in a strange land which few westerners have ever visited, Harrer was befriended by the young Dalai Lama, and was asked to tutor the religious leader in English, geography and the ways of the Western world. He would eventually spend seven years in Tibet, during a period of tremendous political upheaval in that country, graced with the friendship and the spiritual enlightenment of the young Dalai Lama. As the deep and abiding bond between these two isolated , lonely people evolved, the selfish and egotistical Harrer experienced selflessness for the first time, allowing him to complete the emotional transformation which began on his way to Lhasa.

SEVEN YEARS IN TIBET

Brad Pitt stars as Heinrich Harrer in Seven Years In Tibet, a Reperage and Vanguard Films / Applecross Production for Mandalay Entertainment, released in the United Kingdom by Entertainment Film Distributors. The film is produced by Jean-Jacques Annaud, John H. Williams and Iain Smith. Richard Goodwin, Michael Bessman and David Nichols are the executive producers, with Alisa Tager serving as associate producer. The screenplay, based on Heinrich Harrer's memoir, is by Becky Johnston.
Also starring are David Thewlis (Naked, Dragonheart) as Harrer's partner Peter Aufschnaiter, B.D. Wong (Jurassic Park, Father of the Bride) as Tibetan courtier, Ngawang Jigme, Mako (Conan the Barbarian, Tucker, The Man and his Dream) as Tsarong and Indian film star Danny Denzongpa, known for his villainous roles in countless films, as the

How do the media portray Buddhism?

AO1+AO2 skills ACTIVITIES

Think/pair/share
Think of all the examples you can where you have seen or heard Buddhists in the media. With a partner, decide how accurate these images have been. Decide as a class whether you think the media give a fair representation of Buddhism.

Buddhism in the media

Buddhism only appears rarely in the Western **media**. Buddhist countries are rarely involved in wars or major political events, so do not often attract media attention. Even when Buddhist countries do get mentioned in the news, their religious background is rarely important to the story being covered, and often does not get mentioned.

The major exception to this is coverage of the activities of the Dalai Lama. The Dalai Lama is the exiled leader of Tibetan Buddhism. He lives in India, but speaks and writes in English, and often travels to Europe and America to speak to Buddhists there. The Dalai Lama is a charismatic figure, and attracts large crowds to his meetings, so news programmes therefore often cover his activities. In fact, so much attention is given to the Dalai Lama, and so little to other forms of Buddhism, that it would not be surprising if some Western audiences assumed he was the leader of all Buddhist schools.

Most media coverage of Buddhism is seen in adverts, television programmes or films, or the specific religious programming required of the television and radio stations by the Government. Although the specific religious programming about Buddhism tends to be accurate and informative, it probably does not reach a wide audience. It will tend to be viewed primarily by those with a religious interest rather than the wider public, so does little to change the general perceptions of Buddhism.

Many of the adverts, television programmes or films that feature Buddhists do so for comic effect. Often the Buddhist will be meditating obliviously while those around them are running around, or engaged in frantic activity. This caricature of Buddhist **meditation** ignores the Buddhist requirement to be aware of the world around them. In fact, Buddhists often meditate with their eyes open or half open, to maintain their awareness of the world around them.

In other media presentations, Buddhists may be portrayed as advocating peace whatever the circumstances: for example, trying to talk about the value of peace as a man with a machine gun walks towards them shooting. Again, this is a caricature of the Buddhist teaching of **ahimsa**.

Most Buddhists do not seem to be offended by these portrayals. Instead, there seems to be a general acceptance that the media tend to caricature most religious followers. However, some Buddhists have expressed a desire to see the Buddha portrayed as less of a figure of fun. They find such portrayals of the Buddha to be disrespectful, and would like his image to be treated with the same respect as most programmers do for, say, Jesus or Muhammad ﷺ.

Some films made in the West focus on Buddhism. The two most famous are *Little Buddha*, starring Keanu Reeves as the Buddha, and *Seven Years in Tibet*, starring Brad Pitt as a German meeting the young Dalai Lama in Tibet. Both films have been popular at times and, while Buddhists may query their historical accuracy, they have generally accepted them as a welcome way in which to bring Buddhism to a wider audience.

Within other countries, such as India and Thailand, films and comic book presentations of the life of the Buddha are popular. The previous lives of the Buddha are often presented in comic-book form for children and are seen as a positive way to engender their interest in Buddhism.

RESEARCH NOTE

Find out the last time the Dalai Lama was in the UK, and the highlights of his visit.

REMEMBER THIS

Ahimsa is the principle of non-violence and respect for all living things.

ACTIVITIES

AO1+AO2 Skills

- Should Buddhists be offended by the often-comedic presentation of Buddhism in the Western media? Why/why not?
- What duties do the media have to present religions accurately? Does this vary for different types of media?

Buddhism:
Religion and the media 2

The next two pages will help you to:

- investigate Buddhist attitudes towards the media
- explore the Buddhist concepts of censorship and freedom of speech.

Buddhism using the media

Some Buddhists have embraced the media as a way to inform others about Buddhism. The Dalai Lama has often used his presence in the media to highlight issues he wants brought to attention. In learning and speaking English, he has ensured he can provide 'sound bites' which can be readily used by the news media, rather than relying on them having to find a translator. He has also used the influence of other Buddhists for the same purpose. For example, the actor Richard Gere (who is a practising Buddhist) generally avoids media attention outside of his film career. However, he has been filmed and photographed with the Dalai Lama and has spoken publicly against the Chinese invasion of Tibet.

The Internet and other media

Other Buddhists have used the Internet as a way to spread the teachings of Buddhism. Many Buddhist texts have been made available, often in English, free of charge, in their entirety on the Internet. For example, the Buddhist website accesstoinsight has made available the Pali Canon along with a wealth of other Buddhist material. Another organisation, The Clearvision Trust specialises in making resources available to teachers and students. On their website it is possible to listen to talks given to A Level students, read articles by university lecturers, and buy videos and DVDs suitable for children.

Censorship

There is no one attitude to censorship within Buddhism. As with most other issues within Buddhism, it is a matter of the interpretation of Buddhist teachings from the five precepts and the Eightfold Path which determine Buddhist attitudes.

Some Buddhist countries have very strong censorship rules. For example, Thailand has banned the film *The King and I* because it was felt that the film was derogatory towards the King of Thailand. This might be seen as an interpretation of the first precept of non-harming, as the film may harm the reputation or feelings of the King. However, the attitude of Buddhist countries towards censorship is probably more influenced by cultural expectations and attitudes than it is by Buddhist teachings.

Is it right for media stars such as Richard Gere to try to influence the views of others about political or religious matters?

Many Buddhists have been embracing new technology as a way to inform others about Buddhism.

In the five precepts, Buddhists are told to avoid 'false speech'. In the Eightfold Path, they aim to use 'right speech'. Both of these teachings appear to lead to a duty to control and self-censor speech in order to avoid harm to others, so it may appear that Buddhists would tolerate some censorship in order to prevent harm. On the other hand, the same Buddhist teachings, combined with the Buddhist teaching of right action, might require people to speak out to prevent harm as well. This means that censorship which restricted people's ability to speak the truth or help others would not be compatible with Buddhism. It might seem that a limited form of censorship might be compatible with Buddhist teachings. In essence these teachings are designed to help people to control their own behaviour, in order to avoid negative kammic consequences. It could be argued that the media should censor itself, rather than have censorship imposed upon it.

Do films like this encourage people to be violent?

Sex and violence in the media

Again, Buddhists will have different attitudes to the portrayal of sex and violence in the media.

Some may see the media images of sex and violence as no more than harmless entertainment, providing they are seen as what they are – a fantasy world. In this sense, seeing them as unreal, relegates their importance and influence on the life of the viewer.

However, most Buddhists would like to see sex and violence in the media moderated. Some may feel that seeing casual sex or violence in the media might desensitise people to its effects, and make them less likely to act appropriately when they face similar situations in real life. Alternatively, people may actually believe that such behaviour is 'normal' and seek to emulate it. This could lead them to break the first or third precepts. At the least, it might be seen as adding to the confusion that people face about the correct model of behaviour, thus increasing the ignorance or delusion in the world.

 **ACTIVITIES**

- Do Buddhists use the media effectively? Give some suggestions as to how they could use it better.
- Are Buddhists right to be concerned about the portrayal of sex and violence in the media? Explain as fully as possible.
- Write to the government from a Buddhist point of view explaining what censorship rules you think they should impose on the media.

GradeStudio

AO1

QUESTION
Explain Buddhist attitudes towards the portrayal of violence in the media. **[6 marks]**

Level 1
A basic response might mention that Buddhists do not generally approve of violence, and therefore are likely to disapprove of its use in the media.

Level 2
A more thoughtful response might explore the concept

of ahimsa in more depth. It might then explore whether violence in the media that was likely to cause harm – for example, violence in children's programmes – might be disapproved of more strongly.

Level 3
You might continue by exploring whether violent portrayals in anti-drink-driving campaigns, which are designed to reduce accidents, and therefore harm to others, might be approved of.

Christianity:
Religion and the media 1

The next two pages will help you to:

- identify a variety of media and evaluate the influence that they have
- examine the way in which Christianity and religious figures are portrayed in the media.

What is the media?

The **media** is the external way in which humans **communicate** with each other, and it influences every part of modern life. Any form of communication can be used in a good or a bad way, and Christians do not agree with each other about which different forms and uses of the media are acceptable.

The media includes television, radio, film, print, the Internet, computers and advertisements, as well as the performing arts (dance, drama, music). All of these have an influence on those who use them.

The influence of broadcasting media, print and film

With the development of cable and satellite television, there has been an increase in the number of channels that are broadcast. Most people only watch a few of their favourites but, even so, the majority of people spend quite a few hours each week watching television.

Christians may be concerned about the messages that are given through television and film. For example, regular viewing of a number of soap operas might give a biased outlook on what is acceptable in everyday life. Young people can see things on television that may be unsuitable for them, and have a negative influence on them. The use of the **watershed** in television is not as effective as it was in the past, as many young people watch beyond that time.

Christians may feel that the way in which different lifestyles are portrayed in television programmes encourages us to waste money, or to spend it in ways that are unacceptable for believers. They might also feel that, by devoting too much time to television, they are not concentrating enough on their religion. This is also true of the way in which celebrity lifestyles are shown in magazines and newspapers.

The attitudes of sports celebrities can give cause for concern if they are not behaving in a positive manner; their lifestyles can encourage people to behave in a manner that is not acceptable to Christians.

ACTIVITIES

Make a chart to show all the different forms of media you can think of, with an example of how each one is used in life today.

MUST THINK ABOUT!

- How many television channels are available to you?
- How many do you watch regularly?
- How many hours a week do you spend watching television?

ACTIVITIES

Choose either a soap opera character or a celebrity and explain how their lifestyle might go against Christian beliefs. You will find it useful to look at previous Topics in this book.

> **Colossians 3:23**
> *Whatever you do, work at it with all your heart, as working for the Lord, not for men.*

The influence of the Internet

Technology is developing rapidly. Many Christians are concerned that chatrooms and social networking sites can have a dangerous influence on young people. Of course, they can also be used to promote religious beliefs and to enable Christians to access religious teachings at home. There are also concerns about the way in which fanatics can use the Internet to persuade others to accepts beliefs that might be against Christian teachings.

The influence of performing arts

Music is a part of 21st-century culture and can be heard on radio, through MP3 players and the Internet, and on television channels. It can be used to influence our moods when shopping, and is generally a powerful tool. Many Christians feel that the emphasis on love and sex in popular music, rather than relationships, gives a false message. There may also be concerns about the way that music can encourage rebellion or undermine society.

How are Christians and Christianity portrayed in the media?

Films about the Christian faith can be seen as a good way to promote Christian beliefs, but can also be considered to show the faith in the wrong way. Martin Scorcese's 1998 film *The Last Temptation of Christ* caused concern as it was thought to show the events leading to the death of Jesus in a violent manner.

Television evangelism provides faith programmes for those who cannot go to church or join a faith community. One of the most popular is BBC1's *Songs of Praise*.

Cable and satellite television broadcast a number of religious programmes that promote the faith in a positive way.

AO2 skills ACTIVITIES

A number of comedy shows use Christianity as their theme. Some of these might be considered inappropriate by Christians as they show religious figures in a way that mocks the faith. Two popular programmes that can be researched:

- *The Vicar of Dibley*
- *Father Ted.*

Taken from the film **The Last Temptation of Christ.**

AO2 skills ACTIVITIES

Investigate any two religious programmes and write a news report to show how they portray Christianity.

Christianity:
Religion and the media 2

How can we balance censorship and freedom?

Many societies feel that there is a need to restrict what is shown or published in the media in order to prevent obscene (offensive) material being available. Some Christians would like to see greater control over the media, especially since the development of many unrestricted social networking sites.

It is considered important to protect vulnerable members of society from material that might influence them adversely, or corrupt or upset them. However, this is a difficult issue, as people have widely differing views on what is actually acceptable.

Methods of censorship

- The watershed is designed to alert adults that some programmes unsuitable for children may be broadcast.
- The Press Complaints Commission deals with any complaints against the press.
- For the Internet, there is an Internet Watch Foundation, and many social networking groups operate their own independent monitoring restrictions.
- There are restrictions on films and computer games which offer guidance as to the suitability for different age groups. In the past, this was much more rigorous than it is today.
- The Advertising Standards Authority (ASA) regulates advertising.

These groups only respond to a problem after the material has been screened or published or appeared online, and this means that vulnerable people might have already been exposed to or influenced by them. For example, the boys who abducted and killed two-year-old James Bulger in 1993 were later said to have been influenced by video and film material.

However, too much restriction prevents freedom of speech, which is seen as an important right in society. Countries that operate strict **censorship** are often oppressing their people and denying human rights. In the past, censorship has resulted in books being burnt, sometimes by Christians who felt that they contained **immoral** ideas, and at other times by repressive governments. Many people feel that this is unacceptable.

The next two pages will help you to:

- explain how censorship and freedom of belief might conflict
- identify how Christian beliefs inform their response to the portrayal of violence and sex in the media.

AO1 skills ACTIVITIES

Think about films or DVDs you have seen in the last year and decide which, if any, might have been age restricted. Discuss in your group why this has been done, and explain why you agree or disagree with it.

Should people have the right to express any opinion in public?

 RESEARCH NOTE

Find out more about the role of the ASA at their website.

REMEMBER THIS

Immoral means not conforming to accepted standards of behaviour.

What might Christians think about the portrayal of sex and violence in the media?

If Christians agree that sex outside marriage is wrong, it is likely that they will find some current themes portrayed on television and in the media offensive and against their beliefs. Some of the more traditional churches will condemn all material that **condones** promiscuity or sexual relationships outside marriage.

All Christians would agree that humans are 'made in the image of God' (Genesis 1) and so each individual should be treated with respect. Christians also believe

> **1 Corinthians 6:19, 20a**
>
> *that your body is a temple of the Holy Spirit, who is in you, whom you have received from God?… honour God with your body.*

Anything in the media that promotes the **degradation** of human beings would go against Christian teaching and so would be unacceptable to Christians. This would include scenes or images containing pornography. Media containing violence, or where war or fighting is glorified or encouraged, would also be frowned on, although there might be a different opinion about news programmes that highlight violence in order to inform people about what is happening in the world.

It is often difficult to make a clear ruling about what is unacceptable for Christians, but general principles enable believers to follow the teaching of their faith.

REMEMBER THIS

What do Christians believe about sexual relationships? Refresh your memory by looking back to Topic 1.

AO2 skills ACTIVITIES

What would you censor in the media? Explain why you have these views. Use examples from recent news items, films and the Internet to support your argument.

GradeStudio

AO2

QUESTION

'There should be no censorship in the media.'

Discuss this statement. You should include different, supported points of view and a personal viewpoint. You must refer to Christianity in your answer. **[12 marks]**

Level 1

First, show that you understand what the question is about, and state an opinion. For example, some Christians do believe that there are occasions when censorship may be necessary, particularly when women or children are exploited for pornography.

Level 2

Next, justify this point of view by referring to a religious teaching. For example, the Bible teaches that Christians should look after the poor and helpless, and this applies very clearly to occasions when people are exploited for money.

Level 3

Next, offer a deeper explanation. For example, some Christians may be concerned about how far censorship should go. During the Second World War, the Nazis burnt books to stop ideas spreading. Most Christians would be very concerned with this course of action because it limits freedom of speech. Remember to give your own opinion.

Level 4

Finally, offer a deeper explanation of the second viewpoint and give reasons for your own opinion. For example, you might say that issues of censorship and freedom of speech also affect the way in which we treat the beliefs of other faiths. You might believe that censorship is almost always wrong because it can limit freedom of speech and may also push these things underground. However, you might think that there are occasions when people must respect the beliefs and principles of others.

Hinduism:
Religion and the media

The next two pages will help you to:

- explain the attitudes Hindus have to the media
- evaluate how Hindu beliefs influence their actions concerning the media.

The Mahabharata *was successfully adapted for television in India, some reports claiming that 99 per cent of all Indians saw at least some of it.*

How do you communicate in a digital age?

We live in a world of many different types of communication. How can Hinduism be effectively represented in the age of the Internet, television and cinema?

The **media** are interested in telling stories. Hinduism is a faith that has developed its teachings by using stories. In India, the *Mahabharata* was successfully adapted into ninety-four parts for television, running for two years. When it was shown on the BBC, it attracted the highest ever audience for a subtitled programme. It has also been adapted for the stage in a nine-hour re-telling by the director Peter Brooke.

Film

There have been many attempts to portray India in cinema, such as *A Passage to India* (1984). In 1982, the film *Gandhi* won nine Oscars for its portrayal of the Indian Hindu religious leader. Some people objected to the way he was presented and felt that the image put across was a little too saintly. However, this was important in spreading his ideas across the world and reaching new audiences.

India has one of the largest film industries in the world, nicknamed 'Bollywood'. Many films take ancient Hindu stories or ideas and put them into a new context. They are often bright and vibrant, with lots of music and songs. Films such as *Bride & Prejudice* and *Moulin Rouge* have been greatly influenced by the Bollywood style.

Music

Music that has its origins in Hinduism has also become popular. The Indian classical musician Ravi Shankar was a major influence on the Beatles and other pop/rock musicians. He plays ragas, which are often Hindu religious tunes. The growth of bhangra and Bollywood soundtracks that are sampled has had a major effect in promoting Hindu culture in the West.

New media

The Internet has become crucial in spreading the Hindu faith, and various Hindu communities across the world have a presence there. Many of these are quite critical of other media such as television, which they see as too **secular** (not religious) in their reporting of events. They believe that, as India is about 80 per cent Hindu, this should be reflected in the programmes made and the presenters used.

The growth of satellite and digital stations has also caused concern, as many traditional Hindus see these as encouraging the younger generations to follow fashions and develop attitudes that do not fit with the faith. However, these developments have also created an opportunity for religious groups to develop their own television stations to celebrate Indian and Hindu culture.

Concerns about the media

Television and cinema have been criticised for promoting un-Hindu behaviour. Indian television stations have screened soap operas from the UK and the USA. There is particular concern about some of the attitudes to sex and sexuality contained in these programmes.

Some Hindus believe that the media can sometimes be a distraction to pursuing the religious life. The media may also encourage criticism of tradition and may, some believe, encourage the abandonment of a sense of **dhamma**. The media can also encourage people to think about their individuality rather than the fact that they belong to communities of faith. Some Hindus are concerned about the **stereotypical** depiction of faith that television and the cinema might give, which they say are unfair and do not encourage faith.

Many Hindus might also fear that the media – especially through advertising – may encourage people to become too attached to the world around them of sense, rather than seek the high calling of **moksha** – spiritual liberation. In order to be effective, moshka has to create a sense of want in people.

REMEMBER THIS

Dharma means religious duty in Hinduism.
Moksha is the release from the cycle of reincarnation (**samsara**).

ACTIVITIES

- Could you use an advertising campaign to encourage people to become Hindus? What problems might you face?
- Research in detail one Hindu story. How might you re-tell this in such a way that a modern audience might understand its themes?
- Watch one edition of a popular soap like *Eastenders* or *Hollyoaks*. Write down what happens in the plot. How far do the characters in these shows live their lives by values that would fit with Hindu teaching?
- Find out about how Indian classical music has influenced the development of pop music in the UK and in the USA.

Islam:
Religion and the media 1

The next two pages will help you to:

- explore the portrayal of Islam in the media
- investigate Muslim attitudes towards the media.

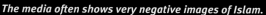
The media often shows very negative images of Islam.

Islam in the media

Unfortunately, on many occasions when Islam appears in the news media it is because of problems in particular countries such as Afghanistan or Iraq, or their relationship with the Western world. Often these news items may appear to be very negative and critical of Islam. However, there are many occasions when Muslims themselves appear in the media which have nothing to do with this.

Portrayal of Islam and of important religious figures in the media

In recent years, some parts of the media have been accused of **Islamophobia** – hatred of Islam and Muslims.

Most Muslims believe that there should be no representation of Allah nor of any living thing that Allah created – to do so would be **shirk**. Therefore, Muslims are understandably cautious about the story of Islam being represented on the television or in film. Although Muslims do not worship Muhammad ﷺ, many feel that any attempt to portray him would be disrespectful and quite possibly inaccurate.

However, there have been films about Islam that have met with the approval of Muslims. *The Message* (1976) and *Muhammad: the Last Prophet* (2002) were both made by Muslims. In both films, the Prophet himself is not shown and the films are made as though he were the cameraman. In this way, no disrespect is shown.

AO1 skills **ACTIVITIES**

Think/pair/share
Think of some of the occasions when you have seen or heard about Muslims in the media. With a partner, decide how accurate these portrayals have been. Decide as a class whether you think the media give a fair representation of Islam.

AO1 skills **ACTIVITIES**

Watch or find out more about *The Message* (1976) or *Muhammad: the Last Prophet* (2002). Write a review explaining how Islam and Muslims are represented in the film.

RESEARCH NOTE

There are two versions of *The Message*. Find out why.

Muslim attitudes towards films, books and comics that focus on religious messages

For some religious people, nothing related to their religion should be represented in the media in the form of films, books or comics.

In 1988, Salman Rushdie wrote a book called *The Satanic Verses*, which caused offence to many Muslims. The courts in the United Kingdom decided that laws about blasphemy offered protection only to the Church of England.

At the same time, the Ayatollah Khomeini issued a fatwah (a religious opinion on Islamic law issued by an Islamic scholar) against Rushdie. Many people asked whether authorities in Muslim countries had any right to declare a fatwah against Muslims living in non-Muslim countries.

Comics and cartoons can cause problems for some people because they are often just intended to make people laugh or can be very violent.

The case of the Danish cartoons

In September 2005, a major Danish newspaper, the *Jyllands-Posten*, published a series of cartoons including drawings of Muhammad ﷺ as a terrorist. Obviously Muslims found these highly offensive and asked for an apology. Ten ambassadors to Denmark from Muslim countries complained to the Danish Prime Minister. The Indonesian ambassador to Denmark wrote: 'We hope there will be understanding of Muslims' feelings about Mohammad. And we hope there will be an apology from Jyllands-Posten.'

However, the newspaper published a statement in which it said:

'We must quietly point out here that the drawings illustrated an article on the self-censorship which rules large parts of the Western world. Our right to say, write, photograph and draw what we want to within the framework of the law exists and must endure – unconditionally!'

As a consequence there were riots in Denmark and elsewhere, and many other European papers republished the cartoons as a response to what they saw as **censorship**.

RESEARCH NOTE

Find out about the establishment of the State of Israel or the troubles in Iraq and why there are problems there today. Make sure that you look at different sources and try to get a balanced view.

AO2 skills ACTIVITIES

- Choose either *The Satanic Verses* or the Danish cartoons. Research the events they triggered and write no more than 300 words explaining what happened.

- Should Muslims be offended by the stereotyped way in which Islam is often presented in the media? Why/why not?

- What duties do the media have to present religions without using stereotypes or causing offence? Does this vary for different types of media?

The Danish cartoons provoked protests from Muslims across the world.

Islam:
Religion and the media 2

The next two pages will help you to:

- investigate how Muslims use the media to represent Islam
- look at Muslim attitudes to censorship and freedom.

Using the media to represent Islam

As so much media coverage of Islam has tended to be negative, in recent years Muslims have worked towards obtaining more positive coverage of their faith and lifestyle on the television.

Recently a new channel has been launched to cover Middle Eastern events and reflect the news from this perspective:

Al Jazeera English, the 24-hour English-language news and current affairs channel, is headquartered in Doha, the capital of Qatar.

The organisation is the world's first global English language news channel to be headquartered in the Middle East.

From this unique position, Al Jazeera English is destined to be the English-language channel of reference for Middle Eastern events, balancing the current typical information flow by reporting from the developing world back to the West and from the southern to the northern hemisphere.

The channel aims to give voice to untold stories, promote debate, and challenge established perceptions.

With broadcasting centres in Doha, Kuala Lumpur, London and Washington DC and supporting bureaus worldwide, the channel will set the news agenda, bridging cultures and providing a unique grassroots perspective from under-reported regions around the world to a potential global audience of over one billion English speakers.

The station broadcasts news, current affairs, features, analysis, documentaries, live debates, entertainment, business and sport.

Building on Al Jazeera Arabic channel's ground breaking developments in the Arab and Muslim world that have changed the face of news within the Middle East, Al Jazeera English is part of a growing network that is now extending this fresh perspective from regional to global through accurate, impartial and objective reporting.

AO2 skills ACTIVITIES

'All religions should have their own news channels.' Discuss.

Remember to give your own opinion and support it.

Censorship and freedom of speech

Censorship is when someone is prevented from publishing or broadcasting something which might be offensive to other people. The ancient Romans had two censors who oversaw the rules of the city.

Censorship is a difficult issue because on the one hand people want to protect vulnerable members of society, while on the other they do not want to limit people's individual freedom. Freedom of speech and freedom of the press are also very important means of making sure that countries do not become dictatorships or police states.

Advertising is seen by many as a valuable part of the media. However, there have been occasions when religious people, including Muslims, have petitioned the Government when they have found particular advertising offensive – this is often because of the way in which they are portrayed in adverts.

The issue of censorship was raised earlier in this Topic showing the reaction to cartoons in a Danish newspaper. Islam does not support censorship, but does believe that all people should show respect towards the religious beliefs of others.

Because Islam does not approve of the portrayal of its religious figures does not mean that Muslims do not have a sense of humour about themselves.

Censorship and the portrayal of violence and sex

Many religious people object to the portrayal of violence and sex in the media, particularly when this is accessible to children. Many Muslims do not believe that violence and sex are suitable topics for entertainment.

Although Islam is not a pacifist religion, it teaches that even during war the aim must always be to re-establish peace.

Muslims also believe that sex is a gift from Allah and that women should be protected. Pornography exploits women and suggests that they exist just to be used by men.

In 1979, after the Shah was deposed, women in Iran returned to wearing the veil. However, times change and in 2000 many of the daughters of the women who had welcomed wearing the veil as a protest against the corruption of Western society were protesting themselves for the restrictions on clothing to be lifted.

Sexual images are often used in advertising.

Oh yes... There will be blood.

Many religious people object to violent films such as **Saw.**

Muslims in Tehran protesting against American involvement in Israel.

AO1+AO2 skills **ACTIVITIES**

Try to watch the film *East is East*, or one of the films by Gurinder Chadha such as *Bend it like Beckham*. Write a review of the film you have watched and research Muslim reactions to it.

AO1+AO2 skills **ACTIVITIES**

- In pairs, write a handout for a meeting protesting about the amount of violence and sex on the television. Include supported religious viewpoints as well as your own.

- 'If religious people want to talk about their faith in public, they should not try to stop other people from saying anything they want or writing anything they want.' Discuss. Write an answer to this question, making sure you look at both sides of the discussion.

Judaism:
Religion and the media 1

The next two pages will help you to:

- explore the portrayal of Judaism in the media
- investigate Jewish attitudes towards the media.

Judaism in the news

When Judaism appears in the news, it is often because of political problems concerning the State of Israel and its relationship with the West Bank and the Gaza Strip. The images that appear can be very negative and critical of Jews.

The other main area where you may see stories about Jews in the **media** is in relation to the Holocaust or Shoah of the 20th century. Here, Jews are seen as the victims of the Nazis.

Many famous Jewish comedians such as Sarah Silverman (left) make jokes about being Jewish.

AO1+AO2 skills ACTIVITIES

Think/pair/share
Think of all the examples you can of where you have seen or heard Jews in the media. With a partner, decide how accurate these images are. Decide as a class whether you think the media give a fair representation of Judaism.

RESEARCH NOTE

Find out about the establishment of the State of Israel and why there are problems there today. Make sure that you look at different sources and try to get a balanced view.

However, there are many other occasions when Jews themselves appear in the media on their own account, with individual stories about their own lives. Often, these stories have nothing to do with the fact that they are Jewish – the fact that they are may not be mentioned, and may not even be apparent.

Portrayal of Jews

The media has produced **stereotyped** images of Jews throughout history. One particularly strong stereotype can be found in characters such as Fagin in Charles Dickens' *Oliver Twist*.

One of the issues that arises in entertainment is when fun is made of religion. Much comedy relies on stereotypes for its humour, and many jokes are made about Jews and Jewish customs – by Jews and non-Jews alike. Most Jews treat humour as harmless, provided that it is not intended to hurt or offend people.

Portrayal of important religious figures

Many Jews believe that G-d cannot be represented by an actor, and should not appear as a character or even a voice. They believe that this is against the third commandment:

> **Exodus 20:7**
> *You shall not swear falsely by the name of the Lord your G-d; for the Lord will not clear one who swears falsely by His name.*

Another view is that G-d and, sometimes, other people should not be represented at all because of the teachings of the second commandment:

> **Exodus 20:4–5a**
> *You shall not make for yourself a sculptured image, or any likeness of what is in the heavens above, or on the earth below, or in the waters under the earth. You shall not bow down to them or serve them.*

Jewish attitudes towards films, books and comics that focus on religious messages

For some religious people, nothing related to their religion should be represented in the media in the form of films, books and comics. However, most Jews would not take such a severe position, provided that no disrespect is shown or harm intended.

Many films have been based on the stories found in the Jewish Scriptures: for example, *Moses the Law-giver*, *The Ten Commandments*, *David and Goliath* and even Disney's *Prince of Egypt*. *Joseph and the Amazing Technicolor Dreamcoat* by Tim Rice and Andrew Lloyd Webber started on the stage, but is now a film too. These have not caused problems because they are attempts at telling stories from the Bible while being careful not to cause offence.

There are also many films about Judaism and Jewish life, such as *Fiddler on the Roof*, *Yentl* and *Sixty-six*.

Jewish actors, directors and producers

Although there have been many famous actors, film directors and producers who are Jewish, often people are unaware of this because the films they make are not about Jews. One exception to this is *Schindler's List*, Stephen Spielberg's film of Thomas Keneally's book, set during the Holocaust in the Second World War. Stephen Spielberg and many of the cast were Jewish, even though the writer Thomas Keneally and the person the film is about – Oskar Schindler – were not.

Comics can cause problems for some Jews because they are often only intended to make people laugh, or can be very violent. However, many children are given religious comics that tell the stories from the scriptures in comic strip form, without giving offence.

So most Jews do not have any particular problems with representations of their religion in the media, whether they are serious or funny, provided that they are not disrespectful.

FOR DEBATE

What was the reason for the instruction given in the third commandment?

ACTIVITIES

AO1 skills

Watch or find out more about one film about Jewish life. Write a review explaining how Judaism and Jews are represented in the film.

ACTIVITIES

AO1+AO2 skills

- Should Jews be offended by the stereotyped way in which Judaism is often presented in the media? Why/why not?
- Are the news media right to focus so much on Jews in Israel? Why/why not?
- What duties do the media have to present religions accurately? Does this vary for different types of media?

Judaism:
Religion and the media 2

The next two pages will help you to:

- look at the way in which Jews use the media to represent Judaism, and to educate people about it
- understand Jewish views on censorship and freedom of speech.

Poster advertising the anti-semitic film, Der ewige Jude *(The eternal Jew), Germany 1940.*

Using the media to represent Judaism

Some religions actively use the media and, in particular, television and the Internet to spread their faith to others, as well as to encourage their own members.

Judaism is not a missionary or **proselytising** religion – Jews do not try to convert other people to their religion because, according to the Torah, anyone who follows the **Noachide Code** (see page 144) is already doing all that G-d wishes of them. It is only Jews who have to follow the 613 **mitzvot**.

However, there is some advantage in using the media to show people what Jewish life is like and what they believe, as this can promote understanding within communities and help to fight ignorant prejudice. There are many television programmes about Jewish life and about particular Jewish communities.

One Jewish Rabbi, Lionel Blue, has become a well-known radio personality. Best known for his contribution to the *Thought for the Day* spot on BBC Radio 4's *Today* programme, he has been heard by tens of thousands of people, most of whom are not Jews.

REMEMBER THIS

The **mitzvot** are the 613 commandments by which Jews should try to live their lives.

Showing what Judaism is really like

Since the BBC started regular television broadcasting in 1946, there have always been regular religious programmes on Sundays. These periods were known as the 'God Slot' and were almost always Christian. The amount of this programming has decreased in recent years.

Some people now feel that it is not appropriate to have worship on the television unless all religions are represented.

Jews have lived and worked in the United Kingdom for a thousand years and have been involved in the media from the beginning. As Judaism is not involved in trying to convert people who belong to other religions, it does not need to use the media in this way. However, there are often documentary programmes that aim to explain aspects of Judaism and Jewish history.

Censorship and freedom of speech

Censorship is when someone is prevented from publishing or broadcasting something that might be offensive to other people. The ancient Romans had two censors who oversaw the rules of the city.

Censorship is a difficult issue because, on the one hand, people want to protect vulnerable members of society while, on the other, they do not want to limit people's individual freedom. Freedom of speech and freedom of the press are also very important means of making sure that countries do not become dictatorships or police states.

Even well-intentioned work can raise difficult issues. For example, people viewing *Schindler's List* might get the impression that Jews are pacifists, going like lambs to the slaughter. However, on the whole, Judaism is not a pacifist religion: during the Holocaust, the victims had little or no choice but to obey their captors.

Censorship and 'family values'

Many people, including Jews, have expressed concerns about the amount of violence and sex that appears in the media, particularly on television and now in some computer games.

Traditional family values are very important in Judaism. Jews are naturally concerned about programmes in the media which suggest that alternative lifestyles are equal to or better than these family values.

Propaganda and privacy

Many people in the Western world and, in particular, Jews, are suspicious of censorship because they remember the Nazi propaganda in the 1930s and the censorship in communist countries such as the former Union of Soviet Socialist Republics, where atheism was the established view and there was a one party state.

Today it is generally accepted that religious belief and worship are private matters and that people should not be stopped from holding public office because of their religion.

ACTIVITIES

- 'If religious people want to talk about their faith in public, they should not try to stop other people from saying anything they want or writing anything they want.' Write an answer to this question making sure you look at both sides of the discussion.

- In pairs, write a statement from a major broadcaster in which you explain how and why matters of censorship and freedom of speech should be dealt with in the news and other programmes.

Sikhism:
Religion and the media

AO1+AO2 skills ACTIVITIES

In pairs, think carefully about programmes or films that have a religious theme. Make a list of everything you can think about.

Now make three columns in your book:

Name of film/programme	Negative aspects	Positive aspects

Discuss how each entry portrays religion in a positive and negative manner. Try to put some brief details about your views.

The next two pages will help you to:

- express understanding of how the media can promote positive and negative stereotypes about Sikhs and their faith
- explore the message and intent of a number of films which focus on Sikh religious and philosophical messages
- analyse how Sikhs are portrayed in the media and the effect of the media on Sikh lifestyles
- evaluate your own views about the relationship between the media and religion.

Images of Sikhs are becoming commonplace in mainstream media.

Sikhs in the media

There is not a great deal of portrayal of Sikhs in the media. Some of the better-known recent portrayals are through productions such as *Bend it Like Beckham* and *Bride & Prejudice*.

These productions look at Sikhism from a cultural rather than religious angle, and include negative and positive images: the young Sikh girl at the heart of *Bend it Like Beckham* is an ardent football player, and much of her playing has to be kept secret from her family because of their cultural attitudes. However, Sikhs are quite open-minded and are active participants in India's national sports teams. *Bride & Prejudice* also has positive and negative images of Sikhs, and a lot of the material is far from being an accurate representation.

The Khalsa Press at Lahore in 1883

Historically, Sikhs have relied a great deal on the media to promote their faith. The activities of the Khalsa Press at Lahore in

1883 have been essential in publishing material to promote Sikhism, especially in the face of threats from the Arya Samaj, who resisted giving the Sikhs a distinct identity of their own.

Modern-day usage of the media to promote Sikhs and their faith

Media in modern society is currently viewed as essential in promoting Sikh values, especially within the Sikh communities living outside India. Channels such as 'Alpha ETC Punjabi' are excellent tools through which Sikhs can address cultural, religious and moral aspects of their faith. 'Alpha ETC Punjabi' even has live gurbani from the Golden Temple at various times of the day. Journals such as *The Sikh Review* and newspapers such as *The Sikh Times* and *Eastern Eye* address issues faced by the British-born generation of Sikhs too.

  GradeStudio

AO1

QUESTION
Explain how the media can be a useful tool for Sikhs to promote awareness of their faith. **[6 marks]**

You could build an answer like this:

Level 1
Firstly, make the examiner aware that you know what you are talking about. You could begin your answer as follows: 'Historically, Sikhs have relied on the media to promote an awareness of their faith. Promoting their distinct identity is an issue that Sikhs have had to grapple with throughout the development of the Sikh religion.'

Level 2
Next go on to discuss the activities of the Khalsa Press at Lahore in 1883. An explanation of the activities of the Arya Samaj could also be undertaken here. Continuing on a historical note, the use of the media by Bhai Vir Singh could be used.

Level 3
Finally, move on to the modern-day use of the media by Sikhs. Negative images of the Sikhs arose post-1984 with the bombing of the Golden Temple in Amritsar and the subsequent assassination of Indira Gandhi. Channel such as 'Alpha ETC Punjabi' are excellent tools. Also look at publications such as *The Sikh Times* and their impact on society.

MUST THINK ABOUT!

Sikhism is the youngest of the six major faiths.

 **ACTIVITIES**

In groups of four of five, imagine you have been commissioned by a group of British Sikhs to produce a film about their lives and adaptation to British society. Generally, Sikhs fit in well within British society. What makes them most visible from other minority groups is their outward appearance with the turban. How are you going to go about beginning your film, what theme will it have and what representations of the Sikhs do you wish to portray? What central message will your production have? Think of a suitable and eye-catching title and visual promotion too.

GradeStudio

Welcome to the Grade Studio

Grade Studio is here to help you improve your grades by working through typical questions you might find on an examination paper. For a fuller explanation of how Grade Studio works, and how the examiners approach the task of marking your paper, please see p. 30.

AO1

Question

Explain Christian attitudes towards the portrayal of violence in the media.

[6 marks]

Student's answer

Christians believe that violence is wrong and should not be shown in the media because it goes against the Ten Commandments. Some Christians might also believe that portraying violence in the media might encourage people to be more violent.

Examiner's comment

The candidate has given a satisfactory answer to the question. There are two relevant points but only one of them really relates to Christianity. In order to reach Level 3 the candidate needs to give more information and examples. The candidate could also use more technical terms from the specification to show the breadth of their knowledge and understanding.

Student's improved answer

Christians believe that violence is wrong and should not be shown in the media because it goes against the Ten Commandments. Some Christians might also believe that portraying violence in the media might encourage people to be more violent.

Some people might say that showing violence just to make the programme more exciting is never justified, but that sometimes it is necessary to portray violence in order to explain the story, for example, the whipping of Jesus in the Passion of the Christ.

Many Christians might say that the portrayal of violence is something that has to be judged on a case-by-case basis.

Examiner's comment

This is now a good answer to the question. The candidate has shown a clear understanding of the question. There is good description and explanation of a variety of different responses to the portrayal of violence. The candidate has shown some analysis in dealing with the question. The information is presented clearly and there is good use of technical terms.

AO2

Question

'People should never be allowed to make fun of religion in the media.' Discuss this statement. You should include different, supported points of view and a personal viewpoint. You must refer to Christianity in your answer.

[12 marks]

Student's answer

Some Christians might say that it is always wrong to make fun of religion in the media because religion is the most important aspect of their lives. Some Christians might also say that no one would like fun to be made of their religion, so why should people make fun of Christianity.

Examiner's comment

The candidate has given a limited answer to the question. There are two relevant points but they both address the same point of view and neither is expanded. In order to reach Level 4 the candidate needs to give alternative viewpoints and also include a personal response.

Student's improved answer

Some Christians might say that it is always wrong to make fun of religion in the media because religion is the most important aspect of their lives. Some Christians might also say that no one would like fun to be made of their religion, so why should people make fun of Christianity.

Some people, on the other hand, might say that it depends on what is meant by 'fun'. Humour is part of everyday life and, because people who follow a religion are also human, there may be occasions when humour is not hurtful, but just a joke that people can share. Some may say that making fun of individual people and what they do is fine but that this does not include actually making fun of their religion.

My personal opinion is that there are always occasions when we find something funny, but this must be done with respect and should not ever be done with the intention of offending people.

Examiner's comment

This is now a good answer to the question. The candidate has shown a clear understanding of the question and has presented a range of views supported by evidence and argument. The answer explains Christian views, among others, and includes a personal viewpoint, which is also supported.

These specimen answers provide an outline of how you could construct your response. Space does not allow us to give a full response. The examiner will be looking for more detail in your actual exam responses.

These examples only use Christianity but you could use the Grade Studio to apply to any of the religions you are studying and the structure of the answers would work in the same way.

ExamCafé

Tools and Tips

Now you have finished the course, it is time to revise and prepare for the examination. Before this sends you into a flat spin or a panic with all those worries you have about coping in the exam situation, remember that as you have worked through the course you have gained knowledge, understanding and skills. Yes, you will have to refresh your memory and practise your skills but this section of the book is intended to help you to do those things effectively and ensure you do justice to yourself in the exam.

The key to good revision is to 'work smart'. This section will guide you to know what is needed for success and, just as important, what is not. So don't panic! Think positive because the examiner will. GCSE is about what you *can do*, not what you can't.

Key points to note at this stage

1 You revision needs to focus on what the examiners want in your answers so that you can get the best possible marks.

   - In GCSE Religious Studies there are two things that examiners are looking for. These are described in the assessment objectives AO1 and AO2.

   - Each assessment objective is worth 50 per cent of the marks.

2 You need to understand that the exam questions are designed to measure your performance in each assessment objective. This will ensure that you know how respond to the questions so as to reach the highest levels. Each question will have five parts:

   - four assessing AO1 – three questions checking on your knowledge, one measuring understanding and analysis

   - one question assessing AO2 – assessing your ability to put forward different points of view on an issue, weigh them up against each other and express your own views, backing everything up with evidence and good arguments.

If this all sounds rather scary – just hold on. As you work though this section you will see that by knowing what examiners want in each part of the question you can make your revision really count because it will be well focused on success in the assessment objectives.

ow to get started

u do need to have a sound knowledge and understanding of
you have studied, so there is some basic factual learning to be
ne. Techniques for revision are quite personal and will depend
how you learn things best. Here are some suggestions:

- Create summary cards to summarise a unit or a part of unit – a
small card will hold between 5 and 10 bullet points.

- Design memory cards (really good for the visual learner) – use
pictures or other visual prompts to recall key facts or, for
example, the order of events in the marriage service.

- Break your revision time up into intensive revision sessions of
5–10 minutes – give yourself a break (no more than 5 minutes),
then test yourself on what you have revised.

- Write your own questions. Write mark schemes for them.
Answer the questions and use the levels of response to mark
them.

each Topic you need to:

- Set everything you learn in the context of the religion you are
studying, remembering that it is a living faith, practised by real
people in the 21st century.

- Make sure that you cover all parts of each section of the
course.

- Know the meaning of all the technical (religious) words in the
specification. Learn a short definition for each of them, which
you can use in your revision notes and in the exam.

- Make connections in your revision between what you know
and how and why this is important for religious believers. Use
spider charts or mind maps for this, if it helps.

member that only 25 per cent of the marks are awarded for
owledge – a further 25 per cent depend on you showing you
derstand what you know. So although knowledge revision is
portant, it is only the basis for you being able to do well in the
derstanding questions for AO1 and the skills questions for
2.

Exam Café

Revision
Common errors and mistakes

Misreading the question: Of course this will never happen to you, but a surprising number of candidates answer a question which they think has been asked rather than the one that has actually been asked. They see a key word and miss the point of the question, losing most of the marks as a result.

Wasting valuable time: A question worth 1 mark does not need a paragraph response. Match the length of responses to the mark allocations and don't waste time.

Disorganised waffle: AO2 responses in particular need to be planned, otherwise you will waffle and muddle along. In your revision, practise planning responses and then write up your plan so that you get into the habit and feel confident to do this in the exam. If you feel strongly about an issue in an AO2 response, make sure you take a step back and think calmly about other points of view. A long rant about your view will get few marks.

Poor selection of knowledge: Choose good examples that focus on the religious aspect of the topic. For example, the response to the question 'Why do Christians give to charities?' – 'Because they like people to see them being generous' is not a good response from a Religious Studies point of view. 'They are following the teachings of Jesus to "love your neighbour"' is much better and will get more marks.

Using the same information over and over again: Saying in response to different questions, for example, that caring for other people or giving money to a charity bring the believer 'closer to God' may be true, but you should not expect the examiner to credit you with many marks unless you link the comment to each of the Topics. The parable of the Good Samaritan is not the only parable in the Bible; candidates who use it over and over again to justify the beliefs or actions of Christians cannot expect to get many marks.

Getting hung up o your view of an issue: This is a real danger when you feel strongly about the issue in the AO2 stimulus. One point of view expressed with lots of personal feeling will get less than 30 per cent of the marks. You must consider various views and have balance, as well as giving your own opinion on the answer.

Revision checklist

This section covers all six Topics in the Applied Ethics part of the specification, so you need to pick out the ones that you are studying for the examination.

TOPIC 1 RELIGION AND HUMAN RELATIONSHIPS

In this Topic there are a number of different issues that you need to be able to explain. You should be able to write about religious beliefs about **marriage**. Although marriage ceremonies are on the specification, you do not need to describe the details of the ceremony, rather show how they reflect belief. You should also understand teaching about Civil Partnerships. You should be able to explain different religious attitudes towards **divorce** and remarriage. Finally, you need to make sure that you understand religious teaching about different forms of **contraception**.

TOPIC 2 RELIGION AND MEDICAL ETHICS

When you are studying this Topic, all the issues are really concerned with the idea of the **sanctity** of life. You need to understand what is meant by **abortion**, fertility treatment, **cloning**, **euthanasia**, **suicide** and animal research. As well as this, you must be able to explain religious responses to each of these issues. It is possible that you may have strong feelings about some of these but you must still ensure that you present a balanced argument.

TOPIC 3 RELIGION, POVERTY AND WEALTH

This Topic is about the disadvantaged. You need to be able to explain religious beliefs about the existence of **poverty**, famine and disease. You also need to show that you understand religious teachings about how people in these circumstances should be helped, about **charity** and about the right use of money. Finally, you need to consider what might be considered to be a **moral** or **immoral** occupation and be able to explain why.

TOPIC 4 RELIGION, PEACE AND JUSTICE

This Topic is about war, **pacifism** and **justice**. Make sure that you can explain the 'Just War' Theory and apply it to particular conflicts. You should be able to explain Christian attitudes towards war, but it is very important that you remember that the commandment is 'Do not commit murder' and not 'Do not kill' – there is a difference. In writing about pacifism, make sure that you do not simply say something like 'Jesus was a pacifist' unless you can back this up with evidence or argument. Finally, you need to be able to explain the aims of punishment and religious attitudes towards **capital punishment** in particular.

TOPIC 5 RELIGION AND EQUALITY

This is a large Topic with several sections, and in the examination you need to make sure that you have covered all of them. You should be able to explain the ideas of equality, **discrimination** and **prejudice**. You should also be able to explain the religious arguments about **racism** and issues of gender equality. In writing about attitudes towards other religions, you must be sure that you understand this fully and do not write something like 'Christians love everyone and think that all religions are equal'. Finally, you need a good understanding of the concepts of **forgiveness** and **reconciliation**.

TOPIC 6 RELIGION AND THE MEDIA

This is an easy Topic in which to write a lot about nothing. Remember the warning earlier about disorganised waffle. Whatever question you are attempting from this Topic, you need to ensure that your answer is clearly focused on the question being asked and that you are using religious responses in your answers.

ExamCafé

Revision

The details of the course are known as the Specification. It is broken down into the Topics listed above. Here is a summary of the key areas of each unit that you need to know about.

Section of the specification	Key elements
Religion and human relationships	Know the meaning of the technical terms in the specification so that you can answer factual questions such as 'What is meant by contraception?'
	Know and understand the importance of each topic in this section and how these beliefs might affect their lifestyle.
	Know and understand how marriage ceremonies reflect Christian teaching. Also be able to explain attitudes towards Civil Partnerships.
	Be able to explain different attitudes towards divorce, remarriage and contraception.
Religion and medical ethics	Know and understand religious teachings about the sanctity of life and how this belief is reflected in the issues in this Topic.
	You need to be able to explain different religious attitudes towards issues of abortion, fertility treatment, euthanasia, suicide and the use of animals in medical research.
Religion, poverty and wealth	You must focus on religious understandings of the causes of hunger, poverty and disease, not just general ones.
	You need to be able to explain religious responses to these issues, including giving money to charity as well as practical responses.
	You should know religious teachings about the use of money and ways in which it should not be used: for example, gambling or lending at interest.
	Finally, you need to be able to explain what is meant by 'moral' and 'immoral' and what religious believers might consider moral and immoral occupations.
Religion, peace and justice	Be able to give a detailed explanation of the 'Just War' Theory and religious attitudes towards war.
	Explain religious approaches to the use of violence and different attitudes towards pacifism.
	Understand the concept of justice and punishment.
	Be able to explain the aims of punishment and religious responses to capital punishment.
	Understand religious responses to the treatment of criminals.
	Be able to explain beliefs about social justice and injustice.

Religion and equality	Be able to explain religious teaching about equality.
	Be able to explain religious attitudes towards racism and gender issues.
	Show understanding of religious attitudes towards other religions, including beliefs about spreading the teachings of the religion and conversion.
	You need to be able to explain the words forgiveness and reconciliation and explain beliefs about these.
Religion and the media	You need to know about different types of media and be able to explain their influence.
	You need to be able to explain religious attitudes towards the media and the way in which religious figures may be portrayed in the media.
	You should be able to consider the use which religion can make of the media.
	Also you should be able to explain the issues that are raised by the concepts of censorship and freedom of speech.

Spot-check – Christianity

Can you answer the questions in the table below?

Question	Response	Mark
What is meant by an abortion?		1
What is contraception?		1
State two reasons why Christians might be opposed to war		2
State three ways in which Christians might use the media		3

Look at the table below. If these are the answers, what were the questions?

Answer	Question	Mark
To help a woman to have a baby		1
Is a form of euthanasia		1
Stopping people from reading or looking at something		1
To prevent someone from becoming pregnant		1
Discriminating against someone because of their skin colour		1

Exam preparation
Sample answers and questions

Now you have done some serious revision it is time to see what sort of response to the questions will get good marks in the exam. Here are some examples of responses, with comments from the examiner to show you what is good about them and how they could be improved.

Remember that examiners will use levels of response for part **d** which is AO1 and part **e** which is AO2. For parts **a–c** responses will be point marked. This means that if there is one mark allocated for the question, only one point is expected, if two marks are allocated, then two points are expected and so on. Part **a** is worth one mark, **b** two marks and **c** three marks.

AO1 a–c

Here are some AO1 point-marked questions and example responses from Topic 1: Religion and human relationships.

What is a divorce?

Ending a marriage.

> Check that you write about 'religious' aspects.

Examiner says
Correct.

Give two religious aspects of a Christian marriage service.

1) the ring 2) the vows 3) confetti

Examiner says
Responses 1) and 2) are correct, but response 3) is not a religious aspect.

Why might Roman Catholics not want to be divorced?

It breaks their vows. Marriage is a sacrament with promises made to God. They will probably not be able to be remarried in church.

> Here, although there is only 1 mark per point, a one-word answer is impossible. You will need to be precise and concise in your response.

Examiner says
Three good reasons given.

Let us look now at some responses to the AO1 part **d** of each question, which is going to be marked by levels of response. These questions are worth six marks, but this does not mean that examiners are looking for six points or three points with some development. Examiners are looking for depth of understanding that the response displays. This could be shown by referring to several points and developing each of the points a little, or by developing one or two points fully.

AO1 d

Here are some AO1 questions and example responses from Topic 2: Religion and medical ethics.

Explain how Christians might respond to someone who wants to commit suicide.

When answering this question, ask yourself the question 'why?' as soon as you have written down a reason. There are different levels of explanation, and the examiner is looking for depth not for a superficial level.

Response 1

Christians might say that it is wrong to commit suicide because it is killing, which is against the Ten Commandments. They might say that only God has the right to take life. They might try to cheer the person up by talking to them.

Examiner says
This is a satisfactory response, reaching Level 2. The information given is relevant, and accurate reasons have been chosen. However, the response is not well developed and is essentially one-sided, giving only one explanation.

Response 2

Christians might say that it is wrong to commit suicide because it is murder, which is against the Ten Commandments. They might say that only God has the right to give life and to take it away.

Some Christians might try to talk the person out of it by showing them how much God loves them.

They may also persuade them to speak to an organisation like the Samaritans who help people in these situations. Also, they might show people how much they are loved and that there are still good things in life.

Examiner says
This is a good response. It contains much of the satisfactory response but it is much more developed. The reasons for different views are explained. This response would reach Level 3.

ExamCafé

Exam preparation
Sample answers and questions

AO2

And now to part **e** – AO2. This part of each question is worth 12 marks, or 50 per cent of the total. It is really important that you learn how to respond to the statements in a way that will ensure you get the best marks possible and hit the highest level. There are four levels for AO2. Remember that AO2 is about expressing views, including your own, about an issue, and backing those views up with good evidence and argument.

Here is an AO2 question and some example responses from Topic 5: Religion and equality.

> **'Christians should try to convert everyone to their religion.'**

Response 1

Christians believe that it is their duty to make everyone join their religion so that they can go to heaven. Some people might say that this is wrong and people should be left to decide their religion for themselves.

Response 2

Christians believe that it is their duty to make everyone join their religion so that they can go to heaven. This is because Christianity is a proselytising religion and 'Gospels' are the 'good news' which they have to spread.

Some people might say that this is wrong and people should be left to decide their religion for themselves. It is wrong to try to persuade someone to join your religion just because you believe in it.

Examiner says
This is Level 1. Two relevant viewpoints are stated but there is little support to back them up. This is a simplistic response and shows limited understanding of the question. There is no use of technical terms.

Examiner says
This is Level 2. This is a better answer as it explains to the examiner what the candidate understands the question to be about. However, although two viewpoints are stated and slightly developed, the response is still rather limited.

Response 3

Christians believe that it is part of their duty as followers of Jesus to make everyone join their religion so that they can go to heaven. This is because Christianity is a proselytising religion and 'Gospels' are the 'good news' which they have to spread. They also believe that becoming a Christian is the only way in which people can reach heaven and the presence of God.

Some people might say that this is wrong and people should be left to decide their religion for themselves. It is wrong to try to persuade someone to join your religion just because you believe in it.

Others may think that everyone can listen to whatever they like and can then make their own decisions. My opinion is that it is very difficult for Christians not to try to persuade people to join their religion

Response 4

Christians believe that it is part of their duty as followers of Jesus to make everyone join their religion so that they can go to heaven. This is because Christianity is a proselytising religion and 'Gospels' are the 'good news' that they have to spread. They also believe that becoming a Christian is the only way in which people can reach heaven and the presence of God.

Some people might say that this is wrong and people should be left to decide their religion for themselves. It is wrong to try to persuade someone to join your religion just because you believe in it.

Others may think that everyone can listen to whatever they like and can then make their own decisions.

My personal opinion is that it is very difficult for Christians not to try to persuade people to join their religion because they believe it is part of their religious duty. However, I do not like people knocking on my door trying to persuade me to join their faith and I think it should be left to individuals to come to their own decisions.

Examiner says
This is a satisfactory response and meets the criteria for Level 3. It is reasonably well organised and contains some significant views that are explained well and have evidence to justify them. There is a balance of views. There is good use of technical terms. However, there is no argument in support of the personal opinion and this limits the response to Level 3.

Examiner says
The personal response presents a new view and comes to a conclusion. The candidate has grasped the significance of the issue. The personal view is backed up by evidence. There is good accurate use of specialist terms and the response is reasonably well organised. This will take the response to Level 4.

ExamCafé

Exam preparation
Understanding exam language

Examiners try to keep questions short, clear and easy to understand. To do this they use certain words to show what you should do in order to respond to the question. Sometimes a particular word is used to tell you what is required. We call these flag words because they act like flags telling you simply and clearly what is required. Examples of flag words used in Religious Studies exams are:

State	Usually used in AO1 questions worth 1–3 marks. This means write down a fact about something. For example, 'State one condition of a Just War.' – response 'called by a recognised authority'.
Give	This is used instead of 'state' and requires the same sort of response.
Describe	This is used in AO1 questions and means, tell the examiner factual information about the item or idea. For example, 'Describe Biblical teaching used in a discussion about abortion' means 'Write down factual information about what teachings of the Bible are used when discussing abortion.'
Give an account of	This is asking for the same sort of response as 'describe'.
Explain	This means show that you understand something. For example, 'Explain why many Christians do not approve of divorce' means the examiner wants you to show that you understand the reasons many Christians give for not approving of divorce. An 'explain' response will include some knowledge, but the best responses will give reasons and show an awareness of different views on an issue.
Why	This word is used as shorthand for 'explain'. Put the word explain in front of it and you will know what to do. For example, 'Why do many Christians not approve of divorce?' is the same as 'Explain why many Christians do not approve of divorce'.
How	This can be used to ask you for factual information: for example, 'What do Christians believe about euthanasia?' It can also be used for questions that are asking for understanding where a mixture of fact and understanding is required. For example, with 'How do Christians react to the issue of euthanasia?', the response can be factual about how Christians might respond, or it could be about how Christians will be determined to support hospices because of their beliefs, which is explanation.
Important	This word is used in AO1 part **d** questions and it indicates that you should say why people should or should not do or believe something. For example, 'Explain why opposing racism is important to Christians' means 'Give reasons to explain why some Christians make the fight against racism a main part of their religious life.'
List	This is used instead of 'give' or 'state' and requires the same sort of response.

Examiner Tips

When answering these questions, ask yourself the question 'why?' as soon as you have written down a reason. There are different levels of explanation and the examiner is looking for depth not for a superficial level.

'What is?' just means describe something.

Check that you know what the word 'pacifism' means.

For questions that are awarded 1 mark per point, a one-word answer may be sufficient. You will need to be precise and concise in your response.

Planning and structuring an answer

In some of the grade studios you have seen how to build a response. This is really important for the AO1 responses to part **d** (6 marks) and the AO2 responses to part **e** (12 marks). In each case, follow this structure.

- Check that you really know what the question is about. In the AO2 questions, work out the key word or words in the statement. For example, in 'Working to help the poor is more important than worship', the key words are 'more important than'. If the response does not address this, it will not get many marks.
- Make a note of key points to include in AO1 responses and use a spider diagram to note down viewpoints for AO2.
- Begin your response with a brief reference to what the question is asking you to do.
- Write clearly, concisely and in orderly fashion about the topic or debate. Check all the time that you have explained everything and have referred where appropriate to Christianity.
- Come to a conclusion. In the case of AO1 this may just be – 'so we can see why Christian love is so important'. In the case of AO2, the conclusion should include your personal view, a summing up of the views you have expressed and an evaluation of their significance.
- Write clearly. Manage your time in the exam, so that you can read your responses through to check for sense and accuracy.
- Check spellings and make sure you have used grammar and punctuation correctly. Written communication marks are included in the levels of response.

Glossary

abortion: the deliberate termination of a human pregnancy

adultery: sex between a married person and a person who is not their spouse

ahimsa: Buddhist and Hindu term for non-violence and respect for all living things

AID: Artificial Insemination by Donor, where a sperm donor other than the husband is used for a fertility treatment

AIH: Artificial Insemination by Husband, where the husband's sperm is used for a fertility treatment

Aqd Nikah: Muslim marriage contract

atman: the soul, or real self

Beth Din: the Rabbinical court that decideds on matters of Jewish law

bhikkhunis: Buddhist nuns

bhikkhus: Buddhist monks

bodhisattva: a being destined for Enlightenment, who chooses to remain in the world of samsara in order to help living beings

capital punishment: the legally authorised killing of someone as punishment for a crime

caste system: class divisions in Hindu society based on heredity

censorship: preventing publication or broadcasting of something, usually because it might be offensive to others

charity: to give help or money to people in need

cloning: making identical copies of a living creature by cultivating DNA

commitment: an engagement or obligation

compassion: sympathy and concern for others

condones: overlooks or accepts

contraception: use of artificial or natural methods to prevent conception

covenant: promise or agreement

dalits: the oppressed, outside the four varnas, previously known as the 'outcasts' or 'untouchables'

daswandh: Sikh practice of giving 10 per cent of surplus money to the poor

degradation: humiliation

denomination: strand of Christianity, such as Baptist, Anglican, etc.

dhan: the Sikh word for helping others through giving to charity or giving time to help those in need

dharam yudh: Sikh belief in the Just War

dharma: religious duty in Hinduism; in Buddhism dharma means universal law or ultimate truth

discrimination: unjust or prejudicial treatment because of race, age or gender

divorce: legal dissolution of a marriage

dukkha: loosely translated as suffering or unsatisfactoriness

ecumenical movement: people who work to improve understanding between Christian groups

Eucharist: the Christian ceremony commemorating the Last Supper, in which bread and wine are consecrated and consumed

equality: treating people as equals regardless of gender, race or religious beliefs

euthanasia: killing a patient suffering from an incurable disease or who does not want to live but cannot kill themselves; illegal in most countries

evangelism: persuading others to share your faith

fitrah: the teaching that Islam is the only true religion and that all people are born to be Muslims

forgiveness: to forgive (stop feeling angry towards) someone who has caused you hurt

Harb al-Muqadis: Islamic Holy War

iddah: the period when attempts are made to reconcile before a Muslim divorce

immoral: not conforming to accepted standards of behaviour

interfaith dialogue: discussions and work to help understanding between different faiths

Islamaphobia: negative attitudes to Islam based on fear

IVF: short for *in vitro* fertilisation, where an egg is fertilised in laboratory conditions, then implanted in the womb

jihad: the personal struggle of a Muslim against evil in the way of Allah

justice: just (fair) behaviour or treatment

kama: sensual pleasure in Hinduism

kamma: intentional 'action' in Buddhism

karma: in Hinduism, the law of cause and effect (in Buddhism, this is known as **kamma**)

kirat karna: Sikh belief in earning a living honestly

Khalsa: literally means the 'Pure Ones' and refers to those Sikhs that have taken initiation and agree to live by the rules and regulations of the Rehat Maryada

lesbianism: same-sex relations between women

lex talionis: the passage in Exodus that talks about taking 'an eye for an eye, a tooth for a tooth'

live in poverty: to be extremely poor

mahr: Muslim dowry, or money given by the groom to the bride

marriage: formal, legal union of two people

media (pl.): the means of mass communication (singular is **medium**)

meditation: a state of concentrated calmness

mikveh: a ritual bath for Jews, which is usually part of the synagogue complex

mitzvot (pl.): the 613 commandments by which Jews should try to live their lives (singular is **mitzvah**)

moksha: in Hinduism, the release from the cycle of reincarnation (**samsara**)

moral: accepted standards of behaviour

nibbana: in Buddhism, a state free of greed, hatred and delusion, and thus free of dukkha

niddah: Jewish purity laws

Noachide code: seven commandments given to Noah by G-d after the flood

ordination: the process by which individuals are consecrated, or set apart, as clergy to perform various religious rites and ceremonies

pacifist: someone who believes that war is always wrong

prejudice: making judgements not based on reason or actual experience

procreation: conceiving and having babies

proselytising: trying to convert people to one's own religion

racism: prejudice, discrimination or ill treatment against someone because of their race

reconciliation: restoring friendly relations

reincarnation: the **rebirth** of a soul in a new body in Hinduism and Sikhism (the Buddhist concept of rebirth, although often referred to as reincarnation differs significantly from this in that there is no unchanging 'soul' to reincarnate)

repentance: sincere regret or remorse from one's actions

Sabbath or **Shabbat:** Jewish day of spiritual rest, starting at sunset on Friday and ending at nightfall on Saturday

sacrament: something which cannot be undone

sacred: holy, special

sadaqah: extra charity that Muslims give to the poor

sanctity: to be holy or sacred

samsara: 'everyday life' – the continual round of birth, sickness, old age and death which can be transcended by following the Eightfold Path and Buddhist teaching. In Hinduism this means 'The world' – the place where transmigration (the soul's passage through a series of lives in different species) occurs

secular: not religious

sewa: Sikh idea of service to the community

sexism: prejudice, stereotyping or discrimination, typically against women, on the basis of sex

Shari'ah: Islamic law based on the teachings of the Qur'an

sila: ethical action (or morality) in Buddhism

social justice: the concern that everyone should be treated fairly regardless of their background

stereotype: a fixed, over-simplified image or view of a person or group

suicide: killing oneself

tithe: the Christian act of giving a tenth of your income to charity (formerly taken as a tax by the Church)

tzedaka: an act of charity in Judaism, for example the practice of giving part of your income to help the poor

ummah: worldwide community of Muslims

vand chhakna: the Sikh principle of sharing one's wealth and goods with those who are less fortunate

varnas: Hindu social classes believed to have existed since the beginning of the world

watershed: the time after which programmes that are unsuitable for children are broadcast (9 p.m.)

zakah: paying money to the Muslim community to help the poor

zulm: Islamic term for doing something wrong against Allah, other people or yourself

Index

Single User Licence Agreement: GCSE OCR B RS Applied Ethics ActiveBook

Warning:

This is a legally binding agreement between You (the user or purchasing institution) and Pearson Education Limited of Edinburgh Gate, Harlow, Essex, CM20 2JE, United Kingdom ('PEL').

By retaining this Licence, any software media or accompanying written materials or carrying out any of the permitted activities You are agreeing to be bound by the terms and conditions of this Licence. If You do not agree to the terms and conditions of this Licence, do not continue to use the GCSE OCR B RS Applied Ethics ActiveBook CD-ROM and promptly return the entire publication (this Licence and all software, written materials, packaging and any other component received with it) with Your sales receipt to Your supplier for a full refund.

Intellectual Property Rights:

This GCSE OCR B RS Applied Ethics ActiveBook CD-ROM consists of copyright software and data. All intellectual property rights, including the copyright is owned by PEL or its licensors and shall remain vested in them at all times. You only own the disk on which the software is supplied. If You do not continue to do only what You are allowed to do as contained in this Licence you will be in breach of the Licence and PEL shall have the right to terminate this Licence by written notice and take action to recover from you any damages suffered by PEL as a result of your breach.

The PEL name, PEL logo and all other trademarks appearing on the software and GCSE OCR B RS Applied Ethics ActiveBook CD-ROM are trademarks of PEL. You shall not utilise any such trademarks for any purpose whatsoever other than as they appear on the software and GCSE OCR B RS Applied Ethics ActiveBook CD-ROM.

Yes, You can:

1 use this GCSE OCR B RS Applied Ethics ActiveBook CD-ROM on Your own personal computer as a single individual user. You may make a copy of the GCSE OCR B RS Applied Ethics ActiveBook CD-ROM in machine readable form for backup purposes only. The backup copy must include all copyright information contained in the original.

No, You cannot:

1 copy this GCSE OCR B RS Applied Ethics ActiveBook CD-ROM (other than making one copy for back-up purposes as set out in the Yes, You can table above);

2 alter, disassemble, or modify this GCSE OCR B RS Applied Ethics ActiveBook CD-ROM, or in any way reverse engineer, decompile or create a derivative product from the contents of the database or any software included in it;

3 include any materials or software data from the GCSE OCR B RS Applied Ethics ActiveBook CD-ROM in any other product or software materials;

4 rent, hire, lend, sub-licence or sell the GCSE OCR B RS Applied Ethics ActiveBook CD-ROM;

5 copy any part of the documentation except where specifically indicated otherwise;

6 use the software in any way not specified above without the prior written consent of PEL;

7 subject the software, GCSE OCR B RS Applied Ethics ActiveBook CD-ROM or any PEL content to any derogatory treatment or use them in such a way that would bring PEL into disrepute or cause PEL to incur liability to any third party.

Grant of Licence:

PEL grants You, provided You only do what is allowed under the 'Yes, You can' table above, and do nothing under the 'No, You cannot' table above, a non-exclusive, non-transferable Licence to use this GCSE OCR B RS Applied Ethics ActiveBook CD-ROM.

The terms and conditions of this Licence become operative when using this GCSE OCR B RS Applied Ethics ActiveBook CD-ROM.

Limited Warranty:

PEL warrants that the disk or CD-ROM on which the software is supplied is free from defects in material and workmanship in normal use for ninety (90) days from the date You receive it. This warranty is limited to You and is not transferable.

This limited warranty is void if any damage has resulted from accident, abuse, misapplication, service or modification by someone other than PEL. In no event shall PEL be liable for any damages whatsoever arising out of installation of the software, even if advised of the possibility of such damages. PEL will not be liable for any loss or damage of any nature suffered by any party as a result of reliance upon or reproduction of any errors in the content of the publication.

PEL does not warrant that the functions of the software meet Your requirements or that the media is compatible with any computer system on which it is used or that the operation of the software will be unlimited or error free. You assume responsibility for selecting the software to achieve Your intended results and for the installation of, the use of and the results obtained from the software.

PEL shall not be liable for any loss or damage of any kind (except for personal injury or death) arising from the use of this GCSE OCR B RS Applied Ethics ActiveBook CD-ROM or from errors, deficiencies or faults therein, whether such loss or damage is caused by negligence or otherwise.

The entire liability of PEL and your only remedy shall be replacement free of charge of the components that do not meet this warranty.

No information or advice (oral, written or otherwise) given by PEL or PEL's agents shall create a warranty or in any way increase the scope of this warranty.

To the extent the law permits, PEL disclaims all other warranties, either express or implied, including by way of example and not limitation, warranties of merchantability and fitness for a particular purpose in respect of this GCSE OCR B RS Applied Ethics ActiveBook CD-ROM.

Termination:

This Licence shall automatically terminate without notice from PEL if You fail to comply with any of its provisions or the purchasing institution becomes insolvent or subject to receivership, liquidation or similar external administration. PEL may also terminate this Licence by notice in writing. Upon termination for whatever reason You agree to destroy the GCSE OCR B RS Applied Ethics ActiveBook CD-ROM and any back-up copies and delete any part of the GCSE OCR B RS Applied Ethics ActiveBook CD-ROM stored on your computer.

Governing Law:

This Licence will be governed by and construed in accordance with English law.